WAR BY OTHER MEANS

Also by John Yoo

The Powers of War and Peace

WAR BY OTHER MEANS

AN INSIDER'S ACCOUNT
OF THE WAR ON TERROR

John Yoo

Atlantic Monthly Press
New York

Published simultaneously in Canada
Printed in the United States of America

FIRST EDITION

Library of Congress Cataloging-in-Publication Data

Yoo, John.
War by other means / John Yoo.
p. cm.
Includes bibliographical references and index.
ISBN-10: 0-87113-945-6
ISBN-13: 978-0-87113-945-0
1. Terrorism—Government policy—United States.
2. War on Terrorism. 2001-3. War and emergency powers—
United States.   I. Title.
HV6432.Y66 2006
363.325'15610973—dc22
2006048972

Atlantic Monthly Press
an imprint of Grove/Atlantic, Inc.
841 Broadway
New York, NY 10003

Distributed by Publishers Group West

www.groveatlantic.com

06 07 08 09 10   10 9 8 7 6 5 4 3 2 1

CONTENTS

INTRODUCTION

A lmost every day brings some new revelation in the war on terror-ism, from tales of mistreatment of al Qaeda detainees held at the U.S. Naval Base at Guantanamo Bay, Cuba, to the National Security Agency's wiretapping of suspected terrorist calls into the United States without a warrant, to the Supreme Court's June 2006 *Hamdan v. Rumsfeld* decision rejecting military commission trials for terrorists. And every day brings some new confusion, exaggeration, or misinformed attack on the government's policies. This book, which draws from my time as an official in the Office of Legal Counsel of the Department of Justice from the summer of 2001 to 2003, seeks to explain the choices that the Bush administration made after 9/11.

These decisions were controversial because the events of 9/11 itself were unprecedented, which forced our government to reexamine old assumptions, to reconsider policies, and to rededicate itself to protecting the national security against a new foe. American policies to stop al Qaeda have come under enormous attack in the media, the academy, and abroad. In this book I explain that these policies were the result of reasonable decisions, made by thoughtful people in good faith, under one of the most dire challenges our nation has ever faced.

The war with al Qaeda has presented difficult and close calls, and no doubt another administration might have reached different answers, but overall these decisions have been successful in preventing another 9/11-type attack on the United States.

Two mutually antagonistic parties have created the controversy today over terrorism policy. On one side, human rights advocates, academics, and pundits fear that the Bush terrorism policy will amount to the second coming of Richard Nixon. They view detention or wiretapping programs not as protecting the country from further attack, but as attempting to infringe on civil liberties or spy on innocent Americans. They believe that the methods and rules of the pre–9/11 world will work against post–9/11 terrorism. It is a view understandably colored by the lens of Vietnam and Watergate, which saw the greater threat to freedom coming from our own government rather than a foreign foe.

The other responsible party has been the Bush administration. It has often failed to explain clearly to the public the difficult decisions al Qaeda has forced upon us. Do we adopt aggressive measures against terrorists or allow the chances of another al Qaeda attack to increase? No one in the government wanted to make these choices; they were thrust upon us by the 9/11 attacks. When I joined the administration in the summer of 2001, I never anticipated having to detail the precise meaning of torture in military and intelligence interrogations, or the use of wiretapping to track down terrorists within the country.

Upon confrontation and questioning of its policies, the Bush administration tended to run and hide. It allowed itself to be done in by leaks, and neglected to defend the hard choices it had to make. It allowed the most partisan and acrimonious critics to frame public understanding of terrorism policies.

One controversy that surrounded me—the withdrawal of the legal opinions having to do with interrogation techniques—was really just about politics. A new memo offered in substitution changed little in actual administration policy. Its purpose was to give the White House political cover by making the language more vague, and thus, presumably, more politically correct. It harmed our ability to prevent future al Qaeda attacks by forcing our agents in the field to operate in a vacuum of generalizations. Our intent in the Justice Department's original research was to give clear legal guidance on what constituted "torture" under the law, so that our agents would know exactly what was prohibited, and what was not. It is unfortunate, in my view, that this political game had to be conducted at the expense of our men and women in the field.

On the surveillance issue, the Bush administration had learned, to its credit, a few lessons from the torture controversy. It came out with a full legal justification of its actions. Here it has so far prevailed. Both policies were part of a common, unifying approach to the war on terrorism, which I attempt to explain in this book. It was the willingness of the administration to explain the NSA program that made all the difference.

Because of the Bush administration's reticence, a great deal of media attention has fallen on me and my views. Given my position in the government, I did not expect to be involved in many important decisions. My field of research and writing in the university world was war. Unlike others in the Justice Department at the time of 9/11, I had read about military commissions under the Lincoln administration, I knew how foreign surveillance worked, and I had written several studies on the balance of power between the President and Congress in war and foreign affairs. I had not expected to be too busy, because the Bush Justice Department—like the administration generally—focused primarily on a domestic agenda.

Much of the attention on me is due to the fact that there are few Bush administration veterans who will defend their decisions in the war on terrorism in public. Some inside and outside the administration have chosen to fall silent out of lawyerly discretion, lack of time or energy, or fear of partisan attack. Others have tried to engage in a series of self-serving leaks intended to distance themselves from those decisions. I decided to explain the choices made by the Bush Administration in the very first months of the war.

This was not a role I had ever wanted to play. I came to the government having served in the judicial branch as a law clerk for Federal Appeals Court Judge Laurence Silberman and for Justice Clarence Thomas on the Supreme Court. In the legislative branch, I had served as general counsel of the Senate Judiciary Committee under Senator Orrin Hatch of Utah. As an immigrant to this country, I welcomed the opportunity to serve the nation that had so generously allowed me to join it, and afterward return to academia to continue working on constitutional and international questions. The last thing I wanted to do was devote my career to the study of the issues surrounding terrorism.

I thought we had made the right calls at the time. It was a period when government leaders had to make some tough decisions under demanding conditions. Men and women who put their lives on the line in this war had to carry them out. I feel an obligation to them to explain why they were asked to do what they did and why it was the right thing to do. I served in the government with a number of excellent public servants, both Bush appointees and career civil servants, and I am proud to explain their work. The political and personal criticism of me, I admit, has proven unpleasant at times, ranging from protests at the law school where I teach to outrageous accusations in the press or at public events. But any unpleasantness counts for very little compared with the risks that our soldiers and intelligence officers must undergo to protect our country.

Reevaluation of the administration's decisions was going on even as this book was going to press. On June 29, 2006, a 5–3 majority of the Supreme Court (with Chief Justice John Roberts recused) in *Hamdan v. Rumsfeld* blocked President Bush's military commissions because they did not comport with Congress's rules for military trials. Although its decision was limited only to the trial of terrorists, the Court implied that the Geneva Conventions ought to apply to other aspects of the war on terrorism. I think that the five justices made the legal system part of the problem, rather than part of the solution to the challenges of the war on terrorism. They tossed aside centuries of American history, judicial decisions of long standing, and a December 2005 law ordering them not to interfere with military commissions held at Guantanamo Bay.

As commander in chief, Bush has the authority to decide wartime tactics and strategies. Presidents George Washington, Andrew Jackson,

Abraham Lincoln, and Franklin Roosevelt settled on military commissions, sometimes with congressional approval and sometimes without, as the best tool to punish and deter war crimes by the enemy. Bush used them to solve a difficult problem: how to try terrorists fairly without blowing intelligence sources and methods.

The circus that was the trial of Zacarias Moussaoui shows the dangers in trying to use normal courtroom rules to prosecute terrorists intent on harming the United States. Bush's decision was supported by Congress, which authorized the President to use force in response to the September 11 attacks. Earlier, Congress had recognized commissions in the Uniform Code of Military Justice, and last year it created an appeals process for them.

What the justices did would have been unthinkable in prior military conflicts: intervening in the military decisions of the President and Congress. They replaced his wartime judgment and Congress's support with their own speculation that open trials would not run intelligence risks. Their decision to impose specific rules and override political judgments about military necessity mistakes war—inherently unpredictable, and where our government must act quickly and sometimes secretly to protect national security—for the familiarity of the criminal justice system.

Two years ago, the same justices declared they would review the military's detention of terrorists at Guantanamo Bay. Congress and the President expended time and energy to overrule them. *Hamdan* will force our elected leaders to go through the same exercise again, effort better spent preventing the next terrorist attack.

These questions still confront us, and they are not going to go away. They do not have easy answers, despite the claims of critics. All these questions require a careful balancing of considerations and predictions about the future. Those who must decide in the future, both Republicans and Democrats, need to make their decisions on the merits of the potential outcome, rather than out of fear of political demonization in the press.

During George Washington's administration, the question of whether to ratify the Jay Treaty with Great Britain divided the Framers of the

Constitution. A private citizen at the time, Alexander Hamilton published a series of defenses of President Washington and the treaty under a pseudonym in the newspapers. Thomas Jefferson, a Washington critic, urged James Madison to write against Hamilton in response. "For god's sake take up your pen," he implored Madison. Of Hamilton, Jefferson wrote: "Hamilton is really a colossus to the antirepublican party. Without numbers, he is an host within himself."[1] I decided to take Hamilton as my role model. I spoke and wrote constantly to defend the policies on the war on terrorism, even if the Bush administration would not. Since leaving government, I have written almost twenty opinion pieces in newspapers such as the *Wall Street Journal* and the *Los Angeles Times* discussing terrorism policy, and have spoken at more than seventy panels, workshops, forums, and debates on the subject.

Aside from leaving me tired of traveling, these debates and speeches showed me the need to write this book. I consistently found genuine confusion and misunderstanding about the administration's terrorism policies and the nature of al Qaeda. I also found that many people have an exaggerated view of the role of law. Law is critically important to our society generally, and to the war on terrorism. But the law is not the end of a matter; indeed, it is often the beginning. Sometimes people look to the law as if it were a religion or a fully articulated ethical code that will make these decisions for us, relieving us of the difficult job of making a choice. The law sets the rules of the playing field, but it does not set policy within that field.

Our nation continues to face many tough choices in the war on terrorism. We are not unique; they are the same choices other democracies have had to confront. But there are some things that are different: We (along with Israel) are the first to face a terrorist enemy intent on carrying out the catastrophic destruction of our nation; we also have at our command new technologies that enhance our ability to stop them. Our government must take these changes into account when striking the balance between pursuing terrorists and protecting America, without damaging the civil liberties of the society they are protecting. We need to have a more informed debate to best defend our country. This book is my effort to help us toward that goal.

1

WAR

On September 11, 2001, I switched on the TV in my Justice Department office at the Robert F. Kennedy Building in time to see the second plane, United Airlines flight 175, fly into the World Trade Center tower. Then American Airlines flight 77 hit the Pentagon. Later I learned that my friend Barbara Olson, wife of Solicitor General Ted Olson, had been on it. Rumors of attempted attacks on the White House, the Capitol, the Supreme Court, and the State Department flew around our offices even as the phone lines to the Defense Department and the White House stopped working.

That morning official Washington, D.C. evacuated in the face of a foreign attack for the first time since the British invasion in the War of 1812. I and a skeletal staff of the Office of Legal Counsel (OLC) stayed behind. That night, our country's leaders had to decide whether the United States was at war. FBI officials were already making significant headway in identifying the hijackers, and it soon became apparent even in the hectic aftermath of the attacks that several were al Qaeda operatives. Headed by Osama bin Laden, al Qaeda, which means "the base" in Arabic, had carried out deadly terrorist attacks against Americans for several years, including the bombing of two

American embassies in Africa and the USS *Cole* in Yemen, and had failed at other, even more deadly, attempts.

Uncertainty about whether September 11 started a war is at the root of most of the confusion about the United States' strategy in the war on terrorism. Critics of the Bush administration's terrorism policies believe that terrorism is a crime. They say that terrorism, even attacks as destructive as those on 9/11, by definition cannot justify war, because we are not fighting another nation. Former Clinton Justice Department official and Harvard law professor Philip Heymann states that "war has always required a conflict between nation states."[1] Former senator and presidential candidate Gary Hart and historian Joyce Appleby put the view nicely: "The 'war on terror' is more a metaphor than a fact. Terrorism is a method, not an ideology; terrorists are criminals, not warriors."[2] Yale professor Bruce Ackerman begins a recent book by declaring: "'War on terror' is, on its face, a preposterous expression," and devotes his first chapter to arguing that "this is not a war."[3]

If 9/11 did not trigger a war, as these critics contend, then the United States is limited to fighting al Qaeda with the law enforcement and the criminal justice system, with all of their protections and delays. Lawyers for captured al Qaeda operatives argued before the Supreme Court that it was illegal to detain them. Either the government should charge them with crimes, give them lawyers, and begin a jury trial, or it should let them go.[4] Former Clinton Attorney General Janet Reno filed a brief in support of a petition to release accused al Qaeda agent Jose Padilla on the ground that law enforcement "tools available now provide the Executive Branch with broad authority and flexibility to respond effectively to terrorist threats within our borders," and that no resort to war was needed.[5]

This position would dangerously return us to the more comforting certainties of the pre–September 11 world. For decades, the United States had dealt with terrorism primarily as a crime subject to the law enforcement and the criminal justice systems. In response to previous al Qaeda attacks, the United States dispatched FBI agents to investigate the "crime scene" and tried to apprehend terrorist "suspects."

Federal prosecutors succeeded in putting a few of them on trial in federal court in New York.[6] Ironically, the federal judge issued rulings on the 1993 World Trade Center bombing just weeks before the hijacked planes crashed into the towers. Efforts to capture or kill al Qaeda leader Osama bin Laden throughout the 1990s were shelved, out of concerns that the Justice Department did not have enough evidence to satisfy the legal standard for a criminal arrest.

A return to this state of affairs would be a huge mistake. Bipartisan studies of the failings that led up to 9/11 refer to the inadequacy of the criminal justice approach to deal effectively with an ideologically motivated military organization like al Qaeda. If 9/11 started a war between the United States and al Qaeda, the United States can employ its war powers to kill enemy operatives and their leaders, detain them without trial until the end of the conflict, interrogate them without lawyers or Miranda protections, and try them without civilian juries. No doubt these measures seem unusual, even draconian, but the rules of war provide nations with their most forceful tools to defend their people from attack. We are faced with the difficult task of adapting those rules for the unprecedented appearance on the world stage of an enemy that, while not a nation, can inflict violence at a level once only in the hands of nations. To make wise policy choices, it is essential to understand the difference between, and the appropriate uses of, war as opposed to criminal prosecution. War is too important to be the subject of partisan politics.

Here is how we at the Justice Department sat down to think about September 11. On that clear, sunny day, four coordinated attacks had taken place in rapid succession, aimed at critical buildings at the heart of our national financial system and our nation's capital. The terrorists who hijacked these airplanes in some ways had conventional military objectives—to decapitate America's political, military, and economic headquarters. They failed at the first, partially achieved the second (the American Airlines flight from Dulles Airport to Los Angeles struck a recently modernized and reinforced section of the Pentagon, resulting in far lower casualties and destruction than it would have otherwise inflicted), and succeeded at the third. The attacks killed

more people than the Japanese Navy had killed at Pearl Harbor—
approximately three thousand, with thousands more injured. They
also disrupted air traffic and communications, closed the national stock
exchanges for days, and caused billions of dollars in damage.

The attackers wore no uniforms, carried no arms openly, and did
not operate as part of regular military units. Instead, Mohammed Atta
and his eighteen fellow hijackers disguised themselves as civilians,
used civilian aircraft as weapons, and launched their attacks by surprise from within our borders. Deliberately targeting and killing civilians is deeply immoral, violating the core principle of the law of
war—that combatants are only to target each other and must attempt
to minimize harm to innocent civilians.[7]

The attacks were both vicious and skillful. Al Qaeda's operatives
infiltrated past our immigration and border controls, operated within
our borders for years, and gained the skills needed to fly airplanes into
buildings at schools in the United States without ever being detected
by American intelligence or law enforcement. They simultaneously hijacked four aircraft within minutes of each other, and succeeded in
hitting three of their targets with devastating effect. Even though they
were going to their certain deaths, the hijackers maintained operational security for months, if not years, and managed to take the
United States completely by surprise. Without any conventional
armed forces or the military resources of a nation-state, al Qaeda inflicted a level of destruction on the United States that only a few nations would have been capable of achieving. Evil doesn't necessarily
mean stupid or incompetent.

If a nation-state had carried out the same attacks on the same targets, there would have been no question about whether a state of war
would have existed. If, during the Cold War, the Soviet Union had sent
KGB agents to drive airplanes through American skyscrapers, the
United States would have retaliated, our nation would have gone on a
war footing, and our mutual self-defense agreements with other countries would have come into play. Why should status as an international
terrorist organization rather than a nation-state make a difference as
to whether we are at war?

Who We Fight

The most singular and defining characteristic of the hijackers to a lawyer, the one that makes them unprecedented in our history, is that they fight on behalf of no nation. They launched their attacks on behalf of a network of Islamic radicals who have dedicated themselves to a terror jihad against the West. Many were from Saudi Arabia, one of the United States' closest and oldest allies in the Middle East. While al Qaeda did not immediately claim responsibility for the attacks, American intelligence became certain of its responsibility. Videotape later captured in Afghanistan showed al Qaeda leaders discussing their planning and goals for the operation.

While al Qaeda was not a household word before the September 11 attacks, the United States had suffered repeated attacks at its hands. These include the suicide bombing of the USS *Cole* in 2000, the bombing of American embassies in Kenya and Tanzania in 1998, the attack on a U.S. military housing complex in Saudi Arabia in 1996, and the bombing of the World Trade Center in 1993. Only good intelligence and law enforcement work, helpful allies, and luck had frustrated planned attacks on American airliners over the Pacific Ocean, at Los Angeles airport during the millennium, and at various American embassies and personnel in Europe and Asia.

Public information about the group remains incomplete, but there is much agreement on its basic features and goals. Al Qaeda is a network of terrorists who wish to engineer fundamental political and social change in the Middle East. Some members, including bin Laden, are veterans of the successful resistance to the Soviet occupation of Afghanistan. With the help of Saudi funding, the Reagan administration helped train and arm mujahadeen resistance fighters from many different Arab countries to defeat the Soviets. When the war ended, some of these fighters banded together with the aim of overthrowing Arab regimes at home. They seethed at the rise of the Christian West, the decline of the Islamic caliphate—which had once stretched from India to Spain—the presence of American troops in the holy land of Saudi

Arabia, and at current Arab regimes, which they saw as corrupt and untrue to fundamentalist Islamic principles.

It is as important to understand al Qaeda's ideology as it was to know the worldview of our communist opponents in the Cold War. Al Qaeda members view recent history as a Manichaean struggle between Islam and the West.[8] To them, the United States is the cause of the conflicts and reverses suffered by the Islamic world. Over the long term, al Qaeda thinkers believe America must be forced to withdraw from the Middle East and that U.S. citizens must be converted to Islam. Attacking the United States also serves the near-term objective of undermining its Arab allies in Egypt, Saudi Arabia, and Jordan and replacing them with a fundamentalist Islamic caliphate.[9] "Our fight against these governments is not separate from our fight against" the United States, bin Laden says.[10] Publicity is another goal. Showing the United States to be weak and vulnerable helps al Qaeda to gain new recruits and destabilize secular governments in predominantly Islamic parts of the world. While other Islamic terrorist groups have focused on Israel, for bin Laden and his followers the United States is "the head of the snake."[11]

Al Qaeda had announced its goals at least as early as 1996, when bin Laden issued a fatwa—an interpretation of Islamic law—calling on Muslims to drive American troops out of the Middle East. Two years later, bin Laden and his number two, Egyptian doctor Ayman al Zawahiri, declared war against all Americans, saying that it was "the individual duty for every Muslim who can do it in any country in which it is possible to do it" to kill an American.[12] In an ABC interview shortly thereafter, bin Laden said that "the worst thieves in the world today and the worst terrorists are the Americans. Nothing could stop you except perhaps retaliation in kind."[13] The question was never whether al Qaeda wanted to attack the United States and kill its citizens. The question was only if it had the wherewithal to carry out its threats.

In 2001, al Qaeda had several sources of support. Most directly, it had the shelter of the Taliban in Afghanistan. The Taliban, in turn, received support from Pakistan's military and intelligence services. Al Qaeda gave the Taliban money and a core of loyal fighters; in exchange al Qaeda got a training base and a safe harbor from which to operate. In 2001 as well as today al Qaeda receives its financial support from private and religious charities and individuals, mainly based in Saudi Arabia. It draws its manpower from the pool of disaffected, alienated, or unemployed young men bitter over the Arab world's poverty and decline. It appeals to their fundamental religious beliefs in a time of unsettling change wrought by globalization and social upheaval.

Al Qaeda benefits from our technological age, in which small guerrilla bands, aided by the spread into the global public domain of virulent technologies—chemical, biological, and nuclear—can wreak destruction such as no small group has ever been able to before.

Al Qaeda's terrorist campaign against the United States and its allies continues to this day. It is believed to have been responsible for, or connected with, numerous terrorist incidents following September 11, including the December 2001 attempt by Richard Reid to ignite a shoe bomb on a transatlantic flight from Paris to Boston, an April 2002 explosion at a synagogue in Djerba, an October 2002 explosion on a French oil tanker off the Yemeni coast, a series of bombs on the Indonesian resort island of Bali that same month, and two attacks on Israeli targets in Kenya in November 2002. Al Qaeda apparently carried out the bombings of the Madrid train stations in 2004 that led to the withdrawal of Spanish troops from Iraq, and its operatives are behind some of the attacks on American troops currently in Iraq supporting that country's new government. It may also have been behind the London bombings on July 7, 2005.

Al Qaeda operates in an unconventional and, as strategic analysts like to say, asymmetric manner. Its operatives do not wear uniforms, nor do they form conventional units or force structures. Rather, their personnel, material, and leadership are organized in covert cells. Al Qaeda has no interest in meeting American armed forces on the battlefield, but resorts to surprise attacks, primarily on civilian targets, using unconventional weapons and tactics. Victory for al Qaeda does not mean defeating the enemy's forces and negotiating a political settlement, but demoralizing the enemy's society and coercing it to act in ways that al Qaeda prefers.

Another factor that distinguishes the conflict with al Qaeda from previous wars is jurisdiction, an issue that crops up whenever lawyers become involved. In earlier modern American conflicts, hostilities took place on a foreign battlefield. The United States home front was largely safe between two oceans. Today the battlefield may be anywhere. Possessing no territory, population, or regular armed units, al Qaeda depends on the covert use of global transportation and commercial channels to move its men and resources across borders undetected. This erases the traditional boundaries between the battlefield and the home front.

Why War

The United States has faced violence from non–state actors before. We have used the criminal justice system to handle pirates, domestic terror groups, the Mafia, and drug cartels. But there is a line, however indistinct, between crime and war. In war, nations use special powers to prevent future attacks on their citizens and territory, not to punish past conduct. Law enforcement tries to solve crimes that have occurred in the past. Our military and intelligence agents seek to stop deadly foreign attacks that may happen in the future. The difference in purpose dictates different tools. The FBI and the DEA—not the U.S. armed forces—have prime responsibility for interdicting drug smuggling (although the military sometimes plays a supporting role). They seek to disrupt the operations of drug cartels with traditional tools of law enforcement: interviewing witnesses, collecting physical evidence, and carrying out surveillance. An investigation usually occurs only after a crime has occurred. Deadly force may be used only if necessary to defend the law enforcement agent's life, or another's, against an imminent attack.

Crime is generally committed for personal gain or profit rather than a larger political goal. Drug cartels employ murder, kidnapping, robbery, and destruction to create a distribution network, grab turf from other gangs, intimidate rivals or customers, and even retaliate in military fashion against law enforcement. Al Qaeda resembles organized crime like the Mafia in some respects, but the Mafia is unconcerned with ideology and is primarily out to satisfy its greed.

War involves opposing political objectives. The United States went to war in World War II to achieve regime change in Germany and Japan; they went to war to conquer territory. We resorted to armed force in Korea, Vietnam, and Panama, among other places, to stop the spread of harmful ideologies or to remove corrupt regimes. Like a nation's, al Qaeda's attacks are highly organized, military in nature, and aimed at achieving ideological and political objectives.[14] Crime can certainly be involved in its fund-raising efforts, such as stealing money or defrauding charities, but al Qaeda uses this money for military and intelligence efforts rather than for the mere accumulation of wealth.[15]

Critics of the war on terror often point out that the September 11 attacks began and ended in the United States and are thus only domestic criminal acts. This ignores, however, the fact that the attacks were planned, controlled, and financed by a foreign organization. The domestic site of the 9/11 attacks does not render them acts of crime rather than war. True, the bombing of the Oklahoma City federal building was a warlike attack, but it was carried out by a citizen associated with a group that was far too small and disorganized to suggest any need for war. Domestic violence can sometimes rise to the level of a rebellion or insurrection and qualify as war, like the Civil War. If anything, the domestic focus of the attacks is the most compelling argument for war.

Crime is an endemic, diffuse social problem that has persisted throughout human history. By contrast, war is a set of discrete and violent acts undertaken by a nation or entity for political gain. Were the attacks organized and systematic enough to be considered "armed conflict"? The gravity and scale of September 11 surely crossed that threshold. One international treaty defines armed conflict as attacks that rise above "riots, isolated and sporadic acts of violence and other acts of a similar nature."[16] The Bali, Madrid, and London episodes, together with the bombings in Iraq, are part of a sustained and coordinated campaign against the United States and our allies by a single network in pursuit of an ideological agenda.

Although it seems circular, one way to know if the line between crime and war has been crossed is simply to note whether nations must turn to a military response. Necessity creates war, not a hovering zeitgeist called "law." If only the military has the capability to do what must be done, such as destroying enemy camps in Afghanistan, and it is sent to do it, then it is war. The fact of a military response is one way international law decides if an action constitutes war.[17] In fact, if terrorism were a criminal problem, we could barely use the military at all, thanks to a law called the Posse Comitatus Act, which prohibits the use of the armed forces to enforce our laws except in times of narrowly defined emergencies.[18] Though diplomacy and law enforcement will play important roles, few truly believe that they alone can bring al Qaeda to justice and prevent future attacks. War is violence on a large scale, of the kind we saw on September 11, undertaken for political reasons by a foreign state or entity, which requires a military response.

OLC's thinking culminated in a legal opinion that we issued before the month was out. The White House had asked about the President's authority to carry out military attacks against those responsible for the September 11 attacks and those who harbored or assisted them. On September 25, 2001, I signed an OLC opinion issued to the White House which concluded that a foreign attack had occurred on September 11, the United States was at war, and President Bush had full constitutional authority to launch attacks to destroy the enemy. President Bush had the power "not only to retaliate against any person, organization, or state suspected of involvement in terrorist attacks on the United States, but also against foreign states suspected of harboring or supporting such organizations."[19] This power was not punitive. It included the power "to deploy military force preemptively against terrorist organizations."

As Justice Departments and attorneys general had concluded in the past, we believed that the President could use force abroad alone, if necessary, without Congress's authorization. The constitutional text and structure granted the President this responsibility by making him chief executive of the nation and commander in chief of the armed forces. So had constitutional practice, including wars from Korea to Kosovo and retaliatory strikes against terrorism in Libya, Iraq, and Sudan. As a law professor, I had written that the President could wage hostilities abroad without congressional permission, a position supported by historical practice. I took issue with the views of several leading scholars who were critical of the Vietnam War or the Reagan and first Bush administration's foreign interventions.[20] Nearly all scholars agree that if the United States were attacked, no declaration of war was necessary and the President could immediately respond with armed force. Congressional support was welcome, but in our view it was not constitutionally required.

In the meantime, the President and Congress moved quickly to recognize the state of war between the United States and al Qaeda. In his address to a joint session of Congress on September 20, 2001, President Bush declared: "On September the eleventh, enemies of freedom committed an act of war against our country."[21] And in November 2001, President Bush issued an executive order which stated: "International terrorists, including members of al Qaeda, have carried out attacks on United States diplomatic and military personnel and facilities abroad and on citizens and property within the United States on a scale that has created a state of armed conflict that requires the use of the United States Armed Forces."[22]

Congress agreed. On September 18, Congress enacted an Authorization for Use of Military Force (AUMF)—if not a declaration of war in name, a declaration of war in purpose. It pronounced the September 11 attacks "grave acts of violence" that "pose an unusual and extraordinary threat to the national security and foreign policy of the United States." They justified a military response: "Such acts render it both necessary and appropriate that the United States exercise its rights to self-defense and to protect United States citizens both at home and abroad." (Under international law, the right to self-defense is triggered by an armed attack or the threat of one.) Congress recognized that "the President has authority under the Constitution to take action to deter and prevent acts of international terrorism against the United States."

This wasn't just a nonbinding expression of condemnation of the attacks. The law empowered the President "to use all necessary and appropriate force against those nations, organizations, or persons he determines planned, authorized, committed, or aided the terrorist attacks that occurred on September 11, 2001."[23] The President's authority was not limited to the immediate perpetrators of the attacks but to any nation, entity, or individual who has "harbored such organizations or persons, in order to prevent any future acts of international terrorism against the United States by such nations, organizations or persons." Congress had declared things to be a threat to national security, like drug trafficking or organized crime, but had never before authorized the President to use "all necessary and appropriate force" against these entities.

In October 2001, President Bush ordered the United States military to attack al Qaeda and the Taliban militia harboring them in Afghanistan. This campaign drove al Qaeda and Taliban forces from their strongholds and permitted the installation of a friendly provisional government in Afghanistan.

The Justice Department and the FBI launched a sweeping investigation in response to 9/11. Congress enacted the Patriot Act in October 2001 to expand the Justice Department's powers of surveillance against terrorists.[24] By executive order, the President created a new Office for Homeland Security within the White House to coordinate the domestic program against terrorism. Congress later established a cabinet-level Department of Homeland Security consolidating twenty-two previously disparate domestic agencies into one department to eliminate overlap, turf struggles, and confusion.[25]

Some complain that these measures violate the Constitution because we cannot use military measures against crime. Bush administration rhetoric even seems to suggest this at times. The terminology "war on terrorism" causes confusion by suggesting that we are at war with a combat tactic, not a concrete enemy, as former CIA director James Woolsey has pointed out. He likens a "war against terrorism" to a "war against kamikazes." The war on terror to many ears echoes the avowedly metaphorical "war on drugs" that has always been fought as a criminal matter.[26] Our political leaders have watered down "war" in the interests of mobilizing the nation to solve persistent social problems. However, the United States is not at war with every terrorist group in the world, or all who employ terrorist tactics, or a social problem, but with al Qaeda.

Rhetoric aside, it is perfectly clear that we are now engaged in an international armed conflict with al Qaeda, however much politics may fog the issue. Critics may try to get a federal court to rule that this is not war, or the laws of war do not apply, or that the United States must use only criminal law enforcement tools. But so far, the courts have not upheld this position. It is true that the Supreme Court's 2004 decision on enemy combatants was read by some as dealing a blow to the Bush administration's interpretation of the war on terrorism. *Rasul v. Bush* held that the federal courts would—for the first time—review the grounds for detaining alien enemy combatants held outside the United States.[27] In *Hamdi v. Rumsfeld,* the justices required that American citizens detained in the war have access to a lawyer and a fair hearing.[28]

On closer examination, *Hamdi* actually affirmed the administration's basic legal approach to the war and left the executive branch plenty of flexibility to prevail in the future. Despite enormous political pressure from the media, the academy, and activist litigators, the justices did not turn the clock back to September 10, 2001. They agreed that the United States was indeed at war, one authorized by Congress. As Justice O'Connor wrote for the Court's plurality:

> There can be no doubt that individuals who fought against
> the United States in Afghanistan as part of the Taliban, an
> organization known to have supported the al Qaeda terrorist
> network responsible for [the September 11] attacks, are
> individuals Congress sought to target in passing the [Authori-
> zation for Use of Military Force]. We conclude that detention
> of individuals falling into that limited category we are consid-
> ering, for the duration of the particular conflict in which they

were captured, is so fundamental and accepted an incident to war as to be an exercise of the "necessary and appropriate force" Congress has authorized the President to use.[29]

The justices implicitly recognized in *Hamdi* that the United States may use all the tools of war—including detention without criminal trial—to fight a new kind of enemy that has no territory, no population, and no desire to spare innocent civilian life.

At the same time, the courts unwisely injected themselves into military matters. At one level, these decisions recognize the unique challenges of the war on terrorism. In past wars, it was usually simple to identify a member of the enemy by his uniform. Because our enemy attacks covertly, our system seeks the review of another branch of government to guarantee that an American is actually a threat to national security before he can be detained. On the other hand, we should not extend our constitutional system's checks and balances to benefit aliens captured and held outside the United States in wartime. Both inside and outside the Justice Department, I advocated more judicial deference to the executive branch's constitutional authority over the conduct of war.

One place where we should not look to determine whether war exists is to international organizations like the United Nations. Certainly some alliances, such as the North Atlantic Treaty Organization (NATO), can play a useful role, but that is because they consist of actual governments with populations at risk and real militaries to protect them. NATO immediately recognized that the 9/11 attacks constituted an armed attack, offered to send planes to help defend the United States, and deployed troops to assist in the reconstruction of Afghanistan. The United Nations, however, is another story. A day after the attacks, the UN Security Council issued a resolution recognizing the United States' right of "self-defense," and found international terrorism to be a threat to "international peace and security"[30]—code words in international law justifying the use of military force. The UN's International Court of Justice, on the other hand, has refused to acknowledge that non–state actors have become makers of war against nations. It has repeatedly claimed that nations can only exercise the right of self-defense against other states, most recently in its controversial decision with Israel's construction of its security barrier along the West Bank.[31]

Nations should decide whether war exists. It is their populations under threat, their armed forces that maintain peace and security, and their intelligence and security agencies that will defeat those who threaten them. Al Qaeda's defeat will certainly not come at the hands of the United Nations, nor at the hands of the many nations in the UN General Assembly and other UN institutions that have no assets or forces to contribute.

Implications

If the views of the Bush administration's critics were to prevail, and we were to treat September 11 and other terror attacks as crimes, our system would grant al Qaeda terrorists better legal treatment than that afforded to our own soldiers. The mechanisms of criminal justice forbid government searches of suspects or their possessions without a warrant issued by a neutral magistrate. Police cannot arrest a criminal without probable cause and upon arrest must provide a suspect with Miranda warnings, a lawyer, and the right to remain silent. A suspect has the constitutional right to a speedy trial by jury, and in that proceeding can demand that the government turn over all of its information about the crime and the suspect. He can challenge that information and call his own witnesses in open court. The government must provide all exculpatory evidence to the defendant and access to any witnesses who have information relevant to the trial. A convicted defendant can appeal to higher courts to challenge the verdict and then file for a writ of habeas corpus seeking federal judicial review of any constitutional errors in the trial.

Because the Constitution's Bill of Rights establishes these rules, they are not very flexible. They protect the innocent, but are expensive, tilt in favor of the suspect, and impose high standards of proof on the government. While police can arrest based on "probable cause," a suspect must be released if prosecutors cannot succeed at trial. Courts can convict only if a jury finds that the government has shown "proof beyond a reasonable doubt," which often means something close to certainty. Federal courts and the Supreme Court supervise these rules, which can take years of trials and appeals. If police make a mistake, even in good faith, such as seizing evidence without a proper warrant or failing to read a Miranda warning correctly, the courts will sanction the government by releasing the suspect regardless of the threat he poses to society.[32] As Justice Benjamin Cardozo once observed, "The criminal is to go free because the constable has blundered."[33]

Our founding fathers established this constitutional system because of their concerns over the power of the government. It expresses a worry that the national government would use otherwise unlimited powers to engage in the suppression of political opposition. Sharing that suspicion, many legal conservatives have consistently pressed for the decentralization of power over domestic affairs. But it would be a mistake to believe that the Constitution's framework for criminal justice should apply to war. The former involves the fundamental relationship between the people and its government, and so ought to be regulated by clear, strict rules defining the power given by the principal to its agent. The latter, however, involves a foreign enemy who is not part of the American political community, and so should not benefit from the regular peacetime rules that define it. Applying criminal justice rules to al Qaeda terrorists would gravely impede the killing or capture of the enemy, as well as compromise the secrecy of the United States's military efforts.

According to the Supreme Court, a nation at war is entitled to detain as enemy combatants those "who associate themselves with the military arm of the enemy government, and with its aid, guidance and direction enter this country bent on hostile acts."[34] A nation at war may kill members of the enemy's armed forces. But law enforcement personnel may use force only in defense of their lives or those of others.[35] Once captured, an enemy combatant can be detained until the end of the conflict. Combatants have no right to a lawyer or a criminal trial to determine their guilt or innocence under the usual laws of war. They are simply being held to prevent them from returning to the fight.

While our soldiers are fighting under the rules of war, our enemy thumbs its nose at those rules by attacking in disguise and targeting civilians. As Osama bin Laden declared in 1998 on American television, "We do not have to differentiate between military or civilian. As far as we are concerned, they are all targets."[36] Yet the critics would have us give al Qaeda criminal justice protection precisely *because* it assumed civilian guise on U.S. soil and attacked civilian targets, effectively rewarding al Qaeda for violating every law of war ever devised.

September 11 put America on notice. Once, only nation-states had the resources to wage war. Al Qaeda is able to finance its jihad outside the traditional structure of the nation-state, and this may well extend to nuclear, biological, or chemical weapons. Mere networks of individuals—affinity groups—can now tap military power. Terrorist networks should not, through this loophole, be allowed to evade the laws of armed conflict among nation-states. While we are at war, we must also recognize that it is a different kind of war, with a slippery enemy that has no territory, population, or uniformed, traditionally organized armed forces, and that can move nimbly through the West's open channels of commerce. We must take aggressive action to defeat al Qaeda, while also adapting the rules of war to provide a new framework to address the new enemies of the twenty-first century.

2

THE GENEVA
CONVENTIONS

On a cold winter morning in January 2002, three months after
the United States invaded Afghanistan, we flew through clear
skies over sparkling blue-green waters into Cuba. A gust of warm,
humid air, full of the smell of tropical flowers and trees, embraced us
as we disembarked at the U.S. Naval Base at Guantanamo Bay, nick-
named Gitmo by the military. I couldn't help thinking that it would
all make great beachfront property if Castro ever died.

America had been at war in Afghanistan for three months. One
month before, the military, the CIA, and our allies in the Northern
Alliance had decisively seized control of Afghanistan, forced al Qaeda
from its terrorist bases, and captured hundreds of al Qaeda and Taliban
fighters. We were in Cuba to see the detention facility where many of
those fighters would spend the rest of the war.

I was the junior person on the flight—not quite the bag carrier, but
far down on the agency "org charts"—among the senior lawyers there
from the White House and Departments of Defense, State, and Justice. At the time, I was working for the Justice Department's Office
of Legal Counsel. Although relatively unknown outside the Beltway,
OLC is one of the most powerful legal offices within the federal gov-

ernment. It exists to interpret the Constitution and federal law for the executive branch. In peacetime, OLC usually occupies itself with resolving arcane questions of federal law or resolving interagency disputes. In times of war it advises the President and attorney general on the executive branch's constitutional powers. In the months following 9/11, OLC went into overdrive.

At the beginning of the Bush administration, OLC was an elite office within a government teeming with extraordinarily talented lawyers. Most of OLC's civil service staff were young attorneys just off of or headed to a prestigious clerkship in the federal appellate courts, or even the Supreme Court. Just above them were several experts in foreign affairs, national security, or presidential power with decades of experience. OLC has always been known for attracting deep thinkers on constitutional law, those more interested in figuring out separation-of-powers problems than litigating cases. OLC was often referred to as the attorney general's law firm, or the President's law firm, or the general counsel's general counsel, because when any new or difficult legal question arose, it often found its way there. Its alumni include three Supreme Court justices—Chief Justice William Rehnquist, Justice Antonin Scalia, and now Justice Samuel Alito—several federal appeals judges, attorneys general and solicitors general, and many leading law professors.

As a deputy to the assistant attorney general in charge of the office, I was a Bush administration appointee who shared its general constitutional philosophy. Three of the four other deputies had clerked for Justice Scalia or, like myself, for Justice Clarence Thomas. Other leadership positions within the Justice Department were also held by young conservative lawyers in their early thirties or forties; most had worked for Reagan- or Bush-appointed judges or Republican members of the House and Senate. They were matched by a White House counsel's staff that similarly was composed almost wholly of Supreme Court clerks. Many of us knew each other from going to the same law schools, clerking for the same judges, or working at the same law firms. Heading it all was Jay Bybee, a law professor from the University of Nevada, Las Vegas, who had previously served in the Justice

Department and the White House counsel's office under Presidents Reagan and Bush, and who would soon become a judge on a federal appeals court in Nevada.

Figuring out into which pigeonhole al Qaeda fit under the laws of war fell to the small group of us at OLC who worked on foreign affairs and national security. I had been hired specifically to supervise OLC's work on these issues. Since 1993, I had taught courses in foreign relations and international law at the Boalt Hall School of Law at the University of California at Berkeley. I had taken a sabbatical during that time to serve as a law clerk to Supreme Court Justice Clarence Thomas and as general counsel to the Senate Judiciary Committee under Senator Orrin Hatch, where I gained a first-hand education in the practical workings of the Constitution's separation of powers. Among scholars, I was probably best known for my work on the historical understanding of the Constitution's war power, and I had written a number of articles on the relationship between presidential and legislative powers over foreign affairs. In an administration that arrived in D.C. to focus on domestic issues, like tax cuts, fetal tissue research, and faith-based policies, I was one of the few appointed Justice Department officials whose business was national security and foreign affairs. As the administration moved to adapt the rules of war to this new kind of enemy, OLC's lawyers would play a central role in almost every issue raised by the war on terrorism.

The group of us who landed that day in Cuba surely had no idea then that the "front" in the war on terrorism would soon move from the battlefields of Afghanistan to the cells of Gitmo and the federal courtrooms. Warfare is not limited to military strategies and tactics on a battlefield. In this war, the detection of terrorist networks, detention, interrogation, and covert action are key. The goal is to prevent a terrorist attack—akin to the 9/11 attacks, or the Madrid and London bombings—before it happens. We had to decide what status to accord captured members of al Qaeda and its allies. Ultimately, OLC would advise the White House that the conflict with al Qaeda was not governed by the Geneva Conventions and that its members were not legally entitled to prisoner of war (POW) status. We would also advise that members of the Taliban could lose their right to POW status by refusing to obey the laws of war. President Bush would accept that advice in a decision in early 2002.

Ever since then, human rights lawyers, liberal interest groups, and political activists have attacked the administration for allegedly violating domestic and international law in the war on terrorism. Their criticism intensified after the release of photos depicting the abuse of Iraqi detainees at the Abu Ghraib prison in the spring of 2004. Charging administration officials with violating international and American law, they claim that Abu Ghraib is only the tip of an iceberg of systematic torture by the Defense Department and the CIA.[1] They rail that White House and Justice Department lawyers are guilty of war crimes for daring to find that al Qaeda terrorists are not legitimate prisoners of war. Amnesty International has called for investigations of "high-level torture architects" like Attorney General Alberto Gonzales; David Addington, the counsel to Vice President Dick Cheney; William "Jim" Haynes, the general counsel of the Defense Department; and several lawyers at the Justice Department, including yours truly.[2]

However much political activists repeat the claims of human rights groups, they have no merit. The idea that all the lawyers in the Department of Justice, the White House, and the Defense Department are engaged in a conspiracy to twist the law of the land to authorize an illegal war is simply ridiculous. Al Qaeda is an unprecedented enemy—a covert network of cells with no territory to defend, no population to protect, no armed forces to attack. It operates by launching surprise attacks on purely civilian targets. The only way to prevent future September 11s will be by acquiring intelligence. The main way of doing that is by interrogating captured al Qaeda leaders or successfully breaking into their communications. American policy makers have the unenviable and difficult task of preventing future attacks and adapting the rules of war, written for large-scale conflicts between nations, for this new kind of enemy. Human rights groups undermine their own credibility when they constantly criticize the United States for defending itself against al Qaeda, treating it no differently than they do the real human rights tragedies occurring around the world.

The critics argue that the Geneva Conventions set standards that must apply in all conflicts, big or small, whether nations, insurgents, or terrorists are fighting. They claim that the Geneva Conventions are best read as applying to any armed conflicts that take place on the territory of any treaty signatory (which would be any war, since virtually every nation in the world has joined the Conventions), and that even if the treaties do not strictly apply as a matter of treaty law, they have become customary rules universally accepted through consistent practice by states. While appealing in its simplicity and universality, this argument makes the basic mistake of treating al Qaeda as a nation-state which obeys the rules of war. It ignores what makes al Qaeda unique and unprecedented: the fact that it is a stateless terrorist organization that can attack with the power of a nation. To pretend that rules written at the end of World War II, before terrorist organizations and the proliferation of know-how about weapons of mass destruction, are perfectly suitable for this new environment refuses to confront new realities.

Serious legal and policy choices had to be made in this war. The first and most important question presented to us at the Department of Justice was this: Are al Qaeda and other terrorist organizations entitled to be treated illegal or unprivileged nation-states, or should they be treated as enemy combatants not entitled to the protections of the Geneva Conventions?

The question first arose in November 2001, as U.S. forces began to capture al Qaeda and Taliban fighters in Afghanistan. Pentagon officials had to make basic decisions about the conditions of detention for al Qaeda detainees. The Third Geneva Convention requires that the United States cannot hold a prisoner of war in "close confinement" or "in penitentiaries," but instead "under conditions as favourable as those for the forces of the Detaining Power who are billeted in the same area."[3] In other words, POWs cannot be detained in individual cells, as in a prison, but only in open barracks. A Geneva Convention POW camp is supposed to look like the World War II camps seen in movies like *Stalag 17* or *The Great Escape*. But because Gitmo does not look like this, critics automatically declare that detainees' human rights are being violated.

What the critics usually fail to mention is that the Geneva Conventions are treaties that apply only to international armed conflicts between the "high contracting parties" that have signed them. Al Qaeda is not a nation-state. It has never signed the Geneva Conventions. The Geneva Conventions even allow a warring power that is not a party to the Conventions to benefit from their protections by voluntarily accepting their terms in a specific war. Al Qaeda has not done this. Again, these provisions all make plain who is covered by the treaty, and who is not. The Geneva Conventions are not a law of universal application. They are limited to specific types of situations that arise in wars between nations that are parties to them or that accept their provisions.

Al Qaeda violates every rule and norm developed over the history of war. Flagrant breach by one side of a bargain generally releases the other side from the obligation to observe its end of the bargain. Al Qaeda has made no bargain, and observes no rules resembling those contained in the Geneva Conventions. It does not limit fighting to combatants. It does not spare innocent civilian life. It does not take prisoners. Rather, it kidnaps innocent civilians, such as *Wall Street Journal* reporter Daniel Pearl, and hacks off their heads.

The War Crimes Act of 1996 makes it a federal offense to cause a "grave breach" of the Geneva Conventions, to violate what is known as "common article 3" of the Conventions, and to defy the provisions of another core law of war treaty, known as the Hague Regulations.[4] Because it made elements of the Geneva Conventions part of the federal criminal statute, OLC had to interpret the treaty. No one in the Bush administration, contrary to critics' accusations, wanted to break the law. The very purpose of consulting the Justice Department was to make sure that no one did. Before our military and intelligence agencies could establish policy to address the threats posed by al Qaeda, they needed to know what the law meant first.

When the question on the application of the Geneva Conventions came to OLC, I asked Robert Delahunty to help me with the initial research and drafting of the opinion. Delahunty was one of the three career lawyers in the office who had risen to the level of the Senior Executive Service, the top crust of the civil service. A man in his early fifties, Delahunty had a large white beard, a mane of white hair, a round jovial face, and a hint of an English accent—he often reminded me of a kindly Saint Nick. He had first gone to England to study Greek and Roman philosophy and history, eventually becoming a tenured faculty member at a British university, left to go to Harvard Law School, and joined the Justice Department in the late 1980s. He had drafted many of OLC's opinions on war powers, foreign policy, and presidential-congressional relations under the first Bush and Clinton administrations. He had an encyclopedic knowledge not just of the law and academic works, but of the real lifeblood of international law—the examples of state practice. To my mind, Delahunty was the very model of the career civil servant who applies his or her long years of experience and knowledge to the benefit of the American people.

In an opinion that eventually issued on January 22, 2002, OLC concluded that al Qaeda could not claim the benefits of the Geneva Conventions. The war with the Taliban was covered by the Geneva Conventions because Afghanistan had signed them. But depending on the circumstances, it was possible that the Taliban had forfeited its rights.[5] First, we reviewed the actions forbidden by the Geneva Conventions, and by reference the War Crimes Act. Grave breaches of the Geneva Conventions include "willful killing, torture or inhuman treatment," "willfully causing great suffering or serious injury," or forcing a POW to fight or depriving him of a fair trial.[6] Grave breaches of the Conventions, we believed, could occur only in cases of declared war or any other armed conflict between "two or more of the High Contracting Parties" to the Conventions.[7]

The War Crimes Act also criminalizes violations of "common article 3." Common article 3—"common" because it is repeated in each of the four Geneva Conventions—requires that captured prisoners be treated humanely. It declares that the detaining power—here, the United States—not engage in "violence to life and person, in particular murder of all kinds, mutilation, cruel treatment and torture," or "outrages on personal dignity, in particular humiliating and degrading treatment."[8] Common article 3 applies in "armed conflict not of an international character" that occurs within the territory of one of the signatories to the treaties. The weight of commentary on the drafting of the Geneva Conventions suggested that common article 3 governed civil wars internal to a country.[9] It seemed clear that the drafters—who, after all, had worked in the aftermath of World War II—had anticipated only two types of conflicts: wars between nation-states and civil wars. They did not, and perhaps could not, anticipate the revolutionary change in warfare put on display on September 11, 2001: a non-state actor that could wage international conflicts with all the power of a nation.

Bush administration critics make the erroneous claim that U.S. treatment of al Qaeda terrorists violates common article 3.[10] Some international bodies and human rights critics demand that common article 3's requirements—including its vague prohibition on "outrages on personal dignity"—extend to *all* forms of armed conflict.[11] That reading ignores the text of the Geneva Conventions itself, which says that these requirements apply only to conflicts "not of an international character." It also ignores the context in which the Conventions were written. The clear understanding of nations at the time was to prevent cruelty and unnecessary harm in civil wars, which until that time the laws of war had left unregulated. Many of the nations that signed the Geneva Conventions viewed the emergence of non–state organizations in warfare as a lacuna in the laws of war, and so approved two sets of upgrades to the Conventions in 1977 to explicitly protect them. Tellingly, the United States refused to ratify these add-ons, with President Reagan specifically declaring them objectionable because they gave terrorists the protections in warfare due only to honorable warriors.[12]

The structure of the Geneva Conventions, as ratified by the United States, made clear that al Qaeda could not possibly claim their benefits. Al Qaeda simply was not a nation-state, and it had never signed the Geneva Conventions. Their legal benefits could not extend to al Qaeda, which would not obey them anyway. Common article 3 did not apply to al Qaeda because it is not fighting an internal civil war with the American government. The 9/11 attacks and the struggle with al Qaeda represented an international armed conflict that extended beyond the territory of the United States.

Even if the Geneva Conventions applied, they require that combatants obey four basic principles to receive POW status: They must operate under responsible command, wear uniforms, carry their arms openly, and obey the laws of war. Combatants must clearly distinguish themselves from civilians, and refrain from attacking civilians, so as to reduce the destruction of war on innocent noncombatants. Because of their record of launching deliberate, surprise attacks on civilian targets with no military value and their practice of disguising themselves as civilians, the January 22 opinion concluded, "Al Qaeda members have clearly demonstrated that they will not follow these basic requirements of lawful warfare."

Whether the Taliban deserved the protections of the Geneva Conventions was a much more difficult question, and proved to be the most controversial part of the opinion. Afghanistan had signed the Geneva Conventions, but the question was whether Afghanistan continued as a viable state. The Constitution's recognition of the President as commander in chief and chief executive, long historical practice, and the Supreme Court's view that the President is the "sole organ of the nation in its external relations, and its sole representative with foreign nations,"[13] established that President Bush could suspend treaties with another nation that had ceased to exist. In fact, the Supreme Court had held in a 1947 case that it would not second-guess a decision by the political branches as to whether Germany had ceased to exist as a nation after World War II.[14]

Recent history supplies several cases where a territory lost an effective government and essentially failed. Somalia was the clearest example. Central government authority had collapsed there by 1992, armed gangs fought over control of people and land, and the United States and its allies under the UN's aegis had sent troops. Liberia and Haiti were other examples. OLC's job of defining the law did not extend to uncovering the facts in Afghanistan—that is the job of the

Defense and State Departments and the CIA. The ultimate decision as to whether Afghanistan was a failed state rested with the President. But the U.S. government was already on record. Defense Secretary Donald Rumsfeld had said during the Afghanistan invasion that the "Taliban is not a government. The government of Afghanistan does not exist today. The Taliban never was a government as such."[15] Just before the start of the war, the State Department had said: "There is no functioning central government" in Afghanistan. Rather, it said, "The country is divided among fighting factions" and the Taliban is "a radical Islamic movement" in control of about 90 percent of the territory.[16] A similar judgment about Somalia had allowed the UN Security Council to authorize a military intervention for humanitarian reasons, even though the UN Charter allows the UN to use force only to counter a threat to "international" peace and security, not to mix in internal civil wars.

OLC sought to develop a legal test as to whether a state had "failed." In our view, state failure was marked by "the inability of central authorities to maintain government institutions, ensure law and order, or engage in normal dealings with other governments, and by the prevalence of violence that destabilizes civil society and the economy."[17] Borrowing from the legal test for the birth of a state, OLC recommended that the President consider whether Afghanistan had a defined territory and population, whether it was under the control of a government, whether the government could conduct foreign relations and carry out its international obligations, and whether the government has been recognized by the other nations of the world. If the President found these conditions did not exist, he could suspend our legal obligations with Afghanistan because the Taliban was not a real government running a real country. Government testimony and expert works indicated that "rather than performing normal government functions, the Taliban militia exhibited the characteristics of a criminal gang." According to the UN, it had "extracted massive profits from illegal drug trafficking in Afghanistan and subsidized terrorism from those revenues."[18] Afghanistan itself was subject to the control of warlords and ethnic groups, much of the population had fled

to refugee camps, and all but three countries in the world—Saudi
Arabia, Pakistan, and the United Arab Emirates—had refused to recognize the Taliban.

This part of the memo was advancing the law. The idea of failed
states had not been fully incorporated into international law. There
was a legal test for the emergence of new states (usually from the collapse of an empire), but no settled approach on their collapse. In two
previous conflicts, Somalia and the former Yugoslavia, the United
States and its allies had justified intervention on the collapse of governmental authority. If those states were thought to continue in existence, then American intervention in both places likely violated
international law. If the United States could intervene in Somalia,
Haiti, and the former Yugoslavia, surely it could intervene in Afghanistan to stop al Qaeda.

Failed states pose an international threat because their collapse
creates ungoverned territory. Terrorists and international criminal
organizations can move in and flourish. Warlords and gangs can violate
human rights there on a massive scale. Al Qaeda had been able to establish such deep roots in Afghanistan, where it could gather its personnel, organize its assets, and train for its deadly missions in relative
freedom, exactly because there was no real government there. While
operatives could set up cells in Pakistan or even Germany, they still
needed the support of an area where al Qaeda could establish infrastructure, pool its resources and personnel, and take refuge from the
police.

Critics have responded that Afghanistan was not a failed state because the Taliban effectively controlled most of its territory. No doubt
the Taliban ran a harsh regime, they argue, but it could only have
imposed its fundamentalist religious code because it held authority
throughout the country, which is the most important test of whether
a state exists. On the other hand, much of that effective control
seemed to be exercised by warlords, terrorist groups, and tribal militias, while the Taliban did not perform the basic governmental functions of providing minimal services to the Afghani people. Rather, it
carried out systematic human rights abuses against the population and

committed severe war crimes against its enemies. Afghanistan's status as a state depended on the facts, and we left that question up to the President and his advisers.

In any event, the President did not need to rest his decision only on Afghanistan's status as a failed state. Even if Afghanistan were a functioning state, and the Geneva Conventions applied, the laws of war still required that the Taliban militia meet the basic rules for fighting forces. The Geneva Convention governing POWs extends protection to "members of regular armed forces who profess allegiance to a government or an authority not recognized by the Detaining Power."[19] From everything we knew about the Taliban, it did not operate as a regular armed force. It acted more like a mob, without any clear command structure, and its fighters were more likely to be attached to different tribes or warlords than to Afghanistan.

This does not settle the matter though, because Geneva also protects "members of other militias and members of other voluntary corps, including those of organized resistance movements."[20] To receive POW status, such militia members must observe the four basic principles mentioned earlier: "that of being commanded by a person responsible for his subordinates," "that of having a fixed distinctive sign recognizable at a distance," bearing arms openly, and "that of conducting their operations in accordance with the laws and customs of war." If there is "any doubt" as to a detainee's status as a POW, the Geneva Conventions call for a tribunal, which in American practice had been satisfied by convening three officers together in the field. This decision would depend on the facts in Afghanistan, which we could not determine thousands of miles away in Washington. POW status was either up to the military on the field, or, as we saw it, the President could examine the operation of the Taliban as a whole and reach a determination.

Lastly, OLC wanted to make clear that we were discussing only issues of law, not policy. Even if al Qaeda or Taliban fighters did not deserve the legal protections of the Geneva Conventions, the President could still extend those rights as a matter of policy and goodwill. OLC provided historical examples where the United States had provided POW status when not legally required. At the outset of the Korean War, neither the United States nor North Korea had yet ratified the 1949 Geneva Conventions, but General Douglas MacArthur ordered the troops under his command to follow the "humanitarian principles" of common article 3 and the more detailed requirements of the POW convention. During Vietnam, the United States provided POW status to members of the Vietcong, even though they refused to operate in accordance with the principles of lawful combat. In Panama, the United States chose to treat the followers of General Manuel Noriega according to the Geneva Conventions, without conceding that the law required it. In Somalia, Haiti, and Bosnia, American forces agreed with their allies to apply the "principles and spirit" of the Conventions, even though it was unclear whether the wars were civil or international, and many combatants did not obey the rules of warfare. Our point was that the United States could find it advantageous to follow the Geneva Conventions, even if not legally bound to, but that then again it might not. That would be a question for the policy makers—Powell, Rumsfeld, Ashcroft, Tenet, and Rice—to decide, not OLC.

As the White House held its procession of Christmas parties and receptions in December 2001, senior lawyers from the attorney general's office, the White House counsel's office, the Departments of State and Defense, and the NSC met a few floors away to discuss the work on our opinion. We sat at a large round table in a room in the ornate, Empire-style Old Executive Office Building where secretaries of state once conducted business. Just a few days before, American and British special forces and their Afghan allies had killed many al Qaeda fighters in the mountainous caves of Tora Bora, but had just missed Osama bin Laden and his top lieutenants.

This group of lawyers would meet repeatedly over the next months to develop policy on the war on terrorism. We certainly did not all agree, nor did we always get along, but we all believed that we were doing what was best for the nation and its citizens. Meetings were usually chaired by Alberto Gonzales, now attorney general, then the counsel to the President. A short man with perfectly combed jet black hair, Gonzales was a real-life Horatio Alger story. He had grown up in modest circumstances in Texas and enlisted in the Air Force, which encouraged him to go to college. He went to Rice and Harvard Law School, and then returned to Texas, where as a corporate lawyer he came to the attention of Governor George W. Bush. He served as counsel to the governor, was elected Texas secretary of state, joined the Texas Supreme Court, and then came to the White House as the President's counsel. Gonzales's usual modus operandi was to keep his talking to a minimum, to seek a full discussion of the contending views, and to keep his own views private. He hated conflict and would have preferred that every meeting ended in a consensus, yet I found that when he had to, he could make the toughest decisions a lawyer would face. In private, he loved a good joke and had an easygoing, agreeable manner, which concealed a fierce competitive streak. At the same time, he could never understand why opponents (both inside and outside the administration) would resort to bureaucratic maneuvers, personal attacks, leaks, or exaggerations and distortions to prevail. Gonzales came to Washington with no agenda but that of providing his client, George W. Bush, with the best legal advice possible.

At meetings, his deputy, Timothy Flanigan, usually played the role of inquisitor, pressing different agencies to explain their legal reasoning or to justify their policy recommendations. I had known Flanigan ever since he had interviewed me for a job when I was fresh out of law school. He was sometimes overweight, sometimes not, with a glint in his eye and always ready with a funny remark, which must be a job requirement for someone with fourteen children. He had gone to the University of Virginia Law School, clerked for Chief Justice Warren Burger, and then worked in OLC before becoming its head at the end of the last Bush administration. Flanigan had worked at a variety of law firms before leaving private practice for a few years to work on a biography of Burger. He had been a critical member of the Bush campaign's legal team during the Florida recount. Flanigan did not shy away from conflict, as Gonzales did, and knew the ways of Washington, whereas Gonzales had no Beltway experience. Flanigan brought the ties to the broader Washington political and legal community, while Gonzales provided the personal relationship with Bush.

The State Department was usually represented by one of the most experienced officials to have served as its legal adviser, William Howard Taft IV. Taft was a thin man who bore little resemblance to his prodigious presidential progenitor. He had already enjoyed a long career as deputy secretary of defense and DOD's general counsel during the Reagan administration. Another regular participant at meetings on terrorism policy was John Bellinger, the legal adviser to the NSC, who would succeed Taft when Rice became secretary of state. An official in the Clinton Justice Department, Bellinger often shared Taft's accommodating attitude toward international law.

William "Jim" Haynes represented the Defense Department as its general counsel. Haynes was a charming, athletic man; D.C.'s legal newspaper, the *Legal Times,* had done an early profile comparing him to James Bond, which prompted no end of teasing from his colleagues. Haynes was a natural leader who inspired trust from those he worked with. He never sought the spotlight, never sought to dominate a meeting, but instead wanted to hear the positions of the different agencies. He saw his mission as preserving the Defense Department's legal and policy options and the prerogatives of his boss, Secretary Donald Rumsfeld. He attended Harvard Law School, served in the Army, and later became general counsel of the Army under Bush 41. After working for defense contractors and law firms during the Clinton years, Haynes was chosen by Rumsfeld to help transform the military, which made him a target of military lawyers, just as Rumsfeld had encountered resistance from the military brass. Haynes would later be nominated for a federal judgeship in Virginia, but his nomination would be held up by senators critical of the Bush administration's terrorism policies.

Some in the media have become obsessed with another lawyer, David Addington, then counsel to Vice President Cheney, now his chief of staff.[21] No doubt the fascination with Addington is part of a broader effort to claim that Cheney is really in charge of the White

House rather than merely fulfilling the vice president's traditional role as the defender of the President and his party. The punditry's fixation on Addington is, I believe, in large part a response to his colorful personality. In the usual sea of colorless, blue-suited, white-shirted, stripe-tied bureaucrats, men and women whose main goal is to create no waves and make no enemies, Addington stands out. A tall, white-bearded man with a booming voice and a confident, combative manner, Addington always does his homework—he reads voraciously, not just cases, laws, and treaties, but the daily flow of memoranda that course through the White House. He never declines the opportunity to press agency general counsels on whether they are interpreting the law or making policy.

He was the equal of any other lawyer in experience, having served as DOD general counsel under Cheney, special assistant to President Reagan, and lawyer for the House Intelligence Committee. Yet, Addington was always conscious of his position. He enjoyed saying that the vice president "was not in charge of anything" so all he could do "was ask lots of questions"—which often flowed in a torrent, replete with references to CIA practice, military jargon, Marshall Court opinions, and sometimes sarcastic comments. Various media reports claim that his influence was so outsized he even had a hand in drafting Justice Department legal opinions in the war on terrorism. As the drafter of many of those opinions, I find this claim so erroneous as to be laughable, but it does show how wrong the press can get basic facts.

The State Department and OLC often disagreed about international law. State believed that international law had a binding effect on the President, indeed on the United States, both internationally and domestically. Following its traditional view since at least Bush 41, OLC usually argued that international law that did not take the form of a treaty was not federal law because it was not given such authority by the Constitution's Supremacy Clause. In our arguments, State would authoritatively pronounce what the international law was. OLC usually responded "Why?"—as in why do you believe that, why should we follow Europe's view of international law, why should we not fall back on our traditions and historical state practices?

OLC's conclusion that the Geneva Conventions did not apply to al Qaeda did not ruffle any feathers. But it is no secret that the State Department disagreed with our view that the Taliban were not owed POW status. It argued that a territory could not lose its status as a nation-state, even though this had justified American intervention in places like Somalia and Haiti. Taft predicted that a presidential decision that Afghanistan was a failed state would cause the heavens of international law to fall. If the Geneva Conventions did not apply to a failed state, no treaties at all would apply to a failed state. Afghanistan's inability to be a party to any treaties "would have far-reaching implications for the conduct of U.S. foreign policy toward other States with questionable governing regimes."[22] If Afghanistan was a failed state, it would no longer be a member of the United Nations, International Monetary Fund, or World Bank, or a party to the nuclear nonproliferation treaty. The ownership of assets, liability for claims and debts, and "diplomatic relations and the status of our embassy" would be in question. Taft argued that maintaining Afghanistan's status as a state would keep these treaties in place, "to ensure the protection of the population." We thought these arguments were fundamentally ones of policy—they sketched the implications of a finding of a failed state—but did not actually come to grips with the question: Does a state really exist when its territory is gripped by civil war and subject to the control of warlords? Does a state exist when basic services are denied the population, and terrorists can freely roam throughout the land? In this respect, we thought Taft's memo represented the typically conservative thinking of foreign ministries, which places a priority on stabilizing relations with other states—even if it means creating or maintaining fictions—rather than adapting to new circumstances. It reminded me of the decision of the first Bush and Clinton administrations to claim that the ABM Treaty of 1972 still existed even after the collapse of the Soviet Union.

Military lawyers from the Pentagon had a policy concern. Known as "JAGs," short for judge advocates general, they worried that if the United States did not follow the Geneva Conventions, our enemies might take it as a justification to abuse American POWs in the future.

They believed that the Geneva Conventions were now "customary international law"—applicable not by treaty, but by custom developed through the practice of states over time. Most rules of civilized warfare, such as the ban on targeting civilians, had been accepted through custom long before taking the form of a treaty. It did not matter whether al Qaeda had signed the Geneva Conventions or not, the JAGs argued; the principles applied to any war and to anyone that the United States fought. Some, such as Senator Lindsey Graham (himself a JAG), have suggested that the JAGs were shut out of the decision process. From what I saw, the military had a fair opportunity to make its views known. Representatives from the Joint Chiefs of Staff, including uniformed lawyers, were present at important meetings on the Geneva question and fully aired their arguments.

The Justice Department disagreed. Whether to treat captured al Qaeda or Taliban fighters as we would soldiers captured fighting for France or Germany is a matter of policy. The law does not require us to provide them all with similar treatment, because the law cannot predict everything that may occur in life or war. It did not anticipate a war fought with a non-state terrorist organization with the destructive power of a nation. That does not mean that we recommended the administration do everything the law allowed. Setting policy within the limits of the law would depend on the circumstances.

It was far from obvious that following the Geneva Conventions in the war against al Qaeda would be wise. Our policy makers had to ask whether it would yield any benefits or act as a hindrance. Although the United States had obeyed the Geneva Conventions scrupulously in previous wars, our enemies in Korea, Vietnam, and the first Persian Gulf War abused American soldiers anyway. Mistreatment of prisoners is another form of "asymmetric warfare" that weaker opponents use against their stronger enemies. There is no reason to think that al Qaeda or the Taliban would act any differently than had communist China, North Vietnam, or Saddam Hussein. If anything, al Qaeda shows no desire to take prisoners at all, or provide them with humane conditions—but rather instantly executes them (a Geneva Convention violation). Nations at war with the United States will treat

American POWs humanely or abuse them based on the imperatives of war, not on what we do against al Qaeda.

OLC concluded that the Geneva Conventions had not assumed the status of customary international law that bound the United States, nor, for that matter, all nations in the world. Even if the Geneva Conventions could be seen as universal, and not just applicable to signatories, they only governed either conventional wars among nation-states using regular armed forces or rebel groups in a civil war. There was no customary international law on terrorist organizations like al Qaeda that could launch a devastating international attack. No clear customary international law on megaterrorism like 9/11 existed.

The United States has never in its history consented to the idea that the laws of war protect terrorists. In the wake of the wars of decolonization and independence in the third world, several nations sought to extend the protections of the Geneva Conventions to those who did not fight on behalf of states—freedom fighters, rebels, liberation movements, or even terrorists (as the saying goes, "One man's terrorist is another man's freedom fighter"). In 1977, Additional Protocols to the conventions extended POW protections to the fighters of non–state actors, and were signed by President Jimmy Carter. President Reagan decided in 1987 against seeking Senate approval. Reagan criticized the first protocol because it "would grant combatant status to irregular forces even if they do not satisfy the traditional requirements to distinguish themselves from the civilian population and otherwise comply with the laws of war. They would endanger civilians among whom terrorists and other irregulars attempt to conceal themselves."[23] He concluded that "we must not, and need not, give recognition and protection to terrorist groups as a price for progress in humanitarian law." In a sign of how much the world has changed, the editorial page of the *New York Times* praised Reagan's decision.[24]

What clearer evidence could there be that the United States has *not* agreed to give terrorists the protections due to honorable warriors? That it has *not* agreed to an international practice of considering war with terrorists to be covered by the Geneva Conventions. *This* is the law of the land.

Customary rules of international law can develop even without a written treaty, but only through the long practice and agreement of states. There is no world government that legislates and enforces rules on nations. At this moment in world history the United States' conduct should bear the most weight in defining the customs of war. Our defense budget is greater than the defense spending of the next fifteen nations combined.[25] We are the only nation that consistently fights wars around the world to protect its interests, to maintain peace in unstable regions, and to prevent human rights catastrophes. American troops helped keep the peace in Europe after World War II, maintained a delicate balance of power in Asia, and prevented any foreign intervention in the Americas. We have sought with less success to bring a better world to parts of Africa and the Middle East. Our NATO allies could not even stop the fighting along their border, in the former Yugoslavia, without American participation. Even while fighting two wars simultaneously in Afghanistan and Iraq, our military strength remains unrivaled.

Whether nations should adapt the Geneva Conventions to international terrorist organizations like al Qaeda under international law, which arises largely by the practice, agreement, and custom of states, is decided by the nations that actually fight wars. That critical question should not be decided by taking an international opinion poll, where many of the votes are cast by nations that are not democracies, or don't have to face the tough choices demanded by war. The United States has used its dominant military position to create and maintain a liberal international order based on democracy and free trade. U.S. practice in its wars—to maintain global peace and stability—have primary authority in setting international law on the rules of warfare.

Nevertheless, other nations and human rights groups fiercely attacked the United States for its Geneva Convention decision. Normally stalwart European allies, like the Germans, have called for Gitmo to be closed down. None of these nations have the responsibility of holding large numbers of dangerous al Qaeda operatives. They are happy to criticize the United States, but privately they don't want the United States to release their own al Qaeda citizens, who could return home to wreak havoc. Some commentators, like Robert Kagan, have suggested that the differences over the war on terrorism stem from wholly different political cultures. "Europe is turning away from power, or to put it a little differently, it is moving beyond power into a self-contained world of laws and rules and transnational negotiation and cooperation."[26] The United States, on the other hand, has chosen to rely more on power than international law, on military force as much as on persuasion, and sees a world of threats, not peaceful cooperation. "Americans are from Mars, and Europeans are from Venus," Kagan says. Jeremy Rabkin believes that Europeans are engaged in a misguided and dangerous project to degrade national sovereignty and replace it with global governance by international institutions.[27]

Looking back, I would put Europe's criticism of the United States' position on the Geneva Conventions down to old-fashioned rational, but short-term, self-interest. It is no secret that some European countries, particularly France, wish to restore the balance-of-power system that prevailed before World War II. Criticizing the United States for its terrorism policies inflicts political costs on us, seeks to unify world opinion under European leadership, and attempts to turn other nations against American policy. Meanwhile, these nations benefit from our fight against al Qaeda, just as they did during our struggle against the Soviet Union. Some European allies make significant contributions to the war on terrorism, but the U.S. carries by far the greatest burden. France, Germany, and other European nations have large immigrant Muslim populations which have not assimilated—witness the 2005 riots in France and the location of the operational leaders of the 9/11 attacks in Hamburg, Germany. They do not want to provoke their Muslim communities by pursuing an openly tough terrorism policy.

Our January 2002 memo represented an effort at consensus. On our flight to Gitmo, I sat next to Taft and sought to make clear that the President could choose to leave aside the failed state theory. He could decide instead that the Geneva Conventions would apply to Afghanistan, but that members of the Taliban could lose their POW status if they failed to obey Geneva's requirements for an armed force. State wanted to hold thousands of informal hearings in the field for captured

Taliban fighters. OLC maintained that the President could decide whether the Taliban militia as a group met Geneva requirements based on his constitutional authority to interpret treaties. The President could decide, if he chose, that Geneva's rules would apply as a matter of policy, including common article 3's guarantee of basic humane treatment of detainees.

A few weeks after the Gitmo trip, the lawyers met again in the White House situation room, a surprisingly small but ultrasecure room in the basement of the West Wing (one can even see photos of it on the White House Web site), to finally resolve the issues for presidential decision. If Geneva Convention rules were applied, some believed they would interfere with our ability to apprehend or interrogate al Qaeda leaders. We would be able to ask Osama bin Laden loud questions, and nothing more. Geneva bars "any form of coercion" and POWs "may not be threatened, insulted, or exposed to unpleasant or disadvantageous treatment of any kind." This is more restrictive than domestic criminal procedures used in American police stations, where every day police officers get into suspects' faces and try to cut plea bargains in exchange for cooperation. Geneva's rules were designed for mass armies, not conspirators, terrorists, or spies.

Consensus eluded the group. Gonzales had the unenviable task of summarizing the different positions for President Bush and attempting to forge a consensus. On January 18, 2002, the President decided that neither al Qaeda nor Taliban fighters would receive POW status under the Geneva Conventions. According to a leaked State Department memo, Secretary of State Colin Powell asked President Bush to reconsider this decision. Powell wanted not just the Taliban covered, but al Qaeda too.

With al Qaeda we face a dangerous network of conspirators who can inflict mass casualties. Preemptive attacks or arrests based on intelligence are our most important tool. This became the central issue as the President reconsidered. According to a leaked draft of a memo to the President dated January 25, 2002, Gonzales took the position that the nature of the al Qaeda threat rendered "obsolete Geneva's strict limitations on [the] questioning of enemy prisoners, in addition to its requirements that captured fighters receive commissary privileges, pay, athletic uniforms, and scientific instruments."[28] Why? According to the leaked draft the United States must be able "to quickly obtain information from captured terrorists and their sponsors in order to avoid further atrocities against American civilians." Applying different standards to al Qaeda does not abandon Geneva, but only recognizes that Geneva does not reach an armed conflict against a stateless enemy able to fight an international conflict.

Gonzales's leaked draft summarized the policy considerations raised by different agencies. In our conflict with al Qaeda, information was our primary weapon against future attack: it made no sense to follow Geneva when the need for intelligence is so great. Finding Geneva did not apply would also effectively eliminate any threat of domestic prosecution under the War Crimes Act, which might impose an unwise and unnecessary straitjacket on U.S. troops in a war whose "circumstances and needs" were unpredictable. The memorandum emphasized that "the war against terrorism is a new kind of war," not "the traditional clash between nations adhering to the laws of war."

Gonzales has been caricatured as calling the Geneva Conventions "obsolete" or "quaint." This plucks words out of context and misrepresents the leaked draft. Its argument was that Geneva did not apply as a matter of law, and that it was far more important as a matter of policy not to fatally hamstring intelligence-gathering by imposing a legal process never meant for the case, even if diplomacy would seem to counsel otherwise. Appearances and the massaging of international sensibilities could wait.

Gonzales's draft presented Colin Powell's objections. The United States had consistently applied the Conventions in previous conflicts, even when the law did not require it. Refusing to apply Geneva would weaken the United States' future ability to demand POW treatment for captured Americans. Our allies and some domestic groups would condemn the decision. Failing to apply Geneva "could undermine U.S. military culture which emphasizes maintaining the highest standards of conduct in combat, and could introduce an element of uncertainty in the status of adversaries." It was a good argument, and from precisely the person—the secretary of state—who must be concerned with world opinion.

Gonzales's draft memo recommended that the President find that neither al Qaeda nor the Taliban were covered by Geneva. It observed that in past conflicts, the United States had found the Conventions did not apply legally. This would be particularly appropriate in regard to "terrorists, or with irregular forces, like the Taliban, who are armed militants that oppressed and terrorized the people of Afghanistan." It also argued that as a matter of policy the United States should still provide captured enemy combatants with humane treatment, which would provide a minimum standard for interrogation or any other detention conditions. Military regulations governing detainees would still apply, but the draft memo pointed out "our adversaries in several recent conflicts have not been deterred by [the Geneva Convention on prisoners of war] in their mistreatment of captured U.S. personnel, and terrorists will not follow [Geneva Convention] rules in any event." Any concerns about a decline in military discipline were cured by President Bush's order that the detainees be treated humanely. Gonzales's memo conceded that other nations would criticize our decision, and might even withhold cooperation, but said it was important to apply international law only where it was actually binding.

Gonzales's description of the policy pros and cons neatly summed up the choice before the President. It answered the primary objection of those who argued that the military ought to continue to follow the Geneva Conventions because otherwise other nations would abuse our captured soldiers. Would U.S. refusal to provide POW status to al Qaeda and the Taliban influence the conduct of a future opponent? Who knew? In a future conflict, say over Taiwan, China might violate the Geneva Conventions, citing America's previous refusal to apply them to al Qaeda. Such prediction is inherently uncertain, however, and if one were going to decide based on the past, China has not been a stickler for Geneva Convention rules anyway. It seems safer to predict that in deciding POW policy, China's primary interest would be in the treatment of Chinese prisoners, not the treatment of al Qaeda prisoners from a previous war that never involved China. Suffice it to

say that citing precedents about the enemy's treatment of other nations' prisoners in other wars wouldn't drive America's POW policies,
much less China's or any other hypothetical adversary's.

According to yet another leaked memo, Powell responded the next
day. Powell's leaked memo conceded that al Qaeda were not POWs,
and that the Taliban individually or as a group might also lose their
entitlement to that status.[29] To Powell, the important question was
that the United States publicly declare that the Geneva Conventions
applied to the war in Afghanistan. His memo argued that following
Geneva would permit the same "practical flexibility in how we treat
detainees including with respect to interrogation and length of the detention," while the cost of the opposite policy would generate "negative international reaction," "undermine public support among critical
allies," and lead to legal challenges in U.S., foreign, and international
courts. Following the Conventions, Powell's memo maintained, "pre-
sents a positive international posture, preserves U.S. credibility and
moral authority by taking the high ground, and puts us in a better
position to demand and receive international support." Publicly declaring support for the Conventions "maintains POW status for U.S.
forces," and "generally supports the U.S. objective of ensuring its
forces are accorded protection under the Conventions." According to
this leaked memo, State had decided to cut its losses, but still hoped
to maintain the application of the Geneva Conventions, in theory, to
Afghanistan.

In a letter to the President on February 1, 2002, John Ashcroft
weighed in. While Ashcroft usually worked from documents prepared
by staff, as every cabinet member must do in the interests of effi-
ciency, he wrote this one personally. If the President determines that
Afghanistan is a failed state, Ashcroft observed, "various legal risks of
liability, litigation, and criminal prosecution are minimized."[30] This
finding would provide "the highest assurance" under domestic law
that no American military, intelligence, or law enforcement officer
would later be prosecuted for violating Geneva rules because the
President's decision that the treaty was not in force would be conclu-
sive. Ashcroft also thought it unlikely that the failed state option would

come back to haunt the United States in a future war because "it would be far more difficult for a nation to argue falsely that America was a 'failed state' than to argue falsely that American forces had, in some way, forfeited their right to protections by becoming unlawful combatants." He pointed to the North Vietnamese abuse of American pilots as an example of the latter.

On February 7, 2002, President Bush decided to follow OLC's legal advice, but to go with Powell's policy. In a memo to Cheney, Powell, Rumsfeld, Ashcroft, Andrew Card, George Tenet, Condoleezza Rice, and General Richard Myers, President Bush said that the Geneva Conventions only applied to conflicts involving states fighting with regular armed forces. "However," he wrote, "the war on terrorism ushers in a new paradigm, one in which groups with broad, international reach commit horrific crimes against innocent civilians, sometimes with the direct support of states."[31] Bush had accepted OLC's legal conclusion that the Geneva Conventions did not apply to al Qaeda, which was neither a state nor a party to the treaties. He also accepted that he could suspend the Conventions with regard to Afghanistan, but decided not to. Instead, he found that the Taliban were "unlawful combatants" who had lost their POW status. President Bush also found that common article 3 applied only to an "armed conflict not of an international character," and hence neither to the war with al Qaeda nor to the Taliban.

A legal finding that the Geneva Conventions did not apply to al Qaeda, and that the Taliban had lost their POW status, did not answer the question of policy—what standards of treatment to provide. On the one hand, treating the detainees as unlawful combatants would increase flexibility in detention and interrogation, potentially yielding actionable intelligence that could prevent future terrorist attacks and locate al Qaeda personnel and assets. On the other hand, appearing to depart from the Geneva Convention standards could cause negative responses from our allies, international criticism, and a decline in military discipline. President Bush ordered that "as a matter of policy, the United States Armed Forces shall continue to treat detainees humanely and, to the extent appropriate and consistent with military necessity, in a manner consistent with the principles of Geneva." He wrote: "Our values as a Nation, values that we share with many nations of the world, call for us to treat detainees humanely," and this principle applied whether legally required or not. President Bush also said that the United States "has been and will be a strong supporter of Geneva and its principles."

President Bush chose the right policy, one that provided the United States with flexibility to develop the rules that should apply to the new enemy of global terrorism, but which, in treating the enemy humanely, maintained American values. The White House released a list of the conditions provided to the detainees, including adequate food, clothing, housing, shelter, medical care, and the right to practice their religion. I witnessed these humane standards myself at Gitmo. Detainees received clothing, regular meals, the means to practice their religion, housing, and exercise. Some detainees received the first modern medical and dental care of their lives. To be sure, conditions were not those of a hotel—detainees were kept in cells, initially constructed of chain fence until more permanent facilities could be built, and they were guarded 24/7 by marines on patrol and from watchtowers. U.S. armed forces were ordered to treat the al Qaeda and Taliban humanely, and they did so admirably.

Human rights advocates and commentators have criticized Bush's policy decision. Some make an absolutist argument, raising the Geneva Conventions to a high principle.[32] The Geneva Conventions, however, are treaties, and very detailed ones at that. They are not a moral code. Bush's order to treat the detainees humanely, regardless of what they had done to us, regardless of the civilians they had killed and the rules of warfare they had broken, arose from morality. What standards to use toward al Qaeda and Taliban detainees is a question of policy. It demands that we measure the costs and benefits of the policy against other alternatives.

President Bush made his decision only five months after the September 11 attacks. All the available intelligence suggested that al Qaeda planned more strikes against the United States. One could argue that the costs to America's international reputation were greater than the immediate intelligence benefits. I do not think so; as various government leaders have acknowledged publicly, the intelligence gathered from captured al Qaeda and Taliban fighters allowed our intelligence, military, and law enforcement to frustrate plots that could have killed thousands of Americans.[33] Al Qaeda clearly sought weapons of mass destruction capable of increasing the devastation it could inflict by an order of magnitude. What President would put America's image in the United Nations above the protection of thousands of innocent civilian lives?

Far from radical, President Bush's decision drew on traditional rules of war. The customary laws of war have always recognized stateless fighters as illegal, unprivileged enemy combatants. This is a category that has existed for centuries. Pirates were the scourge of the oceans, and any nation could capture them; they were never owed the status reserved for legal combatants who obeyed the rules of civilized warfare. Justice Department opinions dating from the Civil War had distinguished between lawful combatants who wear a uniform, fight for a nation, and obey the rules of war, and "secret, but active participants, as spies, brigands, bushwhackers, jayhawkers, war rebels, and assassins."[34] The latter were "banditti" who were "thoroughly desperate and perfectly lawless." "These banditti that spring up in time of war are respecters of no law, human or divine, of peace or of war; are *hostes humani generis*, and may be hunted down like wolves." This understanding continued to prevail during World War II, when the Supreme Court recognized in a saboteur case that unlawful combatants who had forsworn the laws of war did not enjoy those laws' protections.[35] The Geneva Conventions mention neither illegal combatants nor any attempt to eliminate the concept. No one today is talking about hunting al Qaeda down like wolves, but a hardened operative who targets thousands of innocent civilians for death and disguises himself as a civilian is an unlawful combatant not due the protections given to honorable warriors.

Perhaps the greatest achievement of the laws of war over the centuries has been to make clear that noncombatants are off-limits. Innocent civilians cannot be deliberately targeted. Armed forces cannot use civilians as shields, they cannot deliberately conceal themselves in certain buildings, such as religious or medical facilities, and they must wear uniforms to clearly distinguish their status as combatants. Al Qaeda fights in covert, unconventional ways that play to its strengths and our weaknesses—which are also our strengths: our standards of honor and the protections of our legal system.

When our group of lawyers visited Gitmo, the Marine general in charge told us that several of the detainees had arrived screaming that they wanted to kill guards or any other Americans. Many at Gitmo are not in a state of calm surrender. Open barracks for most are utterly impossible; some al Qaeda detainees want to kill not only guards, but their peers who might be cooperating with the United States. As recently as May 2006, prisoners with makeshift weapons attacked guards who had rushed to save a detainee who had faked a suicide.[36] The provision of ordinary POW rights to these detainees, such as allowing them to cook their own food or conduct research, or to keep their own command structure, is infeasible.

The Geneva Conventions make perfect sense when war involves states. They make a laudable distinction between civilians and uniformed combatants to protect civilians, permit detention of combatants to prevent them from returning to combat, and ensure a minimum level of humane treatment for ordinary foot soldiers, most of whom can be presumed, in a twentieth-century battlefield, to have little valuable information. Today the main threat to peace does not arise from the threat of conflict between large national armies, but from terrorist organizations and rogue nations that don't give Geneva or any other rules the time of day.

Human rights advocates and liberal critics of the Bush administration's terrorism policies pretend that the rules of civilized warfare, including the Geneva Conventions, can safely address terrorism. September 11 proved them wrong. Before, the laws of war classified wars into those between states and internal civil wars. In the 1990s, the threat to global peace and security seemed to come from the latter more than the former. But the 9/11 attacks revealed a new kind of threat: a nonstate terrorist organization that wields the destructive power of a nation while ignoring the rules that guide nations. The candid approach would be to admit that our old laws and policies did not address this new enemy, and that we need to start developing a new set of rules to confront it, and soon.

3

ASSASSINATION

On November 4, 2002, Abu Ali al-Harithi, al Qaeda's top operative in Yemen and a planner of the 2000 bombing of the USS *Cole*, and five other suspected al Qaeda members were driving in a car outside the Yemeni capital of Sana. An unmanned Predator drone, controlled remotely by a CIA pilot from a base in Djibouti and overseen by commanders in Saudi Arabia, located the car and fired a Hellfire missile. All six men were killed. All that was left was the charred hulk of a bombed-out car sitting in the desert. Unnamed government sources boasted of the strike to the *New York Times* as an example of a victory in the war on terror produced by high technology and actionable intelligence.[1]

Among the dead was a naturalized American citizen, Kamal Derwish. Derwish was said to be the leader of an al Qaeda sleeper cell that had been discovered in the Buffalo area.[2] The other cell members, known as the "Lackawanna 6," were arrested and pled guilty in 2003 to providing material support to terrorists. Derwish, however, left the country and ended up in the car in Yemen. Derwish had not benefited from an arrest warrant, lawyers, or a plea bargain. Instead, he escaped the reach of the FBI only to meet his end on the receiving end of a CIA missile. Civil liberties lawyers have complained loudly of the treatment of captured enemy alien combatants held at Guantanamo Bay, Afghanistan, or Iraq. Few have protested the summary killing of an American citizen by remote control.

The Yemen strike was not a onetime event in the war, but an example of targeted killing, or what some see as assassination. During the November 2001 invasion of Afghanistan, CIA Predator drones attacked a high-level al Qaeda meeting in Kabul, missing Osama bin Laden but killing his military chief, Mohammed Atef. In May 2002, the CIA reportedly launched a missile against Gulbuddin Hekmatyar, an Afghani warlord who had joined forces with the Taliban. In May 2005, the CIA reportedly killed al Qaeda leader Haitham al-Yemeni, who had been hiding in the fiercely independent area of northwestern Pakistan out of reach of government troops.[3]

In June 2006, the United States successfully targeted and killed Abu Musab al-Zarqawi. As the leader of al Qaeda's operations in Iraq, Zarqawi was responsible for scores of terrorist attacks designed to drive out American troops and to spark sectarian violence between Iraqi Shiites and Sunnis. American intelligence had been given the location of Zarqawi's spiritual adviser, Abdel Rahman, during the questioning of an Iraqi courier.[4] By tracking Rahman, the United States located Zarqawi in an isolated house, and called in an airstrike by a single F-16. Two 500-pound bombs killed Zarqawi, Rahman, and a man, two women, and a child. American commanders chose a targeted attack from the air because no ground troops were in the area and they did not want to risk his escape.

Washington Post reporter Bob Woodward has reported that all of these strikes were authorized by a secret order signed by President Bush less than a week after the September 11 attacks.[5] President Bush obliquely referred to its purpose on September 17, 2001, when he spoke to reservists. "Do you want bin Laden dead?" a reporter asked. "There's an old poster out West, as I recall, that said, 'Wanted Dead or Alive,'" the President replied.

Woodward has written that the President's order authorized the CIA to kill or capture the leaders of al Qaeda and other allied terrorist organizations. As with all covert activity, the executive order was set down in writing, and a copy given to the House and Senate intelligence committees, reportedly including a list of the leading figures to be targeted, such as bin Laden and al Zawahiri.[6]

Satellite imagery, sophisticated electronic surveillance, unmanned drones, and precision-guided munitions allow American intelligence and its military forces to strike enemy targets virtually anywhere in the world, anytime. Today we can reach beyond the traditional battlefield. We no longer need to rely on strategic bombing of the enemy and its support structure. Once U.S. intelligence agents receive information that, say, an enemy leader is in a safe house in western Pakistan or in a car in Yemen, force can be deployed in hours, if not minutes, rather than the days and weeks it used to take to plan and execute attacks. These capabilities allow the United States to match the unconventional organization and tactics of al Qaeda with a surgical response that can target its leaders without the extensive harm to civilians that has characterized previous wars.

Precision strikes against enemy leaders have lately been the focus of media scrutiny and critical commentary.[7] The critics argue that it violates U.S. law banning assassinations. They also argue that, even if technically legal, such targeted attacks are unwise because they risk reprisals against Americans. Perhaps the most well-known strike was against Saddam Hussein's sons, Uday and Qusay, who also served as two of his top aides. At the outset of the Iraq war, President Bush ordered an acceleration of the invasion timetable to take advantage of intelligence revealing the location of Saddam Hussein and his top leaders. The Air Force attack missed.[8] Once Baghdad fell, a team of elite Army soldiers set out to hunt down the missing leaders of the Hussein regime. In July 2003, U.S. special forces tracked down Uday and Qusay to a house in Mosul and killed them after a long firefight.[9] Flanked by Rumsfeld and Paul Bremer, civilian head administrator in Iraq, President Bush praised the action in a Rose Garden speech.[10]

More recently, significant public protests raged in Pakistan in response to the latest example of targeted killing. In December 2005, a Predator drone fired a missile that killed Hamza Rabia, who was reputed to have become one of the top five al Qaeda leaders in the wake of the deaths or capture of more well-known figures in the terrorist organization.[11] CIA officials followed up that success with another attack in January 2006, targeting a dinner where al Zawahiri was supposed to be in attendance. Apparently he did not show up, and the attack killed at least eighteen Pakistani civilians and reportedly at least one aide to Zawahiri instead. Local rallies broke out in protest.[12]

Critics believe that such uses of force are illegal or just bad policy. Executive Order 12,333 states: "No person employed by or acting on behalf of the United States Government shall engage in, or conspire to engage in, assassination."[13] In the wake of the Yemen strike, the Swedish foreign minister called the attack "a summary execution that violates human rights," a view also espoused by Amnesty International.[14] After the attacks that killed Uday and Qusay, George Gedda of the Associated Press asserted that "pursuing with intent to kill violates a long-standing policy banning political assassination," adding, "It was the misfortune of Saddam Hussein's sons . . . that the Bush administration has not bothered to enforce the prohibition."[15] Intelligence analyst Thomas Powers argued in the *New York Times* that efforts to kill Iraqi leaders would invite retaliation: "Mr. Hussein is not the only figure in danger of sudden death in Iraq at the moment, and it is a toss-up who is in greater danger—Mr. Hussein or Paul Bremer."[16] Some human rights advocates believe that such attacks violate international law because the targets are civilians, not uniformed soldiers, and must therefore be handled by law enforcement—making any preemptive attack illegal.

These criticisms rest on profound misconceptions of the nature of the war on terrorism and the rules of warfare. Because we are at war with al Qaeda, we can certainly use force to conduct hostilities against the enemy's leaders. This does not violate any American law—constitutional, congressional, or presidential—or any ratified treaty. Killing the enemy is what warfare is. Targeted attacks further the goals of the laws of war by eliminating the enemy's leaders with minimal but more effective force and reducing harm to innocent civilians. Because we face an enemy that resembles a network, not a nation, the best strategy is to attack those who comprise the key hubs of that network because there will rarely be armed forces to assault conventionally. Destroying training camps alone will amount to no more than "pounding sand."

Taking out terrorist leaders, whether by Predators firing Hellfire missiles from the sky or by Delta teams on the ground, is ongoing, it is legal, and it is wise policy. The crime approach to terrorism seems to forbid such acts, but this only shows how misconceived this approach is in this war. In the peacetime world of criminal enforcement, pre-emptive attacks against "suspects" are, of course, illegal. But in war our intelligence and military must have the ability to carry out targeted strikes. Despite a great deal of innuendo to the contrary by those who disapprove of this war on policy grounds, no American political leader seriously disputes the legality or necessity of targeting terrorists.

Policy

Under peacetime conditions, a democratic nation like the United States normally would never consider attempting to kill individuals *before* they committed a crime. Our criminal justice system acts *ret-rospectively;* a suspect must commit a crime before the police can arrest him. Under our Constitution and laws, a police officer in times of peace can use deadly force only to save his life or the life of another when it is in imminent danger. Police cannot use force to stop a fleeing suspect, even if they believe he might pose a threat to other lives at some time in the future, or to avert a crime that does not threaten someone's life.

Derwish, as far as we know, was not about to threaten anyone's life. He was killed while sitting in a car in the middle of the Yemeni desert. If authorities in peacetime had suspected Derwish of conspiring to commit terrorism, they would have had to gather enough evidence to show probable cause that he was involved in a crime in order to arrest him, then try him and prove to a jury his guilt beyond a reasonable doubt. Then, only if he were sentenced to death by a jury could he have been executed. These rules represent America's decision as a society that the harms of individual crimes, costly though they may be, cannot be fought by direct preemptive action.

War, however, brings forth a different set of concerns. When a nation goes to war, it seeks to defeat the enemy in order to prevent future harms on society inflicted by enemy attacks. Because war deals with prospective concerns, it relies less on exact information and more on probabilities, predictions, and guesswork. The military bombs a building when it estimates with varying degrees of certainty that enemy soldiers or enemy munitions are there. It does not wait to attack until it has proof beyond a reasonable doubt or even probable cause. That would risk allowing the enemy forces to escape, strengthen their position, and live on to attack another day. War by its nature seeks prevention, not punishment.

When the United States was still treating terrorism as a criminal justice system, it waited until after an attack before attempting a capture. Now that we are at war with al Qaeda, we are entitled to kill the enemy's commanders. This advances classic objectives of demoralizing the enemy, throwing their troops into confusion and disarray, undermining their planning, and removing their most able leaders. All wars, including World War II and the Korean War, witnessed numerous attacks on enemy military leaders.[17] In the 1980s, President Reagan ordered U.S. jets to bomb Libyan locations where Colonel Qadhafi might be living and working.[18]

Launching a missile to kill al Qaeda commanders like Derwish, even though he was an American citizen, was perfectly legal. He was a member of the enemy forces, the equivalent of an officer—Derwish amounted to a captain or major in command of an al Qaeda cell, the equivalent of a military unit. Al-Harithi was even more important, something like a colonel. We are legally and morally free to target them for attack whether they are on the front lines or behind them.

If some readers find this outrageous, consider that killing the enemy commander can better promote the principles behind the rules of civilized war. Over the centuries, the laws and customs of war have developed to try to reduce the harm to noncombatants and limit the use of force to that which is proportional to military objectives. By specifically targeting enemy leaders, the United States can render enemy forces leaderless and minimize casualties, both civilian and military.

Using targeted killing as a primary tactic also takes better account of the new kind of war facing the United States. More tanks, more Army divisions, or more carrier battle groups and submarines won't win this war. This did not bring victory in Vietnam and it will not work against the even more diffuse al Qaeda. Traditional deterrence and the threat of retaliation will not be effective against a network with no territory or conventional soldiers to crush. In military parlance, this war is not about "kinetics." The means needed to frustrate or cripple al Qaeda is quite small, and well within the capabilities of a single division of U.S. troops.

The problem is not America's power, but how and where to aim it. Al Qaeda does not mass its operatives into units on a battlefield, or at least it didn't after its setbacks in Afghanistan in the fall and winter of 2001. Al Qaeda disguises its members as civilians, hides its bases in remote mountains and deserts or among unsuspecting city populations, and avoids conventional military confrontation. The only way for the United States to defeat it is to destroy its ability to function, and the best way to do that is by selectively killing or capturing its key members.

The case for taking out individual al Qaeda leaders is *even more* compelling because al Qaeda is a decentralized network, not unlike the Internet, which gives it remarkable resiliency. A killed or captured leader seems to be quickly replaced by the promotion of a more junior member. While the United States succeeded in killing Zarqawi, he was soon replaced by another terrorist leader, this time an Egyptian. Most nation's militaries would have collapsed after the kinds of losses inflicted by the United States over the last five years: thousands of operatives killed, two thirds of al Qaeda's leadership killed or captured, and all of its open bases and infrastructure destroyed in Afghanistan and elsewhere. Al Qaeda continues to exist as a global, ideologically driven network infiltrating operatives into the United States, as well as carrying out new terrorist attacks in Iraq, London, Madrid, and Bali.

Al Qaeda exhibits the typical characteristics of what is known as a "free-scale network."[19] A free-scale network is not created at random. It is made up of many nodes connected to many other nodes for some purpose, and built around hubs. In terms of the Internet, hubs are highly trafficked Web sites with connections to many other sites, such as google.com, yahoo.com, and msn.com. Users visit them often in order to connect to other sites, and a great many of these other sites connect to them as well. In a social or professional network, hubs are people whom a great many people know, who set trends, or whose work influences many others.

Decentralization is a network's great attribute. It can quickly collect and process information from a myriad of sources and coordinate the collective efforts of thousands of nodes located in different places and connected only by a common interest or affinity. If a node disappears, others simply move their connections. Networks can remain remarkably immune to attack. Randomly destroying its nodes will not bring collapse, and the loss of a single hub will not bring down the whole network. Since it has no real single leader, it can function even after suffering severe losses.

Al Qaeda is just such a network. Nodes are terrorists brought together by a shared desire to promote Islamic fundamentalism in the Middle East by any means necessary, including violence. Its hubs are leaders such as bin Laden and Zawahiri, and facilitators such as Khalid Sheikh Mohammed and Ramzi bin al Shibh. Capturing or killing an al Qaeda member is important for the discovery of other cells and plots.

Targeting al Qaeda hubs must be simultaneous. Random, individual attacks on a free-scale network will not work, in the same way that turning off random Web sites would have almost no effect, but closing down a Google or Yahoo would be very serious. Similarly, the functions of ordinary al Qaeda operatives are easily shifted to others. In order to take down the entire network, the United States must gather timely and accurate information and attack its most important leaders simultaneously rather than just stopping imminent attacks one by one.

This raises an important difference between law on the one hand, and good policy on the other. Simply because we *can* kill a member of al Qaeda does not always mean we *should*. We can interrogate captured leaders to learn not just about tomorrow's bombing, but about other plans for the future, and the identities and locations of other al Qaeda facilitators and commanders. It was far more advantageous for American intelligence that al Qaeda leaders Abu Zubaydah, Khalid Sheikh Mohammed, and Ramzi bin al Shibh were captured in Pakistan rather than killed by missiles. Strong cooperative relationships with other nations to capture and detain hostiles are invaluable in this covert war. They can provide us with intelligence, cultural expertise, and capabilities, which is why effective diplomacy and strong alliances are crucial factors in wartime success. Reducing collateral damage to civilians near terrorists is a high priority not only because of American concern about human rights but because mistakes can undermine popular support for our efforts. But critics forget that some nations, such as Pakistan, Afghanistan, and Saudi Arabia, may make formal political protests to cater to their citizens, while quietly allowing us to conduct targeted strikes.

During the Afghanistan invasion, a missile strike on a caravan of SUVs reinforcing Kandahar was postponed based on a military lawyer's judgment that women and children seemed to be in the convoy, although intelligence reported a high probability that the caravan was indeed an al Qaeda and Taliban unit.[20] Taliban and al Qaeda fighters in Afghanistan were bringing their families onto the battlefield intentionally, knowing that this would lessen their chances of being targeted.[21] Decisions to attack in such circumstances cannot be spelled out in simple rules. Instead, the importance of the target must be balanced against the collateral damage to innocents nearby, by military commanders, in a matter of minutes.

In war, we cannot be 100 percent sure the target is in fact the enemy or that our information is utterly correct no matter how diligent we are. In war, we are always dealing with probabilities about the future. Terrorists' plans can change at the last minute. We may have identified the wrong man, or our intelligence services may have made a simple mistake (as with the erroneous bombing of the Chinese embassy in Belgrade during the Kosovo war). Using force to prevent future harms can never be done perfectly. No military can choose or hit the correct target every time. Noncombatants near enemy locations might be killed. Under the tougher standards of domestic law enforcement, we do not punish a police officer who fires his weapon believing that his attacker holds a gun, even if it turns out after the fact that it was a fake gun. We only ask that our soldiers and policy makers make reasonable decisions under the circumstances. Every such decision must balance estimated effects on allied governments, local populations, and nearby civilians against the benefit of possibly eliminating an al Qaeda leader and frustrating his plans.

All this brings us back to al-Harithi and Derwish. Apparently the United States had good intelligence on the two men—consider that our intelligence agencies were able to locate them in a single vehicle traveling at great speed across a desert. No one has stepped forward, neither the Yemeni government nor any relatives, to claim that al-Harithi or Derwish were not members of al Qaeda or were not in that car. Because they were traveling through the desert, the chances of collateral harm to civilians was extremely low. The odds of capturing al-Harithi were not good, as he had succeeded in evading American intelligence for several years. While Yemen is a U.S. ally, parts of it are like the Wild West, beyond the control of the national government. The United States knew that an attack on the two men would not lead to a breakdown in diplomatic relations. Capturing al-Harithi and Derwish would have been preferable, as they could provide useful intelligence, but if they remained outside the reach of our government and its allies, as was deemed likely, at least we could stop them from carrying out further plots to attack the United States.

A similar analysis applied to Saddam Hussein and his sons. At the outset of the Iraq invasion, an attack on Saddam, Qusay, and Uday Hussein promised a high likelihood of success, with low civilian casualties. The benefits of success were large. Without Saddam or his sons at the top, Iraqi resistance to an invasion might have unraveled and casualties and destruction might have been dramatically reduced. Both Congress and Presidents Bush and Clinton had pursued a policy of regime change in Iraq, in good part because of Saddam's history of

seeking, possessing, and using weapons of mass destruction against both
military and civilian targets. A surprise missile attack on Hussein's compound could have produced that regime change in hours rather than
months. Those benefits outweighed the low probable cost in civilian
casualties. The question is why anyone would treat the al-Harithi/
Derwish case any differently from the Hussein case.

Law

Killing an individual, of course, is not legal in all circumstances. Nor
is it illegal in all circumstances. Killing an individual is legal as capital
punishment imposed on a convicted first-degree murderer. It is legal
when a police officer shoots an attacker armed with a weapon. It is
illegal when it is murder, as are any of the hundreds of premeditated
homicides that occur in the United States every year. It is illegal when
it is assassination, except that killing the enemy in wartime is legal.
The rules are fairly clear, and they leave room for the ordinary exercise of judgment in making policy.

Killing Martin Luther King Jr. was an assassination. Killing a foreign
head of state in peacetime is an assassination. Firing a Hellfire missile
to kill bin Laden is not an assassination. Until September 11, 2001,
our government remained confused about this distinction. Now it is
not an assassination. This has everything to do with the law of war.

In the 1990s, the United States passed up at least three chances to
kill bin Laden. By 1997, the CIA and the National Security Council
had become aware that he was more than just a financier of terrorists;
he was the leader of the terrorist group that posed perhaps *the* most
direct threat to American security.[22] Before the 1998 bombings of the
American embassies in Kenya and Tanzania, the CIA had developed a
plan to work with Afghan tribes hostile to the Taliban to capture bin
Laden at his Tarnak Farms compound. The CIA's counterterrorism
head thought the proposal "the perfect operation," and the military
found no "showstoppers."[23] CIA planning went so far as to hold a re-
hearsal of the operation that stretched across three time zones.

Concerns about the legal and political implications of targeting bin Laden prevented execution of the plan. President Clinton's national security adviser, Sandy Berger, thought that the evidence against bin Laden was not enough to win a conviction in the U.S. court system.[24] A senior CIA official worried that the operation would run counter to the ban on assassination.[25] The cabinet-level principals pulled the plug out of concern that civilian casualties could prove too high and that "the purpose and nature of the operation would be subject to unavoidable misinterpretation and misrepresentation—and probably recriminations—in the event that bin Laden, despite our best intentions and efforts, did not survive."[26]

These concerns continued to paralyze the administration as other opportunities came along. Through 1998, the President's orders to the CIA continued to authorize the capture of bin Laden only. Lethal force could be used against him only in self-defense. These limitations, plus shaky intelligence, led the CIA to pass up a chance to take bin Laden out with a cruise missile when he was traveling to and from Kandahar. A few weeks after the embassy bombings in August 1998, the administration had no trouble launching cruise missiles against suspected terrorist camps in Afghanistan, in the hope that bin Laden would be there. While the cruise missiles hit their targets, bin Laden and his lieutenants were absent.

By Christmas Eve 1998, President Clinton had authorized the CIA to allow America's tribal allies to kill bin Laden if they could not capture him, overriding the objections of some that this order violated the assassination ban. Administration lawyers concluded that the assassination ban would not be broken if the United States acted in self-defense under international law against an imminent threat of attack.[27] But Attorney General Janet Reno warned Clinton that relaxing the assassination ban on bin Laden could invite retaliation against U.S. officials.

These missed opportunities were caused by deep misconceptions about American law regarding assassination and killing in wartime, which many then voiced and some repeat today, even *after* 9/11. Their arguments are unpersuasive. Neither the Constitution nor federal statutes prevent the direct targeting of individual members of the enemy. Only Executive Order 12,333, issued by President Ronald Reagan in 1981, is explicit: "No person employed by or acting on behalf of the United States Government shall engage in, or conspire to engage in, assassination."[28] It continues a similar ban first put into place by President Gerald Ford in 1976, reaffirmed by President Jimmy Carter, and followed by every President since.[29]

While it bans assassinations, Executive Order 12,333 does not define them. Since the 1980s, however, government specialists have borrowed standard dictionary definitions to explain assassination as "an act of murder for political reasons."[30] Murder is a specific legal phrase that includes only intentional and illegal homicides. Deaths that occur by accident or are authorized by law, such as a police officer's use of force to protect the life of another, would not constitute murder, and hence cannot be assassination. Killing an enemy soldier in wartime would not be assassination, because the attack has a lawful military, rather than political, purpose. By contrast, the killings of Presidents Abraham Lincoln, James Garfield, William McKinley, and John F. Kennedy were assassinations. Their assailants killed these men during peacetime and with a political purpose. The attempt to kill Pope John Paul II, if it had succeeded, would have been assassination because the Vatican was not at war and he was targeted for political reasons. While popular conceptions of assassination probably include the idea that the killing take place covertly, that connotation does not appear in Executive Order 12,333's text, the laws of war, or their interpretation.[31]

It is easier to understand the scope of the American ban on assassination by briefly examining its historical context. President Ford issued the prohibition in part to head off congressional efforts to ban assassination by statute. Congress was reacting to revelations during 1970s hearings on the intelligence community, known popularly as the Church Committee hearings, which publicized the CIA's role in assassination plots against Fidel Castro, Congo's Patrice Lumumba, Dominican Republic leader Rafael Trujillo, South Vietnam president Ngo Dinh Diem, and Chilean general René Schneider.[32] Senate leaders were concerned that the CIA had pursued these plots without the approval or knowledge of the President. With the Ford order in place, congressional efforts to ban assassination, some with broader prohibitions, failed.[33] Several observers have concluded from this history that presidents intended their executive orders to ban political killings in peacetime, but not lawful killing in wartime.[34] Clearly, neither President Ford nor Congress thought at the time that the executive order would preclude the targeting of perpetrators of attacks upon the United States.

The United States has a national right to use force to defend itself. However, under the UN Charter, member states must refrain from the threat or use of force "against the territorial integrity or political independence of any state, or in any other manner inconsistent with the Purposes of the United Nations."[35] No exceptions were granted, such as preventing humanitarian disasters or rooting out terrorist organizations, except for two: interventions authorized by the UN Security Council "as may be necessary to maintain or restore international peace and security,"[36] or "the inherent right of individual or collective self-defense."[37] According to long state practice, the right to self-defense applies not only after a nation has suffered an attack, but also in anticipation of an "imminent" attack.[38] Despite the arguments of some well-known scholars to the contrary, every state has, in the words of onetime Secretary of State Elihu Root, "the right . . . to protect itself by preventing a condition of affairs in which it will be too late to protect itself."[39] The United States need not wait until an al Qaeda attack has occurred before it can launch a missile against a terrorist camp or send a special operations team to take out a terrorist leader.

Imminence should not be understood as a purely temporal concept. The concept traces its origins to the 1841 *Caroline* incident, in which British forces in Canada crossed the U.S. border and destroyed the *Caroline*, a ship being used by rebels. British and American officials agreed that a preemptive attack was justified if the "necessity of self-defense [was] instant, overwhelming, leaving no choice of means, and no moment for deliberation."[40] Imminence classically depended on timing. Only when an attack is soon to occur, and thus certain, can a nation use force in preemptive self-defense.

Imminence as a temporal concept fails to deal with covert activity. Terrorists deliberately disguise themselves as civilians, and they attack by surprise. This makes it virtually impossible to use force in self-defense once an attack is "imminent." There is no target to attack in the form of the army of a nation-state. The best defense will occur only in the small window of opportunity we have to take out terrorist leaders. This often becomes available, as in the case of bin Laden, well before a major terrorist attack occurs. Imminence as a concept does not address cases in which an attack is likely to happen, but we are not sure when.

In addition to imminence, we need to account for the degree of expected harm, a function of the probability of the attack and the estimated casualties and damage. According to conventional doctrine, a nation must wait until an attack is imminent before using force, whether the attack comes at the hands of a small band of cross-border rebels, as in the *Caroline*, or by way of a terrorist organization armed with biological or chemical weapons. Expected harm ought to be a factor, just as it ought to be a factor in ordinary acts of self-defense, as when one is attacked with a gun as opposed to a set of fists. At the time of the *Caroline* decision in the early nineteenth century, the main weapons of war were single-shot weapons and artillery, cavalry, and infantry. There was an inherent technological limit on the destructiveness of armed conflict.

The speed and severity of attack possible today means that the right to preempt now should be greater than in the past. Weapons of mass destruction have increased the potential casualties a single terrorist attack can wreak, from the hundreds or thousands of innocent lives into the hundreds of thousands or even millions. This does not even count the profound, long-term destruction to cities, contamination of the environment, and long-term death or disease for large segments of the civilian population. WMDs can today be delivered with ease— a suicide bomber could detonate a "dirty bomb" using a truck or spread a biological agent with a small airplane. Detection is difficult, as no broad mobilization and deployment of regular armed forces will be visible, and imminent attacks will be virtually impossible to prevent using conventional military force. Probability, magnitude, and timing must all be relevant factors in when to use force against the enemy.

This same logic explains why most applauded President John F. Kennedy's decision to blockade Cuba during the 1962 missile crisis with the Soviet Union.[41] President Kennedy did not wait until the Soviet missiles in Cuba were on the launching pad, fueled for flight. Rather, he acted earlier, during a brief window of opportunity, to head off the threat before those missiles could become operational. In doing so he risked a U.S.–Soviet war but used military measures that fell short of an attack. To prevent the potential harm from a terrorist WMD attack, the use of force involved in an assault team or cruise missile to kill Osama bin Laden and his lieutenants may be relatively low, and would fall far short of imposing a naval blockade on Cuba.

Targeted attacks to kill the enemy are one of the primary tools of war. As Hugo Grotius, the father of international law, observed in 1646, "It is permissible to kill an enemy."[42] There is no indication that the presidents intended the assassination ban to prevent traditional military operations. War would be made much more difficult to win, and certainly consume many more lives, if specifically targeting members of the enemy armed forces were prohibited.

In war, enemy forces include foot soldiers and command and control up to the commander in chief. Also included are personnel and assets not directly engaged in hostilities, such as combat support units, administration, communications, logistical personnel, and suppliers. Anyone who is a legitimate military target can be attacked with a variety of means, including aerial bombing, snipers, commando raids, and surprise assaults. "All are lawful means for attacking the enemy," Hays Parks, one of America's most respected authorities on the laws of war, has written. "The choice of one vis-à-vis another has no bearing on the legality of the attack. If the person attacked is a combatant, the use of a particular lawful means for attack (as opposed to another) cannot make an otherwise lawful attack either unlawful or an assassination."[43] Those same rules govern our attacks upon al Qaeda leaders and planners today. If the United States may attack Qadhafi in response to

Libya's terrorism, it should have the same legal right to attack bin Laden or Zawahiri. Of course, under this rule, the targeting of the White House and Pentagon on 9/11 was legal, although the method of the attack was not because of the hijacking of civilian airliners.

Limits

All of this is not to say that American agents have a hunting license on anyone they suspect is an al Qaeda operative. The rules of warfare, which give nations and their militaries the right to use deadly force to defeat an enemy, also impose guidelines. But they are not abstract, sterile, and restrictive. Contrary to the protests from professors and activists every time the United States launches a missile or drops a bomb, the rules of war are not broken when a missile goes astray or nearby civilians lose their lives. The laws of war take into account the harsh reality that war is not a precise science and that unanticipated harms or loss of life ancillary to a military attack will occur.

A corollary of the right to destroy enemy personnel and assets is the fact that the deaths of civilians that occur as a result of legitimate attacks against military targets are not illegal. This is the source of the idea of "collateral damage," which made its controversial appearance in the Vietnam War. But the rule is as old as war itself. The central principle of the laws of war is that innocent civilians should not be targeted. On the other hand, the rules of war accept the death of civilians at or near legitimate military targets. Law recognizes that war does not yet amount to antiseptic surgery where we can zap cancers with lasers that leave healthy tissue nearby unharmed.

Thus, the United States does not commit murder if it bombs a location that contains both bin Laden and his associates, on the one hand, and their family members on the other. It did not commit murder in Iraq when, in the course of a firefight with Uday and Qusay Hussein, who were holed up in a residential building in the middle of a densely populated city, civilians next door were harmed too. Rather, it is the terrorists who violate the rules of war by deliberately hiding themselves and their bases of operation within civilian populations, thereby drawing unwilling and unsuspecting innocents into the fighting. In another example of asymmetric tactics, terrorists multiply their strength by relying on the humanitarian morals of the West not to harm civilians. Terrorists know that American military and civilian leaders are reluctant to launch attacks that might cause civilian casualties.

Killing or disabling enemy personnel does not mean that anything goes. The United States cannot use poison on terrorist leaders, or refuse to accept surrender, or shoot the wounded. One of the early laws of war treaties, known as the Hague Regulations of 1907, prohibits "kill[ing] or wound[ing] treacherously individuals belonging to the hostile nation or army," as well as killing or wounding an enemy who is helpless or has surrendered, or declaring "that no quarter will be given." The U.S. military interprets this provision as "prohibiting assassination, proscription, or outlawry of an enemy, or putting a price upon an enemy's head, as well as offering reward for an enemy 'dead or alive.'"[44] Assassination prohibits killing the enemy using treachery. The United States may offer a reward for information or capture, but it does not place bounties on al Qaeda leaders' heads.

Banning "treachery" does not prevent the targeting of individual enemy soldiers or commanders. This distinction was drawn in the very first effort to codify the rules of war, undertaken by Francis Lieber during the Civil War, and issued as General Order Number 100 in 1863 to the Union armies.[45] Under the laws of war today, "treacherously" refers to deceiving the enemy by disguising your forces in the guise of noncombatants protected from attack, or declaring an enemy outside the protection of the laws of war. It could refer to soldiers disguising themselves as civilians or Red Cross workers,[46] or refusing to accept the surrender of a wounded soldier, or placing a bounty on an enemy's head. It has never been understood to prohibit targeting specific enemy commanders or other personnel, and the laws of war do not prohibit the use of surprise, ruses, commando teams operating behind the lines, or stealthy tactics to kill enemy personnel. American forces could launch special forces assaults to kill bin Laden, but they could not refuse his surrender, they could not dress as aid workers, and they could not shoot him if he were wounded and unable to fight.

Even though al Qaeda members are legitimate targets, and there can be little doubt that al Qaeda would not feel itself bound by any rules, not everything is permissible. Under the rules of war, soldiers must obey the principles of "necessity," "discrimination," and "proportionality." "Necessity" demands that nations engage only in destruction "necessary" to achieve a military objective.[47] "Discrimination" means targeting combatants and, within the limits of military technology, sparing civilians from the cruelty of war. "Proportionality" requires that the means used in an attack and the degree of destruction relate to the military goal.[48] Standards of honor and ethics apply. War is not an excuse to wreak havoc or display vindictiveness against the enemy.

Developed by the practice of armies over hundreds of years, these rules place significant limits on warfare. American bombers could not carpet-bomb towns or cities to destroy a few al Qaeda cells. Attacks are also subject to the prohibitions set forth in various laws of war treaties on weapons that cause "unnecessary suffering," such as certain types of explosive bullets, poison, and of course chemical and biological weapons. But if we have a window of opportunity to target bin Laden or his lieutenants, we should strike. We just must select means that will cause the least damage possible, to surrounding civilians.

Other nations' experiences provide an example of how these principles work out in practice. Israel has conducted a campaign of "targeted killings" since 2000 in response to the second Palestinian intifada,[49] using helicopter gunships and even jet fighters to launch missiles at the leaders of the terrorist groups Hamas and Islamic Jihad and the military wing of the Fatah party. The attacks usually occur on territory transferred to the control of the Palestinian Authority under the Oslo Accords.[50] Israel considers itself to be in a state of armed conflict with these terrorist groups and their leaders legitimate military targets. It strives "to use the minimum force necessary to prevent terrorism, acting in compliance with the principles and practice of armed conflict. It takes care to target only those responsible for the violence and makes every effort to avoid the involvement of innocent civilians."[51] While Israel has received a fair amount of international criticism, it has also succeeded in reducing the number of terrorist bombings and civilian casualties that would otherwise have occurred, using both military and nonmilitary means. In seeking to kill bin Laden and his lieutenants, the United States is taking a page out of the Israeli terrorism playbook.

Advances in military technology allow us to avoid the high civilian death tolls of past wars to reach military targets. To destroy Japan's industrial base and induce it to surrender in World War II, the United States killed hundreds of thousands of civilians in bombing raids on cities such as Tokyo and Osaka, not to mention the loss of life in Hiroshima and Nagasaki. American and British bombers destroyed German cities such as Berlin and Dresden, causing the deaths of tens of thousands of civilians. If the Allies could have killed Adolf Hitler with similarly indiscriminate levels of force, they surely would have done so. During the Cold War, America's strategic air and missile commands were prepared to launch assaults that would have killed millions of civilians to deter an attack on the West.

Today's technology allows us to target enemy commanders with pinpoint accuracy. Satellite reconnaissance and electronic eavesdropping allow the United States to spot the exact location of al Qaeda terrorists. Pilotless drones can circle areas of known terrorist activity for hours on end, permitting the United States to act instantly on that intelligence. Precision-guided munitions can hit targets within a margin of error of only yards, reducing civilian casualties. We used the lethal combination of intelligence and advanced weaponry on al-Harithi's car, Saddam Hussein's compound, and Zawahiri's dinner party. Even when attacks have failed, and only second-tier al Qaeda operatives were killed, civilian loss of life has been light in comparison with previous wars.

What about reciprocity? Attorney General Reno warned President Clinton that attacking bin Laden would make American officials targets. In retrospect, those concerns were misplaced and our exercise of restraint did nothing to avert 9/11. If anything, it seems to have encouraged al Qaeda, by convincing its leaders that the United States would not meaningfully respond to attacks. As 9/11 made clear, all of America, leaders and civilians, are al Qaeda's target. It is absurd to believe that if we refrain from targeting bin Laden and his commanders al Qaeda will refrain from similar attacks on our leaders.

Reciprocity is an important principle at work in law and policy. It underlies the laws of war. The international legal system has no supranational government with a legislature that can make laws on behalf of the world, nor an executive branch with an army or police force to enforce them. Nations at war will restrain their conduct if their opponent will, and if neither gains any advantage by doing so. If a nation violates the laws of war, its enemy is likely to do the same in response.[52] Restraint in an individual instance may be perceived by an enemy as humanitarian[53] and might thereby have a positive effect. But it is reciprocity, both positive and negative, that has historically induced the enemy to obey the laws of war. World War II Germany did not refrain from using chemical weapons out of humanitarian concern for Allied suffering, but because the Allies were fully prepared to retaliate in kind.[54]

Al Qaeda will never follow the rules of war; it gains its only tactical advantages by systematically flouting them. American restraint in the use of force, the methods of attack, or the treatment of prisoners will not change the incentives of al Qaeda members bent on salvation in the next world, not this one. But al Qaeda's fundamentally lawless nature does not free the United States from all constraints. Standard principles of reciprocity counsel that we follow customary rules on targeting and the use of force. Ample historical and legal precedent allow American policy makers to address the unique threat that al Qaeda poses. Law has never been a static system, but an evolving one, rooted in rules and principles that change over time to suit changing circumstances. There may be negotiations with terrorists at some point, the United Kingdom–IRA and the Israeli–Palestinian prisoner exchanges. But it is difficult to see that happening any time soon with al Qaeda. For al Qaeda to agree to play on a level playing field with the United States would be tantamount to its accepting defeat. The legal task for us now is to build on old concepts, like piracy, and adapt to new concepts such as precision targeting through intelligence and technology.

4

THE PATRIOT ACT

In the first few days after September 11, Justice Department attorneys gathered in a conference room in the FBI's Strategic Information and Operations Center (SIOC). The SIOC occupies a floor within the J. Edgar Hoover Building across Constitution Avenue from the Justice Department. It was created in 1989 exactly for a day like September 11. It has a thousand phones, 225 computer terminals, networks, secure rooms, and a control room and watch floor. It serves as a twenty-four-hour-a-day command center. [1] Even as one arm of the Justice Department and the FBI worked furiously in the SIOC to piece together the 9/11 plot, another group nearby was beginning a different mission: to change our laws to prevent another attack. This would produce the Patriot Act, the most vilified and misunderstood piece of legislation to come out of the war on terrorism.

The meetings were chaired by Larry Thompson, the deputy attorney general, or DAG, Justice's chief operating officer. Thompson was a rare bird in Washington, D.C., a conservative African-American who was best of friends with the leader of that flock, Justice Clarence Thomas. In his mid-fifties, Thompson brought a sterling reputation and decades of experience in criminal law to the job. He had been the U.S. attorney for Georgia under the Reagan administration, served as an independent counsel, and was a partner at a prominent Atlanta law firm. He had testified in favor of Justice Thomas and advised him during the confirmation hearings. A natural leader, Thompson was the prosecutor who provided the experience in federal criminal law that Ashcroft lacked. He had a no-nonsense attitude in conducting meetings, listened carefully to all points of view, and always displayed fine judgment. Along with Michael Chertoff, the head of the criminal division, Thompson held the Justice Department together in those first days after 9/11.

Ashcroft relied on Thompson to develop initial proposals, and on Viet Dinh, an assistant attorney general, to guide the package through Congress. Viet and I had known each other since law school. We had both clerked for D.C. Federal Appeals Court Judge Laurence Silberman, and had clerked on the Supreme Court the same year, he for Justice Sandra Day O'Connor. We had gone on to work in the Senate the year after, he in the Whitewater investigation, where he worked closely with Chertoff. We even both became law professors, I at Berkeley, he at Georgetown. Viet had a tough job of stewarding the Patriot Act, along with his other assignment of defending the Bush administration's nominees for federal judgeships, another flashpoint between the President and Congress at the time.

A common misperception promoted by civil libertarians is that the Patriot Act was the product of a Republican administration chafing at the bit to take away civil liberties. Nothing could be further from the truth. Almost all of the first proposals originated with career lawyers at the Justice Department who had worked on national security issues for many years, either in espionage or terrorism prosecutions.

These civil servants helped put together the first outline of the Patriot Act from a "wish list" of amendments to the terrorism laws that DOJ had not gotten the last time Congress passed an antiterrorism package in 1996. The proposals were mostly evolutionary changes to adapt to the new world of cell phones, quick travel, and the Internet. Congress had enacted the Foreign Intelligence Surveillance Act of 1978 (FISA), our primary tool to monitor and intercept the communications of national security threats, in the age of rotary phones, Ma Bell, and expensive air travel. I was asked to work on fixing the most important defect in our intelligence laws—the legal "Wall" that had separated foreign intelligence and domestic law enforcement. Blocking communication between intelligence and law enforcement officials, the Wall had played a role in our failure to stop the 9/11 attacks.

Without understanding FISA, it is impossible to understand the Patriot Act—which is probably one reason why polemicists find it easy to attack. FISA had responded to decades of presidential authorization of electronic surveillance for national security purposes without a judicial warrant. Every president from FDR to Carter had approved wiretaps on suspected agents. In the early years of the Cold War, there was a tremendous concern with communists and their sympathizers subverting national security. In the early 1950s, Senator Joseph McCarthy ignited a controversy and initiated hearings to investigate allegations that communists had infiltrated the U.S. government. McCarthy's accusations and smear tactics went too far and, gradually, there was a shift in the tide of public opinion toward the protection of civil liberties, even at the expense of national security. As the Cold War stabilized into a rough balance of nuclear parity in the 1960s, domestic national security threats seemed to diminish even further.

In the Watergate scandals of the 1970s Nixon invoked national security to conceal his wiretapping of domestic political opponents. Concern over civil liberties hit a high-water mark. When Congress responded, its action was a reflection of more than just the magnitude of Nixon's actions, but a growing concern about government abuse of civil liberties, in particular those of individuals involved in the civil rights and anti-Vietnam movements. In 1978, Congress enacted FISA to replace presidentially ordered monitoring of national security threats with a system similar to that used by law enforcement to conduct electronic surveillance of criminal suspects, but with important differences because of the classified information involved. It was this law, not the Patriot Act, which created a system of secret federal courts that issue secret warrants, based on classified evidence, to monitor potential foreign spies and agents.[2] Imposing a judicial warrant process on what had once been done by presidential fiat was the first in a series of restraints upon the executive branch in favor of civil liberties. Later, the courts and the Justice Department interpreted FISA to prevent the sharing of information gained from FISA warrants—which are easier for the government to receive—with criminal investigators. The concern was that FISA would be used as an end for running around normal criminal procedures. This gave birth to the famous Wall, which separated law enforcement from counterintelligence and counterterrorism.

It was precisely this Wall that every blue-ribbon commission to study our national security problems after 9/11 has said must be torn down. Despite efforts over the years to modernize it, FISA is still a product of the 1970s. It was created specifically to hamstring the executive branch in favor of civil liberties, based on the technologies and enemies in existence at the time. It does not meet today's challenge— a sophisticated, covert, foreign enemy that does not operate out of embassies like the spies of the Cold War, but instead conceals its communications within the billions of innocent phone calls and e-mails sent every day. The reforms that addressed abuses of executive power in the 1960s and 1970s resulted in a shift in favor of civil liberties that created the legal regime in place on 9/11. And 9/11 dramatized how drastically we need to reconsider what was done.

Today, FISA remains the main method by which the United States government conducts surveillance and searches of domestic targets suspected of international terrorism. FISA created the Foreign Intelligence Surveillance Court, known as the "FISC," made up of federal judges located around the country. Upon application by a special office in the Justice Department, the FISC can issue a warrant that authorizes electronic surveillance to obtain "foreign intelligence information" if there is "probable cause" to believe the target is "an agent of a foreign power."[3] The definition of "foreign power" includes international terrorist organizations.[4]

The most important constitutional issue raised by FISA is that the search warrant is not based on the Fourth Amendment's normal standard for a warrant. Under the Fourth Amendment, as it has been interpreted by the courts, a judge can issue a search warrant if there is "probable cause" to believe that the target has been or is involved in criminal activity—not just on speculation that someone has committed or may commit a crime. The government must have some proof—not beyond a reasonable doubt; not even more likely than not—that an individual is involved in a crime. FISA, however, permits search warrants based on a lower standard, on just probable cause that the individual is an agent of a terrorist organization. For agents of a foreign power who are either citizens or permanent resident aliens, FISA also requires that they "knowingly" engage in "clandestine intelligence gathering activities," a standard somewhat closer to that of a normal warrant.[5]

FISA generally is not used to investigate crimes that have already occurred. Instead, it monitors individuals who might harm national security in the future. It seeks to prevent future threats to the national security. Courts and the Justice Department created the Wall to prevent domestic law enforcement from taking advantage of FISA's lower standards to investigate purely domestic crime. But in guarding against Nixonian abuse of national security searches, the Wall also prevented entirely good-faith sharing of information and pooling of knowledge against real foreign threats.

The Patriot Act's fixing of these problems, oddly enough, has probably attracted more criticism than any other Bush administration anti-terrorism initiatives. I say "oddly" because the Patriot Act reasonably responds to the huge challenges posed by al Qaeda. Passed within weeks of 9/11 by large House and Senate majorities, it was a grab bag of modifications to existing law that the Department of Justice under both parties had been requesting for years. Nearly unaltered except for a few minor procedural civil liberties protections, it was renewed in March 2006 by a two-thirds majority in the House and by 89–10 in the Senate—after years of hand-wringing, filibusters, and short-term extensions as well as the Bush administration's low poll ratings.

While the Patriot Act had suffered politically from the growing impatience over the Iraq war, the truth is that the worst thing about it is its Orwellian name. It suggested that the government might be poised to abridge civil liberties under the sheep's clothing of patriotism. Its eventual reenactment suggested that the most scathing criticisms were more rhetorical than real.

Recent history certainly has to make anyone wary of increased state police powers in any form. Yet it is also true that American law and politics have evolved since the days of the Alien and Sedition Acts, which prohibited criticism of the government during the 1798 Quasi-War with France, or the Palmer raids, which rounded up communists after World War I. Abuses that occur today are more likely to be isolated and individual acts—mistakes—rather than wholesale deprivations of civil liberties. And at the risk of seeming Pollyannaish, it is worth noting that our career government officials are, by and large, keenly respectful of law and the Bill of Rights—notwithstanding bad-cop stereotypes that stir media excitement. It is hard to imagine any President ordering the surveillance of political opponents today without numerous government officials reporting it to the press and to Congress.

Many legal academics have warned in books, articles, and hearings that the Patriot Act endangers civil liberties. Most of this criticism amounts to the valid but generalized point that any increase in national security might potentially infringe on civil liberties. The rhetoric intensified with the 2004 presidential campaign. Former Vice President Al Gore, calling for the Patriot Act's repeal, accused the Bush administration of using "fear as a political tool to consolidate its power and to escape any accountability for its use." Then-candidate Howard Dean denounced the Act as "morally wrong" and "shameful." In debate on the House floor Dennis Kucinich claimed that "it has become crystal clear that this administration is currently and will continue to abuse, attack and outright deny the civil liberties of the people of this country in defiance of our constitution."[6] The American Civil Liberties Union convinced several city councils to pass symbolic resolutions to disobey the Act and some librarians to file lawsuits against its expanded surveillance powers.

For its part, the Bush administration defended the Patriot Act as a crucial expansion of executive authority to "detect terror cells, disrupt terrorist plots and save American lives."[7] Actually, the Patriot Act provides limited tools with which to tackle this challenge. The truth is that we do not currently have all of the legal tools we need to fight the new war we have before us. While it has begun the job, the Patriot Act is inherently limited because its underlying structure addresses the war we faced thirty years ago. Our human intelligence in this war has been weak; the CIA has had little success in breaking into al Qaeda's inner circle. Our open society makes it difficult, if not impossible, to intercept every al Qaeda agent who attempts to sneak through our borders. We need to press one of our distinct advantages in this war, America's skill in technology and electronic war–fighting, by allowing our intelligence and military to creatively find, monitor, and attack al Qaeda. Rather than unleashing our cyber-warriors and spies, laws like the Patriot Act keep them trapped in the procedures and mind-set of the Cold War.

One set of Patriot Act amendments sought to give antiterrorism officers the same tools that police and FBI agents now use against drug dealers or organized crime. Section 213 allows law enforcement agencies to provide delayed notice of the execution of a search warrant so as not to alert potential terrorists that they are under investigation.[8] When premises are searched and things seized, the normal rule is that the owner is immediately notified.[9] "Delayed notification" has been used in the past, in drug and organized crime cases, and has been upheld by the Supreme Court.[10] The Patriot Act extended this tool to wiretap terrorist targets, which makes perfect sense. What is the point of telling the target that you are placing a wiretap or bug on him? Federal agents had shown its usefulness by successfully breaking up, in one example, a money exchange used to funnel funds from the United States to terrorists in the Middle East.[11] Still, some House Republicans thought it was a serious threat to the civil liberties of terror suspects and almost succeeded in cutting off funds for it in 2003.

Another area where the Patriot Act sought to bring our capabilities up to par—expansion of search powers over business records—sparked even more opposition. This time, librarians were convinced that their rights were at stake. Section 215 allows the government to obtain a FISA warrant for any business records and papers held by third parties, like credit card purchases, phone records, and travel reservation information. Such records are used to trace terrorists' movements, activities, and sources of support. Law enforcement authorities have been able to obtain them through grand jury subpoenas for years. Libraries have, for instance, been subpoenaed concerning a defendant who researched books on how to build an unusual detonator.[12] If anything, the Patriot Act made it more difficult to obtain a warrant for records by routing the process through an independent federal judge.

Nonetheless, librarians filed suit against Section 215. They raised the specter of government agents armed with subpoenas rooting around in book borrowing records. "Many people are unaware that their library habits could become the target of government surveillance. In a free society, such monitoring is odious and unnecessary," the ACLU declared in July 2003. "The secrecy that surrounds section 215 leads us to a society where the thought police can target us for what we choose to read or what websites we visit."[13] Librarians wanted an exemption for any government request for information, with a warrant or not. The only relationships that enjoy this kind of immunity are those with our lawyers, doctors, priests, and spouses, and some of these can be overridden by a sufficient danger to life and public safety. Librarians apparently wanted to raise their services to book borrowers to the same level of social importance.

Groups like the ACLU never mention why the government might need information from libraries. Justice Department officials were not sitting around a conference table thinking that librarians ought to be taken down a notch. Rather, experience identified libraries as places where terrorists believed they could operate freely. In the lead-up to September 11, the hijackers and their network used public computers in libraries for research and e-mails. Additional information from businesses allowed investigators to piece together the links between the September 11 hijackers—after the fact. To prevent another attack, our agents need the information ahead of time, not afterward.

Librarians seemed to think that Section 215 singled them out. The provision does not even mention libraries. It applies to all businesses that keep records, of which libraries are only one. Business records, unlike personal records at home, are not constitutionally protected, because individuals give up any Fourth Amendment rights when they transfer control of records to a third party.[14] Excluding libraries from Section 215 would tell al Qaeda that libraries remain a safe haven where their activities would be free of government surveillance. In the end, librarians succeeded in winning an exemption from producing records solely on government request, but they must still turn over records upon a FISA warrant.

Obviously we do not want the government to have a free hand in examining any private citizen's library records, yet we know that the terrorists behind 9/11 used libraries to communicate. FISA represents a compromise that allows the government to examine a suspected terrorist's records without infringing on the civil liberties of ordinary citizens.

The Patriot Act also updated FISA to cover the technologies of today, as opposed to those of the mid-'70s, before the advent of cell phones, the Internet, e-mail, and the rapid transportation of people, goods, capital, and data. A FISA warrant covered only the district in which the court was located (there are ninety-four federal district courts, one for each state and major city). Cheap ground and air transport means one can lose track of a terrorist in minutes. Section 219 amended the rules to allow district courts to issue search warrants on a nationwide scope in terrorism investigations.[15] Again, no warrant may issue without a federal judge's approval.

Another provision that expanded prior law was the "roving" wiretap. Its name misleadingly raised the specter of a government following individuals everywhere and listening in on their every communication. According to the ACLU, "These wiretaps pose a greater challenge to privacy because they are authorized secretly without a showing of probable cause of a crime."[16] Before the Patriot Act, a FISA warrant only permitted surveillance of one phone number at a time, despite terrorists' ability to rapidly switch e-mail accounts, cell phones, and locations.

Section 206 of the Patriot Act creates a FISA warrant that is applicable to the suspected terrorist no matter what communication device he uses. While no one wants the government to randomly snoop on its citizens without reason, why force our counterterrorism agents to get a new warrant every time a suspected terrorist changes e-mail accounts and cell phones? The Patriot Act merely made our intelligence laws "technology-neutral"—no matter what technology terrorists use, our laws can keep step. Again, this may only happen with judicial approval.

These changes adapted FISA for terrorism. It was not the revolution bemoaned by civil libertarians. While it ushered in useful improvements, it is a mistake to believe that the Patriot Act marked any major change in the way the government fights terror. In fact, since the Act made only evolutionary changes, it can create the opposite of its desired effect by lulling Americans into an unwarranted sense of security.

We needed a sea change in how we could deal with terrorist information. I was asked to study Patriot Act provisions that raised constitutional issues. Our ability to counter terrorism had been sorely hampered by the Wall between intelligence and law enforcement. It was such an impediment that we began to wonder if it unconstitutionally intruded on the executive branch's national security responsibilities. I worked on bringing down the Wall so that the government could pool its information on al Qaeda. This became Section 218 of the Patriot Act, which changed the legal standard for a FISA warrant from one whose primary "purpose" was to gather foreign intelligence to one that needed only a "significant purpose." This implicitly took down the Wall by making it clear that information on terrorist activities, whether it derived from foreign intelligence wiretaps or criminal investigation, could be shared throughout the government to protect national security. It was a change of only one word, but an important one.

The Wall had clearly delayed the FBI from exploiting an important lead in the days before the September 11 attacks. In August 2001, the FBI's Minneapolis field office opened an investigation into Zacarias Moussaoui. Moussaoui had entered the United States in February 2001 to take lessons at a flight school in Oklahoma. In August he moved to another school in Minnesota.[17] He had no prior flight experience and no apparent interest in becoming a pilot. He held $32,000 in his bank account with no explanation of its source, had traveled to Pakistan, and apparently held jihadist beliefs. After 9/11, we learned from French intelligence that he had connections to extreme Islamic groups. We also learned that Moussaoui had met with and received funds from Ramzi bin al Shibh, one of al Qaeda's facilitators. Immigration and Naturalization Service (INS) officials detained him on the ground that he had overstayed his visa. But FBI headquarters turned down the Minneapolis field office's request for a warrant to search his laptop computer and belongings, which had information that could have led to the discovery of the 9/11 plot—all because of concerns about the Wall.

Strict enforcement of the Wall between law enforcement and foreign intelligence blocked yet another lead that might have led to the capture of one of the 9/11 pilots. In 2000, the CIA had begun tracking Khalid al Mihdhar after he had attended a critical meeting of al Qaeda operatives in Kuala Lumpur. Mihdhar flew to Los Angeles in January of that year with another future 9/11 hijacker, Nawar al Hazmi.[18] The CIA had photographs of Mihdhar in Kuala Lumpur with an al Qaeda planner who was involved in the bombing of the USS *Cole*.[19] But because of the Wall, the CIA wouldn't share those photographs with the FBI agents working on the USS *Cole* bombing, which was considered a criminal investigation and not a foreign intelligence operation.[20]

INS records showed that Mihdhar entered the United States again on July 4, 2001, at New York City. CIA and FBI counterterror agents realized Mihdhar's significance and tried to find him in August 2001, but refused to tell FBI agents in New York because of regulations enforcing the Wall. The FBI agents working on the *Cole* case were clearly upset, and said in an e-mail that "whatever has happened to this—someday someone will die—and wall or not—the public will not understand why we were not more effective and throwing every resource we had at certain problems."[21] As the 9/11 Commission observed, "The criminal agents who were knowledgeable about al Qaeda and experienced with criminal investigative techniques, including finding suspects and possible criminal charges, were excluded from the search."[22] Both Mihdhar and Hazmi had used their real names while in the United States, and might well have been found. Instead, they joined the teams that hijacked the planes on September 11.

Before the Patriot Act, a FISA warrant required that "the purpose" of the surveillance be to gather foreign intelligence.[23] FISA does not permit searches whose *only* purpose would be to gather evidence for a criminal prosecution.[24] In 1995, the Reno Justice Department issued guidelines that FISA information could almost never be shared with criminal investigators.[25] This addressed concerns about the DOJ using national security as a pretext to conduct searches without having to meet full Fourth Amendment standards. The Wall prevented information gathered in the realm of foreign intelligence from finding its way into the criminal justice system. A more natural reading would have found simply that "the purpose" of the surveillance must be to collect foreign intelligence, and that this said nothing about other uses to which the information might be put. In other words, if the executive branch wanted to gather intelligence on a foreign threat to national security, it could do so, under FISA, regardless of whether a criminal prosecution might use the information.

The Wall erected by DOJ's interpretive guidelines was dangerously mistaken. Obviously, terrorists operate both outside and inside the United States. We were aware long before 9/11 that al Qaeda wanted to launch a spectacular attack inside our country. Terrorists had already attacked the World Trade Center, struck the *Cole,* and bombed our embassies and military personnel abroad. Only good intelligence and law enforcement work had stopped attacks on American-bound airliners over the Pacific and millennium bombings in the United States. The whole idea of the Wall had been an overreaction to the events of the Nixon era, but as it percolated into law and practice it had weakened our country against real threats. Pooling intelligence was the only way to obtain a full picture, the "mosaic" of all available information about terrorist plans. Judge Richard Posner argues that we should allow our multiple agencies to compete in analyzing available data in a sort of market-based approach to intelligence.[26] But there is no benefit to segregating—or "stovepiping," to use a word one often hears in the government—the actual data that the government collects. Only when information is shared can intelligence and law enforcement agents follow new leads from new sources, or spot broader patterns and threats whose significance can't be understood without context.

Changing the "purpose" standard to one of "significant purpose" would bring down the Wall. This was a small change, but one that responded to the muddleheaded logic that had produced the Wall in the first place. To make clear to the courts and the bureaucracy that information-sharing was legal, Congress needed to change the standard, even though at first glance the language had little to do with sharing information.

But we also had to be careful not to run afoul of the Fourth Amendment. Diluting the "primary" purpose standard, DOJ and the courts had thought, would cast the FISA net unconstitutionally beyond the narrow zone of national security. This issue had tied the Justice Department up in knots for years. It was clear to me that the Fourth Amendment's warrant requirement for searches and seizures did not apply to actions taken to defend the country from foreign threats. There were two distinct legal regimes. The first was the regular criminal justice system. The second was war. Regular criminal warrants could issue on probable cause against organized crime groups, drug cartels, or terrorists who appeared to be violating federal laws.[27] This was the approach to terrorism up to September 11. In war, the military searches for and, indeed, kills the enemy without any warrants at all.[28] Geography alone should not alter the powers of the government to protect the nation from attack. If enemy forces invaded our territory, the Constitution would not require a search warrant before the military could monitor, capture, or kill enemy soldiers. After all, seizing or searching Confederate soldiers during the Civil War did not require a warrant.

If al Qaeda organizes missions within the United States, our surveillance simply cannot be limited to law enforcement. The Fourth Amendment's warrant requirement should not apply, because it is concerned with regulating searches to stop crime, not with military attacks.[29] This principle has been recognized by the lower federal courts, though not yet by the Supreme Court,[30] which has specifically refused to address whether the warrant requirement covers domestic searches conducted for national security purposes.[31] It has applied the Fourth Amendment's warrant requirement to cases of terrorism by purely domestic groups, out of concern that the government might suppress political liberties. Yet the Court has, so far, explicitly refused to consider whether the warrant requirement also limits the scope of the President's power to protect against foreign national-security threats.[32]

Since the Supreme Court's ruling, every lower court to examine the question has found that when the government conducts a search of a foreign power or its agents, it need *not* meet the requirements that apply to criminal law enforcement. In the leading case on the subject, a Virginia federal appeals court observed in 1980 that "the needs of the executive are so compelling in the area of foreign intelligence, unlike the area of domestic security, that a uniform warrant requirement would 'unduly frustrate' the President in carrying out his foreign affairs responsibilities."[33] A warrant for national security searches would reduce the flexibility of the executive branch, which possessed "unparalleled expertise to make the decision whether to conduct foreign intelligence surveillance" and was "constitutionally designated as the pre-eminent authority in foreign affairs." It would place the decision whether to conduct the search on the judiciary, which "is largely inexperienced in making the delicate and complex decisions that lie behind foreign intelligence surveillance."[34] Several other appeals courts have employed a similar logic, and no others have taken a different view.[35]

Warrantless surveillance to protect national security is fully consistent with the Supreme Court's recent approach to the Fourth

Amendment. Not all searches require a warrant. Rather, the Court found in a 1995 case upholding random drug testing of high school athletes that "as the text of the Fourth Amendment indicates, the ultimate measure of the constitutionality of a governmental search is 'reasonableness.'"[36] When a passenger enters an airport, government employees search his belongings and subject him to an X-ray—undoubtedly a search—without a warrant. When American travelers reenter the country, customs and immigration officials can search their baggage and sometimes their person. They do not need to run to a judge each time. When law enforcement undertakes a search to discover evidence of criminal wrongdoing, reasonableness generally requires a judicial warrant. But when the government's conduct is not focused on law enforcement, a warrant is unnecessary. A warrantless search can be constitutional, the Court has said, "when special needs, beyond the normal need for law enforcement, make the warrant and probable-cause requirement impracticable."[37]

A search must be "reasonable" under the circumstances. What does "reasonable" mean? The Court has upheld warrantless searches to reduce deaths on the nation's highways, maintain safety among railway workers, and ensure that government officials are not using drugs.[38] In these cases, the "importance of the governmental interests" outweighed the "nature and quality of the intrusion on the individual's Fourth Amendment interests."[39] It is hard to imagine that any of these situations are more important than protecting the nation from a direct foreign attack in wartime. "It is 'obvious and unarguable,'" the Supreme Court has observed several times, "that no governmental interest is more compelling than the security of the Nation."[40] The extraordinary circumstances of war require that the government seek specific information relevant to possible attacks on Americans, sometimes in situations where a warrant is not practical.[41]

Before the 9/11 attacks, the Supreme Court observed that the Fourth Amendment's warrant requirement would probably not apply to the special circumstances created by a potential terrorist attack. "[T]he Fourth Amendment would almost certainly permit an appropriately tailored roadblock set up to thwart an imminent terrorist attack or to catch a dangerous criminal who is likely to flee by way of a particular route."[42] To be sure, this 2000 case challenged the constitutionality of a highway checkpoint program that searched cars for illegal drugs, rather than for terrorists. And in this case the Court found that the checkpoints violated the Fourth Amendment because the police were searching for drugs for the purpose of "crime control" and "the ordinary enterprise of investigating crimes."[43] But the Court was still telling us that some warrantless searches were acceptable in the emergency situation of a possible terrorist attack, in which the "need for such measures to ensure public safety can be particularly acute."[44]

FISA offers the executive branch a deal: If you go through the process of obtaining a FISA warrant, other courts will likely agree that the search was reasonable and will admit its fruits as evidence in a criminal case. FISA does not *create* the power to authorize national security searches. Rather, it describes a safe harbor by which searches that obtain a warrant will be deemed reasonable under the Fourth Amendment. If a President proceeds with a search under his own authority rather than under FISA or under ordinary criminal procedure, he takes his chances. A court might refuse to admit evidence that had been obtained without a warrant, or even allow the target to sue the government for damages.[45] Then again, it might not. Strict civil libertarians don't see it this way. To them, FISA limits the President's power to conduct war—even one that occurs on American soil—by requiring that any electronic surveillance conducted in the United States must be authorized by Congress.

Many members of Congress agreed that the Wall needed to come down, even before the botched Moussaoui and Mihdhar leads came to light. They also wanted assurance that more information-sharing than was customary in the past would meet constitutional standards. I worked closely with Jennifer Newstead, the chief deputy in the Office of Legal Policy and the day-to-day manager of the Patriot Act in Congress. I had first met her when she'd interviewed for her clerkship with Judge Silberman as a second-year Yale law student. She went on to clerk for Justice Stephen Breyer and would later work in the White House counsel's office and become general counsel of the Office of Management and Budget. She was a quick study and an effective advocate—she went from zero to sixty on terrorism in the days after 9/11.

Together, we worked on briefing Hill staff on the constitutionality of the Patriot Act. Briefings took place in Senate or House committee hearing rooms, shorn of the cameras, bright lights, and gaggle of press. I stood in the middle of the room, described the proposed Patriot Act change to the FISA standards, and took questions. Congressional staff would spread out all over the hearing room, with the senior staff stationed where the public audience usually sat during hearings, and the interns often amusing themselves by leaning far back in the Senators' deep leather seats. Without the need to perform for the media, congressional staff of both parties asked reasonable and thoughtful questions, and we held detailed discussions about the Fourth Amendment, warrantless searches, and the President's wartime powers.

I also spoke with Senator Orrin Hatch, then the ranking minority member of the Senate Judiciary Committee and my old boss when I had served as general counsel of the committee in 1995–96. Tall, always elegantly dressed, and vigorous, Hatch commanded great loyalty and affection from his staff, present and former, including me. He always joked that he "couldn't believe I had given up a real job," by which he meant working for him, so I "could spend my time only teaching a few hours a week and taking it easy." He wanted to hear from me, in person, that the Patriot Act was constitutional. We were at a public event together, and Hatch asked me to sit with him in the back of a black Lincoln Town Car while he was driven around Washington, D.C. He asked me a series of careful questions about the constitutional issues raised by the Patriot Act as we drove by monuments and government office buildings. No one was tougher on terrorists than Hatch, but he wanted to make sure everything was legal. The Patriot Act's passage was never in doubt; everyone at the Justice Department knew that Senator Hatch would get the legislation through, and he did—another accomplishment in a long and distinguished career.

Congress was only the first hurdle in our effort to create more information-sharing among the agencies. Along with the Reno Justice Department, the FISC judges supported a barrier between law enforcement and intelligence. They would not quietly see their handiwork undone. In the first major set of FISA applications under the Patriot Act, the FISC judges tried to erect an elaborate set of requirements and limitations to replace the Wall. Law enforcement officials could not work with intelligence officers to identify targets for FISA surveillance. Officials in the Justice Department's criminal division couldn't talk about prosecution strategy in any way that might influence decisions about FISA.[46] Every time agents working on FISA met with prosecutors, an attorney from the office that practiced before the FISC had to be present as a "chaperone" to enforce the FISC's rules. While the FISC judges were well-intentioned, this kind of micromanagement disregarded the reasons for the Patriot Act.

After this setback, the Justice Department decided to trigger FISA's appeal procedures for the first time in its history. FISA created a special appellate court composed of three sitting federal judges named by Chief Justice William Rehnquist. Its chief judge was Judge Ralph Guy, who sat on the federal appeals court in Cincinnati; the other two judges were Judge Edward Leavy, who sat on the federal appeals court in Oregon, and Judge Silberman. All three had been appointed to the bench by President Reagan and were at "senior" status, which meant that they no longer carried a full caseload on their own courts. I was worried. The case before these judges was to be argued by two capable career civil servants. They might be no match for these judges. The close statutory arguments they had urged on the FISC judges had failed. I knew we would need to argue on broader grounds of presidential power, the Fourth Amendment, and the 9/11 attacks. The Patriot Act would fail or succeed on this single appeal.

In particular, I worried about Judge Silberman, my former boss. Silberman is one of the leading figures in conservative legal circles. A graduate of Dartmouth and Harvard Law School, he had begun his legal career in Hawaii, where he practiced labor law. President Nixon had appointed him solicitor and then the number two official at the Labor

Department. After the "Saturday night massacre" during Watergate, he became DAG in his thirties, when he helped restore a badly battered Justice Department. He advised President Ford on intelligence matters, served as ambassador to Yugoslavia, and advised the Reagan campaign on legal and national security policy. In 1985, President Reagan appointed him to the D.C. Circuit, the second most important court in the nation and the training ground for Supreme Court Justices. Indeed, he had come within a hair of being appointed to the Supreme Court in the late 1980s. Silberman had written a well-known opinion finding the independent counsel law unconstitutional, a decision that was overturned by the Supreme Court but which made him the darling of the conservative legal community. Silberman was one of the few lawyers in Washington who combined a deep knowledge of the theory and practice of intelligence with a top-flight understanding of constitutional law. He had also given me my first job.

Silberman understood well the separation-of-powers and Fourth Amendment issues, and the perverse effects of the Wall. In researching the Patriot Act, I found that he had testified against the original FISA bill as an unconstitutional infringement on the President's national security powers. At the same time, Silberman sometimes displayed a soft side toward criminal defendants, to the point where some of his colleagues on the bench had given him the nickname "Let 'em Loose Larry." He had a fearsome reputation as a questioner—he had caused two attorneys to pass out cold during oral arguments—and I knew from experience that he was unimpressed by civil servants who could not go beyond the statutes at hand.

Ashcroft had asked me to keep a close eye on the case. We both understood that the key to the Patriot Act's ability to stop a future terrorist attack rested with the special FISA appeals court. Even if the Patriot Act allowed our agents to get warrants for business records, or to follow terrorists across jurisdictions and communication devices—in other words, even if we expanded our collection of data—those gains could be lost unless we were permitted to pool information among the intelligence and law enforcement agencies. As long as the Wall stood, we would not be able to connect the dots.

Ashcroft and Thompson asked OLC to help draft the arguments to be presented to the appeals judges, and sent me to ask the solicitor general, Ted Olson, to argue it in person. Thompson understood what was riding on this case.

Olson's participation would signal the importance of the Patriot Act's proper interpretation to the government, and the strength of our disagreement with the FISC. As the "SG," Olson was ultimately responsible not just for the representation of the United States' interests before the Supreme Court, but for all government appeals throughout the country. The SG focuses his efforts primarily on the Supreme Court and rarely appears before a lower court. At the same time, it seemed likely that the Supreme Court would never hear the case, as the FISA appeals court was created specially for this very purpose.

I first witnessed Olson in action as a law student, when I saw him give a talk on the practical implications of the separation of powers, but I did not get to know him until I interviewed for a job with his law firm. I never went to work for him, but my excuse was an offer to teach at his alma mater, the University of California at Berkeley. He was amused that I, a conservative, should go off to teach in the People's Republic of Berkeley, while he had managed to escape to the more "normal" world of Washington, D.C. Olson had served as head of OLC in the first Reagan administration, where he had been unjustly pursued by an independent counsel for advising other officials to assert executive privilege against congressional investigators. Rather than plea-bargain, Olson fought his case all the way to the Supreme Court and challenged the constitutionality of the independent counsel law itself. He won before the D.C. Circuit panel led by Silberman, lost 7–1 in the Supreme Court, but ultimately was vindicated when the independent counsel dropped the case. After that, Olson became one of the biggest stars in the Washington legal community. In 2000, he argued and won *Bush v. Gore* before the Supreme Court. This won him the permanent ire of the left, which bitterly tried, and failed, to block his confirmation as SG.

Olson would do everything he could to help the government prevail in the war against al Qaeda. His wife, Barbara Olson, had been killed on the plane that had crashed into the Pentagon on 9/11. I had dinner at their home just a few days before the attack. We had walked around the fields outside their Virginia house, where she and Ted had been married. Barbara was a tough, smart lawyer who had embarked on a career as a political pundit. She stayed in close touch with Washington politics, and we talked about the usual inside-the-Beltway gossip, who was up, who was down, the biggest mistakes, the latest rivalries. Terrorism, al Qaeda, and the Middle East were far from our minds. In the months that followed, I often thought of that conversation and of the friend I lost on 9/11. She had boarded the doomed flight for an appearance on a television show later that day. When I talked with Olson in his office about the case, he immediately understood its importance for the war on terrorism and decided to argue it personally.

While our brief discussed the Fourth Amendment, the President's national security powers, and the changes wrought by the 9/11 attacks, the crux of the argument lay elsewhere. For years, the FISA court had been ordering which parts of the executive branch could communicate with each other, to the point where it was now requiring a chaperone for domestic and foreign intelligence officials to talk about FISA-generated information. To us, the courts were unconstitutionally interfering with the operations of an independent and coordinate branch of government. This insight was the core of our brief to the court, and it blossomed into a second argument: that while FISA imposed a warrant requirement on the executive, it did not, and could not, restrict how the President chose to use that intelligence to protect the nation. He could use the information to take covert or military action to stop an attack, or he could use it to launch a criminal investigation. That was a decision for the President, not the courts, to make.

Olson argued the case on September 9, 2002—just a few months after the FISC's original decision, which is moving at light speed for the federal courts. Olson did this in addition to performing his day job, arguing before the Supreme Court, which would open its term a month later. Only government lawyers were there, because FISA hearings proceed *ex parte*—with one side present only (it makes no sense for the target to appear when the government is presenting classified evidence about his links to a terrorist group). Because of its sensitive nature, the court sat in secret at the top of the Justice Department, a building that security personnel constantly sweep for listening devices. Cell phones, laptops, PDAs, and any other electronic devices were forbidden. Arguments took place in a sparse meeting room, far from the ceremonial grandeur of a courtroom, and equipped with furniture that looked like it came from the 1960s. It was surrounded by security that would be the envy of any bank.

More top government lawyers came to this argument than to hear an oral argument of the Supreme Court. The Justice Department sent not just Olson but Thompson too. The White House sent Addington. I represented OLC, and lawyers from the FBI and other parts of the Justice Department were also in attendance. Because of the case's classified nature, there were, of course, no opposing lawyers, but the ACLU filed a brief with the judges, which they referred to in the oral argument.

The hearing started at 9 A.M. It was unlike any oral argument anyone had ever seen. The Supreme Court usually gives each side thirty minutes, and the courts of appeals usually give only fifteen. These judges peppered Olson nonstop for three hours. Olson stood at a small table only a few feet from them. This gave the argument an informal atmosphere, but also gave Olson little room to hide. He performed magnificently—answering the judges' questions directly, describing the state of the law fairly, while always advancing the best arguments on behalf of the United States. His first few words showed both his focus on the key legal issue and his ability to place it in the context of the 9/11 attacks as perhaps no other lawyer in the nation could have: "Unfortunately and sadly, two days from now the entire nation will pause to reflect on how bad things can be if our Government is not prepared with every lawful tool available to protect our country and our people from the immeasurable toll that international terrorism can inflict, and to remember the three thousand lives that were taken from us that day because the resources that we have been given to protect us from such acts either did not work or were not being used effectively." [47]

Olson said that the very purpose of the Patriot Act was to "prevent this sort of thing from happening again." He pointed out, "our intelligence agencies and law enforcement personnel, the President's principal agencies in the war against terrorism, must be able to work together efficiently and effectively and cooperatively." But they could not because of the FISC. Its decision "is the most formidable, the most inexplicable and the most easily removable obstacle to achieving the goal for effective and efficient gathering of intelligence to protect the people of this country and this country itself from international terrorism."

Olson spoke without notes, almost in a tone of sadness. The FISC and the Justice Department had misread the Act, he said. FISA had not restricted what uses the President could make of intelligence information to protect the country—whether for arrest and prosecution, detention at the borders, or even military action. The Patriot Act had changed FISA's "purpose" standard precisely to correct this misreading.

The judges didn't let Olson play Daniel Webster before the Supreme Court. Judges Leavy and Guy asked if the FISC had the power to impose "minimization" procedures, case by case, to filter out information that had nothing to do with the purpose of the warrant—unrelated conversations with innocent third parties, for example. Olson conceded that it did, but maintained that the FISC had used this limited power to reinstate the Wall.

Silberman pressed Olson repeatedly on whether the Patriot Act's change of the "purpose" standard was constitutional: "Is it your view [that] the Government's motivation, in constitutional terms, . . . [in] seeking criminal prosecution is wholly irrelevant . . . ?" Silberman continued. What if the *only* reason the government sought a FISA warrant against a terrorist was to throw him in jail, not because he posed any future threat? Wouldn't that violate the Fourth Amendment? Wasn't that why the Justice Department had built the Wall, observed it for many years, and never challenged it in court? Olson did not directly answer Silberman's hypothetical. Instead, Olson responded with an analogy to illustrate how the Wall hamstrung the executive branch in its fight against terrorism. Suppose a surgeon and an anesthesiologist could not communicate with each other except through a hospital administrator about a patient on an operating table, he said. "Instead of [an] exchange of information [among] people who are attempting to accomplish a result . . . , we have made it virtually impossible." Olson went on, "In order to connect the dots someone has got to have knowledge of those various different dots." He didn't claim that if the Wall had been torn down in time, the 9/11 attacks would have been stopped, "but we do know, I have no doubt . . . , if one [wanted] to make it difficult for us to detect and prevent another September 11th, [the Wall] is the way I'd go about doing it."

There was no way to tell from the judges' questions which way the court was leaning. We all prepared ourselves for a possible setback. But in just nine weeks, the appeals judges issued a thirty-page opinion agreeing that the Justice Department and the FISC had misinterpreted FISA by erecting the Wall. To stop the threat of terrorism, the court observed, "arresting and prosecuting terrorists, agents of, or spies for a foreign power may well be the best technique to prevent them from successfully continuing their terrorist or espionage activity."[48] The court said that the FISC had no authority to prevent criminal investigators and intelligence agencies from discussing FISA surveillance, and that FISA had not sought to limit the use of foreign intelligence in criminal arrests and prosecutions of foreign spies. The court also found that the FISC had ignored Congress's plain intent in passing the Patriot Act to pull down the Wall, which they believed endangered the safety of the country. "A standard which punishes . . . cooperation," the judges wrote, "could well be thought dangerous to national security."[49]

This didn't mean we could use FISA with impunity: FISA specifically "excludes from the purpose of gaining foreign intelligence information a sole objective of criminal prosecution."[50] Because the government usually doesn't know how it will use the information when it begins surveillance, the court observed, it was unlikely that FISA would be used to evade Fourth Amendment standards in ordinary criminal cases.

The judges also agreed that according to the Constitution a warrant was not required if the search was "reasonable" under the circumstances. The court distinguished between criminal prosecution that seeks to "punish the wrongdoer and to deter other persons in society from embarking on the same course,"[51] and war or counterintelligence, which is "overwhelmingly to stop or frustrate the immediate criminal activity. . . . Punishment of the terrorist or espionage agent is really a secondary objective; indeed, punishment of a terrorist is often a moot point."[52] September 11 was "out of the realm of ordinary crime control."[53] Because this case "may well involve the most serious threat our country faces," the court found, FISA searches were reasonable. It also observed that other courts of appeals had "held that the President did have inherent authority to conduct warrantless searches to obtain foreign intelligence information. . . . We take for granted that the President does have that authority and, assuming that is so, FISA could not encroach on the President's constitutional power."[54]

The Supreme Court refused to hear any appeal, and the FISA appeals court decision continues to govern the operation of FISA and the Patriot Act today. We learned about the opinion the minute the FISA appeals court released it. Much of it bore the personal writing style of Judge Silberman, which I knew well (he was unusual among federal appellate judges for writing the first draft of his own opinions, always in longhand on yellow legal pads). The time and effort that we had put into the case were vindicated, and Ted Olson's reputation as a convincing oral advocate was proven once again. But DOJ lawyers were not in a celebratory mood, as is often imagined when your side wins a case. The demands of the war on terrorism came before any celebrations. We read the opinion carefully so that DOJ could put the Patriot Act changes into effect as soon as possible. It was the most thorough opinion ever issued by a federal court on electronic surveillance in wartime, and lawyers throughout the government studied it for weeks to understand its implications.

The Patriot Act was one step in the evolution of law enforcement practices to address the new international terrorist threat. While critics obsessed on details like libraries, or delayed notification of targets, these were nothing new in the law. Even Democratic senators began to complain that the whining about the Patriot Act had gone overboard. In Judiciary Committee hearings in the summer of 2004, Senator Dianne Feinstein stated: "I have never had a single abuse of the Patriot Act reported to me. My staff e-mailed the ACLU and asked them for instances of actual abuse. They e-mailed back and said they had none." Senator Joe Biden said that "the tide of criticism" being directed against the Act "is both misinformed and overblown."

But it would also be a grave mistake to believe that the Patriot Act represents a great leap forward in our abilities to stop terrorist attacks. Military historians say that generals fight the last war. Politicians and government officials suffer from the same problem. After World War I, the French built a set of fixed defenses, the Maginot Line, to stop any future German invasion. The French generals, trapped in an obsolete paradigm of military strategy, expected World War I–style trench warfare, not the blitzkrieg that came. Today, like the French generals then, we are still working within the paradigms of the last war. FISA and the Patriot Act are our new Maginot Line. Our political leaders should consider new ways of addressing the threats posed by the new kind of enemy we now face.

Previous U.S. national security efforts were directed at nation-states, such as the Soviet Union and, before that, Germany, Italy, and Japan. These nations all fielded armed forces, defended territory, and protected civilian populations. They tried to expand their control over territory by military force or political coercion. But al Qaeda is different. Its attacks are the products of technologies, ideologies, and global dynamics entirely unknown twenty-five years ago. To prevent another attack, we must allow our intelligence agencies to "connect the dots," to gather more data, search more broadly, and pool information among more analysts and agencies. Preventing 9/11s depends on spotting, in advance, patterns and connections in communications, travel, and transfers of funds. Once it was safe to assume there was little need for any domestic surveillance because we no longer faced any serious communist threat; instead, such activities imperiled privacy rights.

Excessive worry about civil liberties prevent us from thinking more aggressively about electronic surveillance. The threat of an out-of-control executive seeking to harass its political enemies is not what looms before us. Legitimate political activities and speech by American citizens are not being suppressed. There is no lack of lawyers to defend any sensitive cases involving Islamist ideologues who are American citizens or resident aliens and are only exercising their free speech rights, as opposed to conspiring with al Qaeda.

This is not to say that we should not have organizations like the ACLU that scrutinize government actions for abuses or excess. The ACLU keeps the government honest, and I have a great deal of respect for its president, Nadine Strossen, and its capable group of lawyers. But many civil libertarians are taking an absolutist position that opposes almost every counterterrorism measure. They believe that any wartime reduction of civil liberties creates a "ratchet" effect that will permanently diminish freedoms in peacetime. Others say that panic will lead government to go "too far." Scandals du jour do sometimes cause unwise legislation, and not just in the security context. But FISA and its interpretation went overboard in the other direction too. Others say that majorities will always abuse increased power to oppress minorities.

These are generalities that American history does not consistently bear out. It is true that civil liberties throughout our history have expanded in peacetime and contracted during emergencies. During the Civil War, the two world wars, and the Cold War, Congress and the President restricted civil liberties, and courts deferred; during peacetime, civil liberties expanded.[55]

But there is no evidence of any ratchet effect.[56] History does not show that wars have reduced American civil liberties, either before or after the war. The Union reduced civil liberties during the Civil War, but it also liberated the slaves and expanded individual rights against the states afterward. FDR interned Japanese-Americans during World War II, but civil liberties surged in the decades after. Wars can lead to social and economic upheavals that expand individual freedom. Wartime governments may moderate discriminatory or exclusionary policies to rally the nation.

Some serious scholars argue that the government consistently over-reacts to crises by oppressing dissenters and infringing on individual rights.[57] Historical precedents provide some support for this argument. During the 1798 Quasi-War with France, the Federalists made criticism of the government a crime. During the Civil War, President Lincoln suspended habeas corpus on his own authority and instituted military courts for the trial of civilians. In World War I, the Wilson administration prosecuted individuals for seditious speech. FDR ordered the internment of more than a hundred thousand loyal Japanese-American citizens. War no doubt expands executive power. But it does so for a reason: War must be won. Hate, opportunism, or greed toward minorities of enemy nations occur outside of wartime as well. Slavery and Jim Crow were the products of peace, not war.

History suggests that government is often ill-prepared for emergencies. Bold reaction to a foreign threat doesn't necessarily bring oppression, and it may generate courage and creativity instead. Commonsense changes in surveillance law earlier might have stopped al Qaeda before they murdered three thousand people. Instead, bureaucrats stuck to procedures like the Wall, which they knew were not working.[58] It took the calamity of 9/11 to overcome bureaucratic inertia and fix problems that had been clear for years.

Is the Bush administration using public fear to consolidate political power? If it is, it has only another two years to go, and new security policies generally last only as long as the emergency. Lincoln's military courts and military justice did not last beyond the Civil War and Reconstruction. FDR's internments ended after World War II. The President and Congress usually give up their emergency powers voluntarily, and if they don't, courts step in. Despite a succession of wars and emergencies since the Civil War, civil liberties in our country have expanded steadily. Recurring wars and foreign threats have not produced a permanent national security state. In the United States, it is just as arguable that wartime policies have preserved the peace and our civil liberties.

Fighting a network like al Qaeda will require more information-gathering at home than in previous wars. Reducing the chances of a

future 9/11 justifies some loss of privacy. Nothing like the infringements of civil liberties in past wars has occurred nor are they likely to
under current law.

Critics have exaggerated the threat to civil liberties. This is not to
say that there have not been nor should not be some constraints on
the executive branch in this war. The government's powers have been
expanded. Privacy has been reduced, though much more by the sheer
march of communications technology than by the Patriot Act. The
question is not whether some imaginary perfect world of civil liberties has been destroyed, because we do not live in that world. Have
security policies gone further than necessary? The Patriot Act is a
modest effort to adapt existing surveillance tools and strategies to an
enemy whose unprecedented methods demand that intelligence be
gathered on some civilian activity.

But we sorely need to continue to modernize our enforcement powers and make them more effective than they now are, if we are to prevent new terrorist attacks.

5

THE NSA
AND
WIRETAPPING

On Friday, December 16, 2005, the *New York Times* revealed to the world one of the government's most closely held secrets in the war on terrorism. It reported that the super-secret National Security Agency had intercepted telephone calls and e-mails traveling into and out of the United States, so long as one of the parties to the communication was suspected of being a member of al Qaeda. Surveillance took place without a FISA warrant. President Bush confirmed the existence of the program the next day.

The *New York Times* reporters identified me as the lawyer in the Justice Department who wrote a classified legal opinion on the NSA's surveillance program. *Times* reporters quoted from an internal memorandum I had allegedly written which said that the government could use "electronic surveillance techniques and equipment that are more powerful and sophisticated than those available to law enforcement agencies in order to intercept telephonic communications and observe the movements of persons but without obtaining warrants for such uses."[1] They reported that I identified constitutional problems with the program, but wrote that after the 9/11 attacks "the government may be justified in taking measures which in less troubled conditions could be seen as infringements of individual liberties." The following week, the *New York Times* ran a front-page profile of me that claimed I had written a secret 2002 memorandum giving legal approval to the administration's once-secret terrorist-surveillance program.[2]

Justice Department officials have prohibited me from responding directly to the accounts in the *New York Times* and in other papers. They say that to discuss any aspect of the program or my involvement could reveal sensitive national security information that has not been publicly confirmed by the government. While this rule makes a great deal of sense, it has the perverse effect of giving leakers an advantage. Government leakers will reveal only selected information that places them or their interests in the best light possible. Even if the media publishes incorrect or misleading reports, those who follow the rules cannot respond because the government is concerned that any confirmation or denial would reveal secret information.

I met with Attorney General John Ashcroft at least once every few months, and sometimes every few weeks or every few days, to discuss classified matters related to the war on terrorism. Before 9/11, I had met Ashcroft only a few times—when I interviewed for my OLC job, when I had discussed an issue with him during the summer of 2001, and at various Justice Department functions. We were probably as different as two people could be. I was a law professor at the most famous liberal university in the country, the University of California at Berkeley. Ashcroft had made his political career attacking liberal holy grails such as abortion. I had spent most of my career working and arguing with professors. Ashcroft seemed wary of intellectuals. Before 9/11, Ashcroft led a prayer meeting in his office every morning. I had never gone. Ashcroft seemed most interested in public testimony, speeches, and the give-and-take of politics in Congress and in the cabinet. I tried to focus on the substantive foreign policy issues that I had studied for years. He usually didn't get my jokes; I didn't laugh at many of his.

I would usually make an appointment with his confidential assistant whenever I needed to discuss a matter. I would walk by three layers of very nice and efficient secretaries, through a large, beautiful, wood-paneled room, used for ceremonies or large meetings, and a small waiting room. Ashcroft preferred meeting next door in a smaller, personal office equipped with several uncomfortable sofas and chairs arranged in a large circle. He liked to sit back in his office chair and, in his gravelly voice, swap jokes and stories with his long-time aides and associates. Ashcroft was an oral learner, and preferred to be briefed in person rather than read long memos. He was not shy about expressing his views, and one rarely left a meeting without knowing what he thought. While meeting with Ashcroft alone reflected the importance of the issues, it also placed me in a difficult position. I could not discuss certain matters with my DOJ superiors, or rely on the collective resources of OLC, which usually assigned several attorneys to work on an opinion. Operational security demanded by the war on terrorism changed some of OLC's standard operating procedures.

When the *New York Times* published the stories on the NSA, a firestorm of controversy broke out. Some Democratic congressmen suggested that President Bush should be impeached for violating federal law and the Constitution, a view shared by several liberal commentators. A group of law professors and the Congressional Research Service separately argued that the President had broken the law by acting outside the federal wiretapping statutes. In March 2006, Senator Russell Feingold even introduced a motion in the Senate to censure President Bush for approving "an illegal program to spy on American citizens on American soil."[3] Feingold called the NSA program "right in the strike zone of the concept of high crimes and misdemeanors," referring to the standard for impeachment. Feingold, it should be added, was the only senator to vote against the Patriot Act in 2001.[4]

Fire rained down not only from the left, but also from the right. Well-known conservative columnist George Will wrote in the *Washington Post* that the Bush administration had created a new danger by arguing that "because the president is commander in chief, he is the 'sole organ for the nation in foreign affairs.'" Will continued: "That non sequitur is refuted by the Constitution's plain language, which empowers Congress to ratify treaties, declare war, fund and regulate military forces, and make laws 'necessary and proper' for the execution of all presidential powers," Will continued. "Those powers do not include deciding that a law—FISA, for example—is somehow exempted from the presidential duty to 'take care that the laws be faithfully executed.'"[5]

Will and other critics fail to understand that the Constitution grants the President the leading role in foreign affairs. The statement that the President is the "sole organ for the nation in foreign affairs" was not manufactured by the Bush administration, but in fact comes from a 1936 Supreme Court case that recognized the President's control over diplomacy and the setting of foreign policy.[6] Congress as a whole does not ratify treaties. The Senate participates in advising and consenting to treaties in its executive capacity (treaties are discussed in the Constitution's Article II, where the presidency is established), but only after the President has negotiated and signed the treaty.[7] The President can even choose not to send a negotiated treaty to the Senate, or refuse to "make" the treaty after the Senate has approved it. The treaty power does not belong to Congress. The Constitution's Necessary and Proper Clause gives Congress the power to implement the other powers of the government. It does not allow Congress to change the separation of powers in its favor by reducing the powers of the President. Finally, the President has the duty to take care that the laws are faithfully executed, but because the Constitution is the highest form of federal law, the President cannot enforce acts of Congress which are unconstitutional. Will seems to believe the Commander-in-Chief Clause is substantively empty, and that its sole function is to execute the war policies of Congress. What Will and other critics neglect is the President's war power.

In the *Wall Street Journal*, Richard Epstein, perhaps the nation's leading libertarian legal scholar, also argued that Congress has the upper hand in setting war policy.[8] He believes that Congress's powers to declare war, to make rules for the regulation of the armed forces, and to fund the military allow it even to prohibit the military from using live ammunition in combat. Epstein does have a broader view than Will of the Commander-in-Chief Clause, which he suggests guarantees civilian control over the military and prevents Congress from issuing orders or evading the chain of command. Epstein writes: "The precise detailed enumeration of powers and responsibilities in Article II just do not confer on the president a roving commission over foreign and military affairs. He is a coordinate player, not a dominant one." At best, he would allow the President to interpret, but not override, Congress's decisions when confronting a new situation such as the 9/11 attacks.

Epstein's nuanced arguments are more rooted in the constitutional text, but they are no more convincing. Americans historically have understood the Commander-in-Chief Clause to be more than just a designation of the President as the top of the military chain of command. The Founders would have understood a commander in chief as having authority over when to resort to military hostilities and how to conduct them. Article II of the Constitution also vests the President with "the executive power," which, in Justice Scalia's words, "does not mean *some of* the executive power, but *all of* the executive power."[9] Political theorists at the time of the framing considered foreign affairs and national security as quintessentially executive in nature, and our Constitution creates an executive branch that can act with unity, speed, and secrecy to carry out those functions effectively.[10] Congress has important powers, such as the power to issue rules to regulate and govern the military, which gives it the sole authority to set the rules of military discipline and order. But the Constitution nowhere vests in Congress any explicit authority to dominate national security policy, nor gives it an outright veto over executive decisions in the area.[11]

More broadly, these critics misunderstand the Constitution's allocation of war-making powers. The Constitution vests in the President the authority and the responsibility to prevent future attacks against the United States, a power reaffirmed by Congress with the Authorization for Use of Military Force in 2001. The Constitution does not create a legalistic process of making war, but rather gives to the President and Congress different powers that they can use in the political process to either cooperate or compete for primacy in policy.[12] To exercise that power effectively, the President must have the ability to engage in electronic surveillance that gathers intelligence on the activities of the enemy.

No one seems to doubt that the information gained from the NSA program has led to the prevention of al Qaeda plots against the United States.[13] According to General Michael Hayden, the new director of the CIA and leader of the NSA during much of the program's existence, "this program has been successful in detecting and preventing attacks inside the United States." When pressed by reporters whether it had succeeded where no other method would have, he said, "I can say unequivocally, all right, that we have got information through this program that would not otherwise have been available."[14] Attorney General Alberto Gonzales informed the press that the NSA program was perhaps the most classified program in the U.S. government, and that it had helped prevent attacks within the United States. The main criticism has not been that it has been ineffective, but that it violates the Constitution and cannot be undertaken, no matter how necessary the program is and how successful it has been.

I.

OLC legal work on the program remains classified. But after the leak of the program's existence, in January 2006, Justice released a forty-two page white paper, which defended its legality and explained the DOJ's legal thinking on warrantless surveillance.[15] I agree with most of the explanation. But the crucial question left unanswered was: Why, as a matter of policy, would the Bush administration operate outside FISA, especially after going to great lengths to pass the Patriot Act?

The Patriot Act made valuable improvements in our intelligence laws, but it still only updates the pre–9/11 law enforcement approach to national security. The Patriot Act assumes that the government already has enough information to believe that a target is the "agent of a foreign power" before it even asks for a warrant—just as in the criminal justice system, the police must have probable cause in order to act on the belief that someone is involved in criminal activity. FISA operates within a framework that assumes that foreign intelligence agents are relatively simple to detect. In the past, they were usually foreign embassy officials working for a hostile nation and the goal was to build as large a file on their activities and contacts as possible. FISA's drafters had in mind, as a typical case, a Soviet KGB agent operating undercover as a diplomat.

Al Qaeda poses a very different challenge. We do not have a list of diplomats to work from, or an embassy to watch. An intelligence search, as Judge Posner has described it, "is a search for a needle in a haystack."[16] Rather than being able to focus on foreign agents who are already known, counterterrorism agencies must search for clues among millions of potentially innocent connections, communications, and links. "The intelligence services," Posner writes, "must cast a wide net with a fine mesh to catch the clues that may enable the next attack to be prevented."[17] Our best information about al Qaeda will be scattered and tough to gather, and our agents need to be able to follow many leads quickly, and to move fast on hunches and educated guesses.

Members of the al Qaeda network can be detected by examining phone and e-mail communications, as well as evidence of joint travel, shared assets, common histories or families, meetings, and so on. As the time for an attack nears, al Qaeda operatives communicate to coordinate plans, move and position assets, and conduct reconnaissance of targets, "chatter" on their network will increase. When our intelligence agents locate or capture an al Qaeda member, they must be able to move quickly on whatever new information they gather to find other operatives. It is more important to chase them down quickly inside the United States than outside. NSA critics want to place bureaucratic impediments precisely where the danger to America is greatest and flexibility is most important.

Take the example of the 9/11 hijackers. Links suggested by commercially available data could have turned up ties between every single one of the al Qaeda plotters and Khalid al Mihdhar and Nawar al Hazmi, the two hijackers known in the summer of 2001 to have been in the country.[18] CIA agents had identified Mihdhar as a likely al Qaeda operative because he was spotted at a meeting in Kuala Lumpur and was mentioned in Middle East intercepts as part of an al Qaeda "cadre." Hazmi too was known as likely to be al Qaeda. They had rented apartments in their own name and were listed in the San Diego phone book. Both Mohammed Atta, the leader of the 9/11 al Qaeda cell, and Marwan al-Shehi, who piloted one of planes into the World Trade Center, had lived there with them. If our intelligence services had been able to immediately track their cell phone calls and e-mail, it is possible that enough of the hijacking team could have been rounded up to avert 9/11. Today our task is much more difficult because we might not have even this slender information in hand when the next al Qaeda plot moves toward execution.

As we have pursued the Afghanistan and Iraq wars, we have captured al Qaeda leaders as well as their laptops, cell phones, financial documents, and other instruments of modern high-tech life. This gave us information on hundreds of e-mail addresses, telephone numbers, bank and credit account numbers, and residential and office addresses used by their network. Our intelligence services must be able to follow these leads as fast as possible, before the network of al Qaeda operatives fades. An e-mail lead can disappear as fast as it takes someone to open a new e-mail account. Our agents need to move even faster.

FISA creates several problems. It requires "probable cause" to believe that someone is an agent of a foreign power before the government can get a warrant to collect phone calls and e-mails. An al Qaeda leader could have a cell phone with a hundred numbers in its memory, ten of which are in the United States and thus require a warrant. Would a FISA judge have found probable cause that the users of those ten numbers were al Qaeda agents? Probably not. Our intelligence agencies would not immediately know who was using those numbers—or, for that matter, e-mail addresses—at the time an al Qaeda leader was captured?

In this high-tech world, FISA imposes slow and cumbersome procedures on our intelligence and law enforcement officers. These laborious checks are based on the assumption that we are looking backward in time at crimes in order to conduct prosecutions, rather than looking forward in order to prevent attacks on the American people. FISA requires a lengthy review process, in which special FBI and DOJ lawyers prepare an extensive package of facts and law to present to the FISA court. The attorney general must personally sign the application, and another high-ranking national security officer, such as the President's national security adviser or the director of the FBI, must certify that the information sought is for foreign intelligence.[19] It takes time and a great deal of work to prepare the warrant applications, which can run a hundred pages long. While there is an emergency procedure that allows the attorney general to approve a wiretap for seventy-two hours without a court order, it can be used only if there is no time to obtain an order from the court and if the attorney general can find that the wiretap satisfies FISA's other requirements.[20] Even within seventy-two hours our leads could go stale.

Blindly following FISA's framework will also hamper efforts to take advantage of what is known as "data mining." Data mining combines powerful computers and advanced algorithms to analyze vast amounts of information for patterns of behavior. In the United States, corporations employ data mining techniques to market products, like credit cards and magazine subscriptions, and to identify likely buyers based on their income level, geographic location, and purchasing and travel histories. Financial companies analyze various patterns of behavior to discover suspicious activity that might suggest someone has stolen a credit card or account number, and airline security uses a simple variant when it identifies passengers for extra security screening—a foreign citizen buying a one-way, full-fare ticket, in cash, on the day of the flight would likely trigger a second look from airline security personnel. Government data mining theoretically could compile information from government, public, and commercial databases to allow investigators to search for patterns of behavior that might correlate with terrorist activity.

Data mining is an innovative counterterrorism tactic to detect and prevent future al Qaeda attacks. Rather than merely hoping that an agent will one day penetrate al Qaeda's inner circles, a dubious possibility, or that we will successfully seal our vast borders from terrorists, data mining would allow us to see patterns of activity that reveal the al Qaeda network before it can attack. Computerized pattern analysis could quickly reveal whether anyone linked to al Qaeda had made large purchases of chemicals or equipment that could be used for explosives or chemical weapons, we could learn whether he had traveled regularly to certain cities, and we could discover where he had stayed and who he had called in those cities.

Civil libertarians complain that almost all transactions of this nature—calling, e-mailing, spending money, traveling—are innocent; we engage in them every day. But that is exactly why al Qaeda has trained its operatives to use these as tools to conceal their plots. Al Qaeda's leaders understand that it is difficult to analyze billions of transactions and interactions every day in order to detect their cells, and they realize that Western societies impose legal obstacles on government access to such information. Civil-libertarian critics don't seem to have noticed that our government already employs modest forms of data mining to track down criminals and terrorists. In response to drug cartels and organized crime, our government has used simple data mining to track and analyze money flows for years. Banks and financial institutions provide records of financial transactions to the Department of the Treasury, which searches for patterns of money laundering activity.[21] While the great majority of the transactions are legal, the information can piece together proof of criminal links after a conspiracy has been stopped, or it can help indicate suspicious activity that demands further investigation. Analyzing money flows has also proven to be an important tool in detecting and breaking up terrorist networks.

Civil libertarian overreaction can be seen in the outcry in the wake of a revelation, in May 2006, that the NSA had sought call information from phone companies without a warrant.[22] Apparently the NSA obtained billing information on millions of phone calls within the United States, the same information used by telephone companies for billing and marketing purposes. According to *USA Today*, the data had been stripped of names and addresses, but still contained the phone numbers of the calls. President Bush addressed the country to say that he had ordered the government to do everything it could to prevent a future attack while also protecting Americans' privacy. "Al Qaeda is our enemy, and we want to know their plans," he said, without confirming the program's existence.[23] Senator Patrick Leahy expressed outrage and suggested that the government was watching every American for terrorist ties. "Are you telling me tens of millions of Americans are involved with al Qaeda?" he railed at a hearing the day after the *USA Today* story.[24] Harold Koh, dean of the Yale Law School, called the disclosure "quite shocking" and said the courts would never have approved it. House Democrats called for a special prosecutor to investigate.

Privacy concerns here are exaggerated. The Supreme Court has found that such information does not receive Fourth Amendment protection because the consumer has already voluntarily turned over the information to a third party.[25] It is not covered by FISA because no electronic interception or surveillance of the calls has occurred. Meanwhile, the data is potentially of enormous use in frustrating al Qaeda plots. If our agents locate the members of an al Qaeda sleeper cell by a U.S. phone number found in a captured al Qaeda leader's cell phone, call pattern analysis could allow NSA to quickly determine the extent of the network and its activities when time is of the essence.

Through all the outrage, critics usually downplayed the limited nature of the data provided—it did not provide the content of the calls, only the billing data, devoid of information that could identify an individual. Critics feverishly prepared to use the confirmation hearings for General Hayden, whom President Bush nominated to head the CIA, as a platform to accuse the government of yet another invasion of privacy. I met Hayden several times in various briefings and discussions after 9/11. A soft-spoken man, he does not fit the popular image of a four-star general. He is a conscientious, careful, and honest officer who cares deeply about protecting the nation from attack but understands that security must be balanced with privacy rights. He does not believe that one interest trumps the other. In meetings, he was a straight shooter, clear and up front about the upsides and downsides of any program or idea. He is easier to imagine as a physics professor than a Patton shouting orders on the battlefield. Of course, his battlefield is the ethereal world of the Internet and instant communication, not France and Germany. Members of the Senate Intelligence Committee, who had earlier been briefed on the program, asked Hayden some tough questions, but recommended him to the Senate, which confirmed him before the month was out. For once, common sense had prevailed.

Another example of civil libertarian overreaction is the ill-fated and ill-named "Total Information Awareness" (TIA) program proposed by the Defense Advanced Research Projects Agency (DARPA) under Admiral John Poindexter, who had resigned from his job as Reagan's national security adviser under the cloud of the Iran-contra affair. TIA proposed the use of supercomputers to data mine both government and commercial databases to spot potential terrorist activity. Civil libertarians, both on the left and the right, engaged in a scare campaign against TIA—representing it as a big brother attempt to spy on Americans without any safeguards—before any significant research on the project had even begun. William Safire in the *New York Times* raised the alarm with the claim that the Defense Department would create "computer dossiers on 300 million Americans" and that Poindexter wanted to "snoop on every public and private act of every American."[26] An outpouring of criticism led Poindexter to resign and Congress to cut off funding for TIA before any research on it, which could have included a full analysis of privacy concerns, had begun.

It seems that critics are mostly interested in blindly limiting the powers of the government, even as it fights a tough war. They seem to think that the American government must be presumed to be acting in bad faith, so all its activities must be treated with the highest possible level of suspicion. Meanwhile, data mining technology and databases are exploding in the private sector. It would be ironic if al Qaeda and private individuals were permitted greater legal access to new data technology than our own government, especially in wartime.

Over reaction and plain scare tactics killed TIA, a potentially valuable tool proposed after 9/11 to counter al Qaeda's offensive within the United States. It made little sense to cut off TIA at the research and development stage, out of sheer antigovernment paranoia. There was no chance to see what computer technology could even do, no discussion of whether adequate safeguards for privacy could be installed, and no opportunity to evaluate whether data mining would yield leads on terrorist activity that would be worth any costs to privacy.

Perhaps worst of all, we could never explore the ways that data mining be used to *protect* privacy. Data mining scan many perfectly innocent transactions and activities, but this in itself does not make the search illegal. Even searches of homes and businesses or wiretaps with warrants will encounter many items or communications that are not linked to criminal activity. The understandable concern is that data mining will scrutinize much innocent activity, unless controlled in some way by a warrant requirement. But if computers perform the primary scanning, privacy might not be implicated because no human eyes would ever have seen the data. Only when the computer programs highlight individuals who fit parameters that reasonably suggest further study for terrorist links—say a young man who has traveled to Pakistan several times, has taken flight lessons in the United States, and has received large deposits of cash wired into his account from abroad—would a human intelligence officer view the records. At this point, it is important to emphasize, no one is guilty of anything—all that might be done at this point is to seek more information, deploy more resources, or seek a warrant. It would be foolhardy to prevent our intelligence and law enforcement officers from studying patterns of private behavior to stop future attacks. Police routinely rely on the study of patterns to try to predict future crimes. Police will study the "m.o." of past crimes, or patterns of criminal activity in certain neighborhoods at different times.[27]

This underscores the real problem with FISA, and even the Patriot Act. They depend upon individualized suspicion—searches and wiretaps must target a specific individual already believed to be involved in criminal activity. But catching al Qaeda members who have no previous criminal record in the United States, and who are undeterred by the possibility of criminal sanctions, requires more than that. We have to devote surveillance resources where there is a reasonable chance that terrorists will appear, or communicate, even if we do not know their specific identities. What if we knew that there was a 50 percent chance that terrorists would use a certain communications pipeline, like e-mail accounts on a popular Pakistani service, but that most of the communications on that channel would not be linked to terrorism? A FISA-based approach would prevent computers from searching through that channel for the keywords or names that might suggest terrorist communications, because we would have no specific al Qaeda suspects, and thus no probable cause. Rather than individualized suspicion, searching for terrorists will depend on playing the probabilities, just as roadblocks or airport screenings do. The private owner of a Web site has detailed access to that information every day to exploit for his own commercial purposes, such as selling lists of names to spammers, or gathering market data on individuals or groups. Is the government's effort to find violent terrorists a less legitimate use of such data?

Individualized suspicion dictates the focus of law enforcement, but war demands that our armed forces defend the country with a broader perspective. Armies do not meet a probable cause requirement when they attack a position or fire on enemy troops or intercept enemy communications. The criminal justice system seeks to hold a specific person responsible for a discrete crime that has already happened. Individualized suspicion does not make sense when the purpose of intelligence is to take action, such as killing or capturing members of the enemy, to prevent future harm to the nation from a foreign threat.

FISA should be regarded as a safe harbor that allows the fruits of an authorized search to be used for prosecution. It sacrifices speed and breadth of search, but it provides a path for using evidence in a civilian criminal prosecution. If the President chooses to rely on his constitutional authority alone to conduct warrantless searches, then he should use the information only for military purposes. As General Hayden has said, the primary objective of the NSA program is to "detect and prevent" possible al Qaeda attacks on the United States, whether a repeat of September 11; or a bomb in an apartment building, on a bridge, or at an airport; or a nuclear, biological, or chemical attack.[28] These are not hypotheticals; they are all al Qaeda plots, some of which our intelligence and law enforcement agencies have already stopped. The price to pay for using the NSA to stop such plans may be to lose the chance for a future criminal prosecution.

This gives the President the choice of using the best method to protect the United States, whether through the military or by relying on law enforcement. It also means warrantless surveillance will not be introduced into the criminal justice system, a distinction that the judiciary would have to enforce. President Bush could go some way toward alleviating concern about the NSA program by publicly declaring that no evidence from it would ever be used in any criminal case.

Gathering intelligence has long been understood as a legitimate aspect of conducting war; indeed it is critical to the successful use of force. Intercepting enemy communications has always been a central part of these military intelligence options.[29] Our military cannot attack or defend to good effect unless it knows where to aim. America has a long history of conducting intelligence operations to obtain information on the enemy. General Washington used spies extensively during the Revolutionary War, and as President he established a secret fund for spying that existed until the creation of the CIA.[30] President Lincoln personally hired spies during the Civil War, a practice the Supreme Court upheld.[31] In both World Wars I and II, presidents ordered the interception of electronic communications leaving the United States.[32] Some of America's greatest wartime intelligence successes have involved SIGINT—intelligence based on signals—most notably the breaking of Japanese diplomatic and naval codes during World War II, which allowed the U.S. Navy to anticipate the attack on Midway Island.[33] SIGINT is even more important in this war than in those of the last century. Al Qaeda has launched a variety of efforts to attack the United States, and it intends to continue them. The primary way to stop those attacks is to capture al Qaeda operatives who have infiltrated the United States. One of the best ways to find them is to intercept their electronic communications entering or leaving the country.

As commander in chief, the President has the constitutional power and the responsibility to wage war in response to a direct attack against the United States. In the Civil War, President Lincoln undertook several actions—raised an army, withdrew money from the treasury, launched a blockade—on his own authority in response to the Confederate attack on Fort Sumter, moves that Congress and the Supreme Court later approved.[34] During World War II, the Supreme Court similarly recognized that once war began, the President's authority as commander in chief and chief executive gave him the tools necessary to effectively fight it.[35]

Even legal scholars who argue against this historical practice concede that once the United States has been attacked, the President can respond with force on his own.[36] It is inconceivable that the Constitution would vest in the President the power of commander in chief and chief executive, give him the responsibility to protect the nation from attack, but then disable him from gathering intelligence to use the military most effectively to defeat the enemy. As the Supreme Court declared after World War II, "This grant of war power includes all that is necessary and proper for carrying these powers into execution."[37] Covert intelligence is clearly part of this authority.[38] Several Supreme Court cases have recognized that the President's role as commander in chief and the sole organ of the nation in its foreign relations must include the power to collect intelligence.[39] Intelligence rests with the President because the office's structure allows it to act with unity, secrecy, and speed.

Presidents have long ordered electronic surveillance without any judicial or congressional participation. More than a year before the Pearl Harbor attacks, but with war with the Axis powers clearly looming, President Franklin Roosevelt authorized the FBI to intercept any communications, whether wholly inside the country or international, of persons "suspected of subversive activities against the Government of the United States, including suspected spies."[40] FDR was concerned that "fifth columns" could wreak havoc with the war effort. "It is too late to do anything about it after sabotage, assassinations and 'fifth column' activities are completed," FDR wrote in his order. FDR ordered the surveillance even though a Supreme Court decision and a federal statute at the time prohibited electronic surveillance without a warrant.[41] FDR continued to authorize the interception of electronic communications even after Congress rejected proposals for wiretapping for national security reasons.[42]

Until FISA, presidents continued to monitor the communications of national security threats on their own authority, even in peacetime.[43] If presidents in time of peace can order surveillance of spies and terrorists, executive authority is only the greater now in wartime. This is a view that Justice Departments have not only held under President Bush. The Clinton Justice Department held a similar view of the executive branch's authority to conduct surveillance outside the FISA framework.[44]

Since World War II, courts have never opposed a President's authority to engage in warrantless electronic surveillance to protect national security. When the Supreme Court first considered this question in 1972, it held that the Fourth Amendment required a judicial warrant if a President wanted to conduct surveillance of a purely domestic group, but it refused to address surveillance of foreign threats to national security.[45] In the years since, every federal appeals court to address the question, including the FISA Appeals Court, has "held that the President did have inherent authority to conduct warrantless searches to obtain foreign intelligence information." The FISA Appeals Court did not even feel that it was worth much discussion. It took the President's power to do so "for granted," and observed that "FISA could not encroach on the President's constitutional power."[46]

Congress also implicitly authorized the President to carry out electronic surveillance to prevent further attacks on the United States in the Authorization for Use of Military Force passed on September 18, 2001. AUMF has no limitation on time or place—only that the President pursue al Qaeda. Although the President did not need, as a constitutional matter, Congress's permission to attack al Qaeda after the attacks on New York City and the Pentagon, its passage shows that the President and Congress fully agreed that military action would be appropriate. Congress's approval of the killing and capture of al Qaeda members must obviously include the tools to locate them in the first place.

Senator Tom Daschle's claim that, as Senate majority leader, he rejected White House suggestions to explicitly include operations taking place on American soil does not ring true.[47] In the first days after 9/11, I joined the lead White House negotiator, Tim Flanigan, at several meetings with congressional leadership staff on the AUMF. The White House, not the Senate Democrats, wrote the first drafts. We met for hours on end, often in a large conference room in the Senate or House leadership offices in the Capitol. We would sit around a very long table so that every leader or representative of every relevant congressional committee, both majority and minority, would have a seat. Flanigan and I, and one or two people from White House legislative affairs, would sometimes be the only ones there from the executive branch. When we sat down to haggle over its substance, staff for Dashle and House Majority Leader Richard Gephardt asked only that the law make clear that it was consistent with the War Powers Resolution. A statement we had included that the President had the constitutional authority to use force to preempt future terrorist attacks (which everyone agreed stated the obvious) was moved to the statute's findings. We agreed to both changes, which struck us as window dressing.

No one in the room claimed the statute would prohibit military action to stop an al Qaeda attack if one occurred within our borders. If anyone had, I would have immediately objected. We would never have accepted a law that tried to limit rather than support the President's constitutional authority to respond to an attack on American soil. Indeed, at that very moment the Air Force was flying combat air patrols over the offices at the Capitol. Would Senator Daschle say the AUMF did not allow the Air Force to shoot down, if necessary, the next United flight 93? Why else were our fighters on patrol at all? The closer al Qaeda is to attack, the fuller the government powers should be. With attacks in motion within the United States, the need for the executive branch to use surveillance and force is at its most compelling. Turning common sense topsy-turvy, civil libertarians want to impose more obstacles where the need to stop al Qaeda becomes the most urgent.

Critics have argued that the NSA's electronic surveillance is illegal because the AUMF did not explicitly mention wiretapping or surveillance.[48] Of course, it does not mention detentions either, which the Supreme Court later upheld under the AUMF, despite a law on the books known as the Anti-Detention Act.[49] Critics essentially argue that Congress must enact a grocery list of specific powers to fight war. For instance, FISA prohibits electronic surveillance within the United States without congressional permission. However, in the AUMF, Congress authorized the President "to use all necessary and appropriate force" against those "he determines" were involved with the 9/11 attacks. The power to use force includes by implication the power to use surveillance and intelligence to find targets. According to the critics, Congress authorized the President to pull the trigger, but also ordered him to wear a blindfold.

Obviously, Congress cannot legislate in anticipation of every circumstance that may arise in the future. That is one of the reasons, along with the executive branch's advantages in speed, expertise, and structural unity, that Congress delegates authority. Those who consider themselves legal progressives generally support the administrative state and vigorously defend important grants of authority from Congress to the agencies of the executive branch. Agencies such as the Federal Communications Commission or the Environmental Protection Agency exercise powers over important sectors of the economy under the broad congressional mandate that they regulate in the "public interest." These agencies make decisions with enormous economic effects, such as which parts of the radio spectrum to sell, or how much pollution to allow into the air, with little explicit guidance or thought from Congress.

Yet, when Congress delegates broad authority to the President to defend the nation from attack, the defenders of the administrative state demand that Congress list every power it wishes to authorize. While the threats to individual liberty may be greater in this setting, it makes little sense to place Congress under a heavier burden to describe every conceivable future contingency that might arise when we are fighting war, perhaps the most unpredictable and certainly most dangerous of human endeavors. Rather, we would expect and want Congress to delegate power to that branch, the presidency, which is best able to act with speed to threats to our national security.[50] War is too difficult to plan for with fixed, antecedent legislative rules, and war also is better run by the executive, which is structurally designed to take quick, decisive action. It does not stand the test of reason to think that Congress intended to give the President the power to detain or kill members of the enemy but not to search for them, especially once they had reached our shores.

II.

Prominent senators, including Patrick Leahy, Edward Kennedy, and Harry Reid, as well as the ACLU, not only claim that the NSA surveillance program violates FISA, they charge that it shows that President Bush thinks he is "above the law."[51] More subtle critics might argue that FISA is comprehensive and makes provision for wartime; therefore the President has no residual powers over domestic surveillance. Even accepting, for the moment, the claim that the NSA program and FISA are in conflict, this does not make the program unconstitutional. Everyone would prefer that the President and Congress agree on war policy; it was one of the reasons the Bush administration sought the AUMF in the first place. Our nation will wage war more effectively if it is unified.

But conflict between the branches of government is commonplace in our history. The President and Congress have pursued conflicting war policies in many wars. Congress passed the Neutrality Acts before World War II in a largely futile effort to restrain FDR from assisting the Allies. Vietnam and Kosovo are most recent examples of wars in which Congress tried to frustrate or micromanage executive war policy.

The Constitution not only anticipated this struggle, it was written to ensure it. It does not give the President or the Congress complete control over war, foreign policy, and national security, but instead gives each branch different powers that they can use to cooperate or fight with one another. The President is the commander in chief and chief executive, while Congress has the power over funding, legislation, the creation and discipline of the military, and the power to "declare war." National security is dramatically unlike other government powers, such as passing a statute, appointing a judge, or making a treaty, where the Constitution sets out a precise, step-by-step process for the roles of the different branches of government. We should not find surprising the ongoing partisan conflict over terrorism policy after 9/11.

Critics of the NSA program appeal to the Constitution as it works in peacetime, when Congress authorizes a policy and the President carries it out. They imagine that the Constitution requires the President to check back with Congress on every strategy and tactic in the war on terrorism. The NSA program is thus illegal, they say, because President Bush neglected to get yet another law approving it. It is true that Congress offers more transparency and perhaps greater accountability to the public. But it should also be clear that, over time, the presidency has gained the leading role in war and national security because of its superior ability to take the initiative in response to emergencies.

War's unpredictability can demand decisive and often secret action. John Locke first observed that a constitution ought to give the foreign affairs power to the executive because foreign threats "are much less capable to be directed by antecedent, standing, positive laws" and the executive can act to protect the "security and interest of the public."[52] Legislatures are too slow and its members too numerous to respond effectively to unforeseen situations. "Many things there are which the law can by no means provide for, and those must necessarily be left to the discretion of him that has the executive power in his hands, to be ordered by him as the public good and advantage shall require."

The Framers of the Constitution well understood this principle. They rejected extreme republicanism, which concentrated power in the legislature, and created an executive with its own independent powers to manage foreign affairs and address emergencies which, almost by definition, cannot be addressed by existing laws. The power to protect the nation, Hamilton wrote in the *Federalist Papers*, "ought to exist without limitation," because "it is impossible to foresee or define the extent and variety of national exigencies, or the correspondent extent & variety of the means which may be necessary to satisfy them."[53] It would be foolhardy to limit the constitutional power to protect the nation from foreign threats. "The circumstances that endanger the safety of nations are infinite; and for this reason no constitutional shackles can wisely be imposed on the power to which the care of it is committed."

The Framers placed these responsibilities in the office of the President because of his ability to act with unity, speed, and secrecy. In the *Federalist Papers*, Hamilton observed that "[d]ecision, activity, secrecy, and dispatch will generally characterise the proceedings of one man, in a much more eminent degree, than the proceedings of any greater number."[54] "Energy in the executive," said Hamilton, "is essential to the protection of the community against foreign attacks."[55] Wartime, that most unpredictable and dangerous of human endeavors, therefore ought to be managed by the President. "Of all the cares or concerns of government, the direction of war most peculiarly demands those qualities which distinguish the exercise of power by a single hand."[56]

If ever there were an emergency that Congress could not prepare for, it was the war brought upon us on 9/11. FISA was a law written with Soviet spies working out of their embassy in Washington, D.C., in mind. No one then anticipated war with an international terrorist organization wielding the destructive power of a nation. President Bush headed the institution of our government best able to respond quickly to the 9/11 attacks and to take measures to defeat al Qaeda's future attacks. While everyone would like the certainty and openness of a congressional act, the success of the NSA surveillance program depends on secrecy and agility, two characteristics Congress as an institution lacks.

But, critics respond, Congress foresaw that war might increase demands for domestic wiretapping, and still prohibited the President from using electronic surveillance without its permission. Why shouldn't Congress's view here, as in any other domestic question, prevail? Because the Constitution is the supreme law of the land, neither an act of Congress nor an act of the President can supersede it. If Congress passes an unconstitutional act, such as a law ordering the imprisonment of those who criticize the government, the President must give force to the higher law, that of the Constitution. Jefferson took just that position on the 1798 Alien and Sedition Acts. He wrote that he, "believing the law to be unconstitutional, was bound to remit the execution of it, because that power has been confided to him by the constitution."[57] That does not mean that the President "is above the law," it only means that the Constitution is above the Congress, and the President.

If the critics were right, and presidents are duty-bound to obey any and all acts of Congress, even those involving the commander-in-chief power, Congress could have ordered FDR to cancel an amphibious landing in France in World War II, Truman to attack China over the Korean War, or JFK to invade Cuba in 1962. But presidents such as Jefferson, Jackson, Lincoln, and FDR believed that they had the right to take action, within their own constitutional authorities, according to their interpretation of the Constitution, especially in their role as commander in chief.

Decades of American constitutional practice reject the notion of an omnipotent Congress. While Congress has the sole power to declare war, neither presidents nor congresses have acted under the belief that a declaration of war must come before the undertaking of military hostilities abroad. Our nation has used force abroad more than a hundred times, but has declared war only five times: the War of 1812, the Mexican-American and Spanish-American Wars, and World Wars I and II. Without declarations of war or any other congressional authorization, presidents have sent troops to oppose the Russian Revolution, intervene in Mexico, fight Chinese Communists in Korea, remove Manuel Noriega from power in Panama, and prevent human rights disasters in the Balkans. Other conflicts, such as both Persian Gulf Wars, received "authorization" from Congress but not declarations of war.[58]

Both the President and Congress generally agree that the legislature should not interfere in the executive branch's war decisions. Congress's powers ought to be at their height at the decision to start a war, before troops have been committed and treasure or blood spent. In the Nixon-era War Powers Resolution, Congress attempted to prevent presidents from using force abroad by prohibiting the insertion of troops into hostile environments abroad for more than sixty days without legislative approval. Both sides of the war powers debate today agree that the Resolution has been a dead letter and has not prevented presidents from going to war.[59] Presidents and congresses alike have realized that the War Powers Resolution made little practical sense, and instead represented congressional overreaching into presidential expertise and constitutional authority in foreign affairs.

Presidential leadership has always included control over the goals and means of military campaigns. As the Supreme Court has observed, the President has the authority to "employ the armed forces in the manner he may deem most effectual to harass and conquer and subdue the enemy."[60] President Lincoln did not seek a law from Congress over whether to defend Washington, D.C.; President Roosevelt did not ask Congress whether he should make the war in Europe a priority over the war in the Pacific; President Truman did not seek legislative permission to drop nuclear bombs on Japan. Many of the wars fought since World War II, ranging from Korea to Panama to Kosovo, never received any congressional authorization. Obviously presidents should not ignore congressional leaders. A wise President will consult with them at the right time. But the Constitution does not force the President to get a letter from Congress every time he makes an important decision about wartime strategy or tactics.

Nor is Congress defenseless. It has ample powers to block wartime initiatives. It has total control over funding and the size and equipment of the military. If it does not like a war or a strategy, it can cut off funds, reduce the size of units, or refuse to provide weapons. War would be impossible without Congress's cooperation, or at least acquiescence. This is even more so the case in the age of modern warfare, which requires expensive material, high-technology weapons systems, and massive armed forces dependent upon constant congressional budgetary support.

Critics claim that Congress ought to have the upper hand in war in order to prevent military adventurism, to check war fever, and to guarantee political consensus. This sounds plausible, but it neglects the benefits of executive action during times of foreign threat. When Europe plunged into war, Congress enacted a series of Neutrality Acts designed to keep the United States out of the conflict. In 1940 and 1941, FDR recognized that America's security would be threatened by German control of Europe, and he and his advisers gradually attempted to bring the United States to the assistance of Great Britain and the Soviet Union.[61] FDR stretched his authority to cooperate closely with Great Britain to protect convoys in the North Atlantic and provide the British with "obsolete" destroyers, among other things. American pressure on Japan to withdraw from China helped trigger the Pacific War, without which American entry into World War II might have been delayed by at least another year, if not longer.[62]

The Cold War is another example where consistent presidential leadership promoted our national security. Through their proxies, and often in secret, the United States and the communist bloc fought throughout the world. Congress only authorized the Vietnam War; America and its allies fought Soviet proxies in Korea, Vietnam, and Nicaragua, the Soviet Union fought against American-backed forces in Afghanistan, and the two very nearly came into direct conflict during the Cuban Missile Crisis. Generally, we prevailed through the steady presidential application of the strategy of containment, supported by congressional funding of the necessary military forces, but not through congressional decisions on when and where to wage war.[63]

Critics also ignore that Congress's independent judgment can be flawed on national security matters. Congress led us into two "bad" wars, the 1798 Quasi-War with France and the War of 1812. And Congress does not always bring consensus. The Vietnam War, one of the wars initially supported by Congress, did not meet with a consensus over the long term but instead provoked some of the most divisive politics in American history. It is also difficult to claim that the congressional authorizations to use force in Iraq, either in 1991 or 2002, reflected a deep consensus over the merits of those wars. Indeed, the 1991 authorization barely survived the Senate, and the 2002 authorization received significant negative votes and has become a deeply divisive issue in national politics.

Legislative deliberation can breed consensus in the best of cases, but it also can stand in the way of speed and decisiveness. Terrorist attacks are more difficult to detect and prevent than those posed by conventional armed forces and nations, and WMDs allow the infliction of devastation that once could have been achievable only by a nation-state. To defend itself, the United States may have to use force earlier and more often than at a time when nations generated the primary threats. In order to forestall a WMD attack, or to take advantage of a window of opportunity to strike at a terrorist cell, the President needs flexibility to act quickly. By acting earlier, perhaps before WMD components have been fully assembled or before an al Qaeda operative has left for the United States, the executive branch must be able to engage in a limited, precisely targeted, use of force.

Most opposition to presidential power in war has focused on the decision to start conflicts, not how to fight them. As a law professor, I have argued against the common academic view that only Congress can decide when to start a war. But as a government official, I worked to make sure this question was a moot point. By obtaining the AUMF, we wanted to make sure there could be no claim in the future that the President was acting in the war on terrorism without congressional support. That is why we wrote the law as broadly as we did, to permit the use of necessary and appropriate force against anyone connected with the 9/11 attacks. It was meant to run as broadly as the President's constitutional power to exercise full control over the waging of war.

Critics of the NSA program want to overturn American historical practice in favor of a new and untested theory about the wartime powers of the President and Congress. Our intelligence and military will have difficulty fostering innovation and creativity—and the NSA program is precisely that—if we reject decades of constitutional practice in the middle of a war. For too long, our system retarded aggressive measures to preempt terrorist attacks. But seeking to give Congress the dominant hand in setting wartime policy would render our tactics against al Qaeda less rather than more effective. It would slow down decisions, make sensitive policies and intelligence public, and encourage risk aversion rather than risk taking. It ignores the reality of the al Qaeda challenge to require the President to seek, every time he wants to make an important policy change, congressional permission first.

Claims that the NSA program violates the Constitution appeal, I think, to an entirely different concern, not one about law but about politics. It expresses the worry that if the President is waging a war, and this war has crept into the United States itself, we will centralize too much power in the President over our domestic affairs. The NSA program, however, does not signal that we live under a dictator, nor that the separation of powers has failed, the exaggerated claims of civil libertarians notwithstanding.

Instead, the other branches of government have powerful and important tools to limit the President should his efforts to defeat terrorism slip into domestic oppression. Congress has total control over funding and significant powers of oversight.[64] It could do away with the NSA as a whole. The Constitution does not require that Congress create an NSA or any intelligence agency. It need not engage in anything as drastic as doing away with the NSA, of course. Congress could easily eliminate the surveillance program itself simply by cutting off all funds for it. It could also link approval of administration policies in related areas to agreement on changes to the NSA program. Congress could refuse to confirm cabinet members, subcabinet members, or military intelligence officers unless it prevails over the NSA. It could hold extensive hearings that bring to light the NSA's operations and require NSA officials to appear and be held to account. It could even enact a civil cause of action that would allow those who have been wiretapped by the NSA to sue for damages, with the funds coming out of the NSA's budget. So far, Congress has not taken any of these steps, and instead confirmed General Hayden to head the CIA. Congressional silence does not represent opposition to the President's terrorism policies.[65]

Courts can exercise their own check on presidential power, although one that is not as comprehensive as Congress's. Any effort to prosecute an al Qaeda member or a terrorism suspect within the United States will require the cooperation of the federal courts. If federal judges believe that the NSA's activities are unconstitutional, they can refuse to admit any information discovered by warrantless surveillance. The NSA's activities should remain limited to supporting military and intelligence operations, in order to prevent a direct attack, rather than support law enforcement.

The President can structure the NSA program to enhance public confidence that its fruits will not be used for political or law enforcement goals. While he has the constitutional authority to carry out searches in secret, it may be to the nation's advantage for the President to create a consultation process among the relevant cabinet officials, and then between the executive and legislative branches. This would give the public more confidence that the NSA was not being used to carry out political vendettas. By his own account, President Bush had already put into place an early version of this before the public outcry: Each time he approved the NSA program, he asked the cabinet officers responsible for defense and intelligence whether they believed it was necessary, and he submitted the operation to the review of White House and Justice Department lawyers. An expanded version of this could mirror, or simply adopt, the National Security Council structure, but without the legions of staff. The NSC already includes the vice president, the national security adviser, the secretaries of state and defense, and the head of the intelligence community, among others, and it is responsible for approving all covert actions before they are sent to the President for approval. Operation of the NSA program could come under the NSC's purview, although perhaps with restrictions on staff involvement to prevent leaks of sensitive information.

Presidents could also reach out to Congress along the lines of the current system for covert action. Under the NSA, the executive branch notifies the House and Senate intelligence committees of presidentially approved covert actions. These committees have strong relationships with the intelligence community and hold extensive, classified oversight hearings on the nation's covert action programs and other classified intelligence operations. Again, the Bush administration made initial steps toward such a system with the NSA program by briefing selected congressional leaders. To improve public confidence in electronic surveillance of al Qaeda communications with individuals in the United States, intelligence officials could provide routine briefings to an expanded group of House and Senate leaders on the extent of NSA surveillance, its particular targets, and what value it has produced. The group would have to be kept small, and probably would have to exclude staff, to prevent crucial secrets from leaking, an endemic problem in Washington and one that is especially dangerous in war.

The Constitution creates a presidency whose function is to act forcefully and independently to repel serious threats to the nation. Instead of specifying a legalistic process to begin war, the Framers wisely created a fluid political process in which legislators would use their funding, legislative, and political power to balance presidential initiative. As we confront terrorists, potentially armed with weapons of mass destruction, we should look skeptically at claims that radical changes in the way we make war would solve our problems, even those stemming from poor judgment, unforeseen circumstances, or bad luck. The worst thing we could do when confronted by a capable, shadowy enemy like al Qaeda would be to change our government to make it harder to develop innovative policies like the NSA surveillance program.

6

GUANTANAMO BAY

B efore September 11, and without knowing it, we had already captured our first enemy combatant in the war against al Qaeda: Zacarias Moussaoui. Originally held on immigration violations, Moussaoui was soon discovered to be an al Qaeda operative and charged with federal terrorism crimes. After 9/11 and the invasion of Afghanistan, the capture of other al Qaeda and related fighters followed—John Walker Lindh, Yaser Esam Hamdi, Jose Padilla, and several hundred others were soon brought in by U.S. military forces, the intelligence services, and our Northern Alliance allies. After weeks of discussion between the Defense, State, and Justice Departments, the CIA, and the National Security Council, they were sent to the Naval Station at Guantanamo Bay. There, I witnessed the arrival of the first dozen al Qaeda and Taliban in January 2002. At its peak, Gitmo held almost nine hundred detainees. The Defense Department has since released several hundred to the custody of their own governments. As of this writing roughly four hundred remain.

Even as these detainees arrived, critics of the war on terrorism began to demand that the criminal justice system be used to try al Qaeda and

Taliban prisoners. In the criminal justice world, detention promotes punishment of a criminal, his removal from society, and deterrence of other criminal conduct. But 9/11 ushered in a war. The rules of war permit the capture and detention of the enemy without trial, because the purpose of detention is to remove combatants from action. Critics say that the United States has simply made up the term "enemy combatant." This is untrue. The rules of war have always recognized enemy combatants as those who fight on behalf of the enemy, and warring nations have always been permitted to imprison them. No trial is required because the detainees are not being held as a punishment for a crime; they are held until the end of hostilities, and then released. In the summer of 2004, the Supreme Court recognized this explicitly, when it found that "detention to prevent a combatant's return to the battlefield is a fundamental incident of waging war."[1]

In no earlier American war has our legal system opened the courtroom doors to enemy prisoners. The only exception was for citizens, and only then for the limited purpose of determining that they were in fact in league with the enemy. Hundreds of thousands of enemy prisoners of war were captured in Vietnam, Korea, and World Wars I or II, and their imprisonment was never reviewed by an American court. Imagine the chaos if lawyers descended en masse, demanding that evidence against enemy detainees be preserved under a rigorous chain of custody and that officers and soldiers be cross-examined about their battlefield decisions.

Human rights lawyers, law professors, and activists who oppose the war on terror nevertheless have filed many lawsuits. They argue variously that the United States is not really at war, that captured terrorists ought to be charged and be given American court hearings, and if not, that the law requires their release. They seek a return to the exclusive use of the criminal justice system to fight terrorism, as was the practice on September 10, 2001. In a sign of the pervasive power of the judiciary in our nation, these contentions have in the past few years been litigated all the way to the Supreme Court.

The very fact that such lawsuits arrived at the Supreme Court's doorstep was read by some as a defeat for the Bush administration's view that the war on terror was actually a war. Administration policies were indeed checked in two Supreme Court cases. In *Rasul v. Bush*, for the first time in history, the federal courts reviewed the grounds for detaining alien enemy combatants held not only inside but outside the United States.[2] In *Hamdi v. Rumsfeld*, the Court required that American citizens captured abroad must have access to a lawyer and a fair hearing before a neutral judge.[3]

This was an unprecedented insertion of the federal courts into military affairs, overruling a Supreme Court precedent on the exact point dating from the end of World War II.[4] But these rulings also confirmed as a matter of law that the war against the al Qaeda terrorist network and the Taliban militia was indeed a war, that it was authorized by Congress, and that it was not solely a criminal justice matter. These rulings in fact left the executive branch with great flexibility. The pleas of administration opponents were not granted and the justices had not turned back the clock. Rather the Court recognized implicitly that the United States can use all of the tools of war to fight this new kind of enemy.

But the Court did assert its power rather than defer entirely to the military and the President on the question of due process for enemy combatants. It did not declare such wartime military decisions to require deference to the President and Congress, as, quite frankly, I would have preferred.

Can the judiciary make good factual and legal judgments in the middle of war? I believe this assertion of power takes courts far beyond their normal areas of expertise and risks conflict with the President and Congress. And indeed both branches would soon partially reverse the Court for pushing into matters where it didn't belong.

In the war against al Qaeda, the United States has captured enemies that fall into several categories. In previous wars, such as World War II, the enemy was defined by citizenship; the enemy was Germany, Italy, and Japan. But al Qaeda is stateless. Our enemies don't wear uniforms, and they are not defined by national identity. Al Qaeda's members are citizens of countries with which we are at peace, including citizens of the United States itself and its allies, such as Saudi

Arabia and Pakistan. Thus they are harder to detect. Al Qaeda's state-lessness necessarily means that there will be more uncertainty around detentions, as nationality alone cannot determine enemy status. There must be enough information to know that the individual has acted *in association with* al Qaeda to detain him as an enemy combatant.

Enemy combatants so far have fallen into four types: aliens captured and held outside the United States, such as al Qaeda and Taliban fighters caught in operations abroad; U.S. citizens who are associated with al Qaeda or the Taliban, captured abroad; aliens detained within the United States; and U.S. citizens and permanent resident aliens detained in the United States. The first category includes detainees currently held at the naval base in Guantanamo Bay, Cuba, none of whom are U.S. citizens or resident aliens. John Walker Lindh, an American citizen from the San Francisco Bay Area who was captured in Afghanistan while fighting with the Taliban, and Yaser Esam Hamdi, a Saudi Arabian citizen born in Louisiana and also captured in Afghanistan with the Taliban, fall into the second category. The third category includes Moussaoui, a French citizen convicted of plotting additional 9/11–related terrorist killings. In the fourth category is Jose Padilla, an American citizen who had met with al Qaeda leaders and was captured for attempting to enter Chicago from abroad to explode a radioactive dirty bomb.

Unlike enemies in most previous American wars, al Qaeda is multi-national and its reach is global. We fight everywhere. But enemy captures on U.S. soil are hardly unknown. In the Civil War, every enemy combatant was an American citizen. In World War II, some Americans joined the German, Italian, or Japanese armies. When detained, they were not afforded any rights under the American criminal justice system, but instead were treated as enemy combatants. They were never tried for a crime, but were held until World War II had ended.

So why was John Walker Lindh tried? Lindh, a convert to Islam, journeyed in May 2001 to Pakistan to attend a military training camp run by Harakat ul-Mujahideen, an Islamic terrorist group.[5] He trained in jihad and the use of weapons, and soon expressed a wish to fight with the Taliban against the Northern Alliance in Afghanistan. In June 2001 he arrived at al Farouq training camp outside Kandahar, Afghanistan, a central al Qaeda hub, the same camp that housed several members of the Buffalo cell as well as David Hicks, an Australian now held at Guantanamo Bay. Lindh recieved advance arms and explosives training, as well as training in orienteering, navigation, and battlefield combat. On one of three visits to the camp, bin Laden personally spoke with Lindh for about five minutes. Lindh was asked to participate in operations in the United States, Europe, or Israel, but he reiterated his desire to fight in Afghanistan.

Armed with AK-47s, he and 150 compatriots reached the front line with the Northern Alliance shortly before September 11. In November, he retreated with his unit to Kunduz, where he surrendered to the Northern Alliance. On November 24, he was transported to the prison near Mazar-e-Sharif, where he was interviewed by CIA agent Johnny Micheal Spann but refused to say anything. The next day, several prisoners overpowered their guards and killed Spann. Lindh was shot in the melee. After a week, the prisoners surrendered; Lindh was taken into custody and sent to a medical base for treatment. He was interrogated by the military and the FBI in Afghanistan, where he waived his Miranda rights and was flown to the United States for trial.

Lindh's status as an American citizen, and the circumstances of his capture less than three months after the 9/11 attacks, made him the first enemy combatant of the war who received sustained attention at high levels of the government. He was clearly an enemy combatant, detained under the rules of war along with other enemy forces. But there was never any doubt that the Justice Department would take custody of Lindh and conduct a criminal trial. Attorney General Ashcroft believed it important to show that the criminal justice system could still serve an important function in trying terrorists. Neither the Defense Department nor the intelligence agencies protested. They agreed that an American who had joined to fight on the side of the Taliban and al Qaeda, but did not appear to pose an ongoing threat, would be better handled through trial. Deciding to send Lindh to a criminal trial underscored that war and the criminal justice system are not mutually exclusive. Which system to use depends on context and is not prescribed by law.

Lindh's attorneys argued that combatants in the Afghanistan war should be covered by the Geneva Conventions, which would have ruled out criminal sentences such as the death penalty. The trial judge rejected the claim on the grounds that neither al Qaeda nor the Taliban were combatants entitled to POW status.[6] This ruling confirmed the legal position the Bush administration adopted in January 2002 that Geneva did not apply to al Qaeda or to its allies, the Taliban, who were at best outlaw warlords in Afghanistan.

Lindh could not be tried in a military commission because President Bush had reserved its use only for enemy aliens. As an American citizen Lindh had clearly violated federal laws prohibiting the provision of "material support and resources" to terrorist groups, the federal prosecutor's central tool in domestic antiterror cases after 9/11. Material support includes providing "any property, tangible or intangible, or service, including currency or monetary instruments or financial securities, financial services, lodging, training, expert advice or assistance, safehouses, false documentation or identification, communications equipment, facilities, weapons, lethal substances, explosives, personnel (one or more individuals who may be or include oneself), and transportation, except medicine or religious materials."[7] Convictions carry sentences up to life. Lindh's service to the Taliban against American forces and his involvement in the prison outbreak that led to the death of Agent Spann also made him subject to the charge of attempting to kill Americans, a violation of federal law that could have justified the death penalty.

The decision to prosecute Lindh was a policy and prosecutorial choice. We might have chosen to detain Lindh and hold him as an enemy combatant, since citizens working for the enemy can be detained. But, as far as I know, every member of the Bush administration in this war assumed that any American captured fighting against the United States would be brought back home either to be tried in federal court or to be held as an enemy combatant in military detention, not kept in detainee camps in Afghanistan or at Guantanamo Bay. Any American al Qaeda would remain a citizen, although some of my Justice Department colleagues professed amazement that our law did not automatically strip Lindh of citizenship for fighting against his country.

The Justice Department chose to try Lindh in Alexandria, Virginia, known as the "rocket docket" for its reputation of moving cases along at a speedy pace. This is the federal district court, after all, that includes the Pentagon. Judge T. S. Ellis, who presided over the case, had a reputation as a smart, no-nonsense judge who would not tolerate any publicity stunts or courtroom delaying tactics. Nonetheless, Lindh's lawyers—led by colorful and capable San Francisco attorney James Brosnahan—filed various motions that threatened to tie the case up in lengthy battles, notably with their demands to interview various al Qaeda leaders who were, by then, in American custody.

Delays can be costly. Prosecution can create leverage to obtain cooperation as part of a plea bargain, but to have any value the agreement must be struck quickly. After Judge Ellis rejected the most difficult Lindh defense motions in July 2002, a deal was finally reached in October in which he agreed to cooperate. Lindh pled guilty to providing services to the Taliban and carrying explosives during the commission of a felony. Taking responsibility for his actions and expressing remorse at sentencing helped him get only twenty years rather than life. "I made a mistake by joining the Taliban," he told the court. "I want the court to know, and I want the American people to know, that had I realized then what I know now about the Taliban, I would never have joined them."[8]

The second enemy combatant case that demanded high-level attention was that of Yaser Hamdi. Hamdi said he had gone to Afghanistan in the summer of 2000 to fight for the Taliban and, like Lindh, had received weapons training and joined a unit that engaged Northern Alliance forces near Kunduz, Afghanistan, to whom Hamdi surrendered in late 2001. Like Lindh, he was sent at first to the Mazar-e-Sharif prison, then on to another prison in Sheberghan. There he told U.S. intelligence after interrogation that he was a Saudi citizen born in the United States. In January 2002, the military transferred Hamdi to Guantanamo Bay. A birth certificate was found showing that Hamdi was born in Baton Rouge, Louisiana, where his family had lived temporarily when his father worked in the oil industry. He was transferred to the U.S. Naval Brig in Charleston, South Carolina, on April 5, 2002, a beneficiary of the Bush administration policy decision made at the time of Lindh's capture that all Americans captured in the war on terrorism would be brought back to the United States.

It took the federal public defender in the eastern district of Virginia, who was also defending Zacarias Moussaoui, only a few weeks to file a federal case seeking Hamdi's release. Senior District Judge Robert Doumar was assigned the case. From the start, he seemed determined to make life difficult for the government. Doumar allowed the federal public defender to file an initial habeas corpus petition and ordered that Hamdi meet with a lawyer within days. In the Justice Department, we felt that Judge Doumar was trying to turn the case into his own personal crusade. For one thing, he had allowed the federal public defender to walk into court and claim that Hamdi ought to be freed. Then Doumar found that an enemy combatant had a right to a lawyer and unmonitored communications. We took an emergency appeal. The Court of Appeals for the Fourth Circuit, which includes Virginia, dismissed the case under the doctrine known as "standing," that is, on the grounds that the federal public defender could not represent an enemy combatant because he enjoyed no relationship with Hamdi, did not suffer any personal injury from alleged violation of Hamdi's legal rights, and so could not bring a case on his behalf.[9]

In the meantime, Hamdi's father turned up, perhaps encouraged by lawyers set on challenging the administration's war policies. He filed a habeas petition on behalf of his son, curing the lack of standing. Hamdi's father claimed that his son went to Afghanistan only two months before the 9/11 attacks to perform "relief work," and was trapped in Afghanistan once fighting began.[10] Determined to treat Hamdi like a normal civilian rather than as an enemy combatant, the district judge again immediately ordered that Hamdi have unrestricted access to a lawyer. The Justice Department again took an immediate appeal and again the appeals judges reversed, saying that the civilian court inquiry into Hamdi's status was to be "limited and deferential" and noting "that if Hamdi is indeed an 'enemy combatant' who was captured during hostilities in Afghanistan, the government's present detention of him is a lawful one."[11]

Michael Mobbs, a special adviser to the undersecretary of defense, submitted a declaration recounting the facts of Hamdi's capture that left Judge Doumar unsatisfied. In an August 2002 hearing, Doumar said he would take the Mobbs Declaration and "pick it apart." Doumar then proceeded to question whether "Hamdi ever fired a weapon" and whether Mobbs was in fact a U.S. government employee. He then ordered the government to produce copies of all Hamdi's statements, the notes taken from any interviews with Hamdi, the names and addresses of all the interrogators who'd questioned Hamdi, statements by members of the Northern Alliance regarding Hamdi, and a list of all dates and locations of Hamdi's detention. War or no war, this judge was clearly bent on nitpicking every aspect of the military's decision-making. When again ordered by the appeals panel to focus on the sufficiency of the Mobbs Declaration, Judge Doumar ruled that it fell "far short" of the standard justifying detention, being "little more than the government's say-so."[12]

The Justice Department immediately appealed. Judge J. Harvie Wilkinson, former professor at the University of Virginia Law School and a jurist on many Republican short lists for the Supreme Court, presided. Frank Dunham, the very able federal public defender, represented Hamdi. Paul Clement, the deputy solicitor general, argued on behalf of the government. Clement was an old friend from the year we had clerked together for Judge Silberman. A Wisconsin native, he had gone to Georgetown and then Harvard Law School, and following our year with Silberman had clerked for Justice Scalia. He had served as Senator Ashcroft's counsel on the Judiciary Committee, and Ashcroft's confidence in his legal judgment was unlimited.

Clement served as Ted Olson's deputy during difficult times. When Hamdi was transferred to South Carolina, I had gone to Olson to brief him about the issues. I told him I was certain his case or a similar one would go to the Supreme Court, one way or the other, and that it would eventually involve the question of whether the United States was at war with al Qaeda. We discussed the formation of a special group, using the solicitor general's top-flight litigators, joined by OLC, the criminal division, and the civil division, to take control of the detainee cases. After giving it some thought, Olson agreed and delegated primary responsibility to Clement. It is a testament to Clement's legal skills, hard work, and political acumen that he was promoted to succeed Olson as solicitor general at an incredibly young age, even after Gonzales took the helm at the Justice Department.

The case was argued in early October 2002. Three months later, the Fourth Circuit came back with a victory for the government. Hamdi's detention was upheld because it was "undisputed that Hamdi was captured in a zone of active combat in a foreign theater of conflict." His lawyer had conceded as much at oral argument, which relieved the court of having to hold an evidentiary hearing.[13] The Fourth Circuit also agreed that the power to detain Hamdi derived directly from the President's and Congress's powers to wage war. It observed that judicial restraint in wartime prohibited a federal court from intrusively inquiring into the details of Hamdi's capture. Judge Wilkinson also concluded that Congress implicitly authorized the power to detain Hamdi with its authorization of the use of force, and that Hamdi's status as an American citizen didn't preclude his detention as an enemy combatant. "One who takes up arms against the United States in a foreign theater of war, regardless of his citizenship, may properly be designated an enemy combatant and treated as such."[14] The Supreme Court, however, agreed to hear the case in 2004. This was a surprise to me, and probably to most of the Justice Department.

Even as the judge in South Carolina was attempting to try Hamdi's case, the third and most serious case appeared. Jose Padilla was an American who was born and raised in the United States. He had gotten involved in Miami drug gangs, was convicted of murder in 1983 as a juvenile, served at least two jail sentences, and in 1998 moved to Egypt. Assuming the name Abdullah al Muhajir, he traveled in

Pakistan, Saudi Arabia, and Afghanistan, where he came into contact with top al Qaeda leaders. In a meeting with Abu Zubaydah, al Qaeda's operational planner, Padilla discussed a plan to detonate a dirty bomb in a major American city. Padilla underwent al Qaeda training and conducted research on wiring explosives at an al Qaeda camp. When the United States and its allies invaded Afghanistan, Padilla moved to different safehouses to avoid capture, and eventually escaped to Pakistan. In Pakistan, Padilla met with Khalid Sheikh Mohammed, one of the al Qaeda leaders who planned the 9/11 attacks, and discussed schemes to destroy apartment buildings, hotels, and gas stations in the United States. On May 8, 2002, Jose Padilla flew to Chicago from Pakistan, with an intermediate stop in Switzerland.[15]

Intelligence had provided our agents with not only Padilla's name, but his exact itinerary and plans for attack. Padilla left Pakistan with cash, travel documents, and communications devices. As he stepped off the plane in Chicago, he was arrested pursuant to a material witness warrant issued by a New York federal grand jury investigating the 9/11 attacks. This warrant allows the government to detain an individual who is a witness to a federal crime, but who might attempt to flee. It was widely used in the weeks after the September 11 attacks to detain individuals suspected of ties to al Qaeda. The FBI found no weapons or explosives on him. Government agents transferred Padilla to the maximum security wing of New York City's Metropolitan Correction Center and presented him to Judge Mukasey of the federal district court, which appointed him a lawyer. After meeting with his lawyer, Padilla refused to reveal any information to interrogators and instead moved to have his arrest warrant thrown out.

Of these three cases, Padilla was by far the most important for national security. Lindh and Hamdi could provide information on the structure of al Qaeda and the Taliban, who was in the chain of command, how they recruited and trained, and the identities of other recruits, but their knowledge was limited to operations in Afghanistan and Pakistan. That knowledge turned stale as the invasion of Afghanistan receded further into the past. Ultimately, they were equivalent to privates in al Qaeda.

Padilla, however, was a much greater threat, and an intelligence prize. He came to the United States to carry out a *future* terrorist attack. He didn't enter the country with any equipment or plans, and clearly didn't have the resources or expertise to construct and detonate a dirty bomb on his own. Where was he headed? Who was he to meet? Where would he get the money to buy parts for a dirty bomb? Where would he get the radioactive material? Did he have contacts in a facility with nuclear material? We thought he must have entered the country either to meet with a sleeper al Qaeda cell we had missed in the months after 9/11 or to establish a base of operations for other operatives to follow.

From our reconstruction of the 9/11 attacks, we knew that al Qaeda engaged in meticulous planning, staffed its operations with multiple agents, and spent time and resources to allow its operatives to train, conduct reconnaissance, and move into position. Capturing Padilla opened the possibility that we could roll up a dangerous sleeper cell already in the United States, or use him to lure any operatives following him into the country.

Michael Chertoff, then the head of DOJ's criminal division, was among those who worried that we could lose Padilla if he remained in the criminal justice system. Chertoff was one of those rare combinations in Washington: hypercompetent and intellectually brilliant, with a nonpartisan reputation. He had gone to Harvard for college and law school. Legend has it that Chertoff was so intense in law school that he became the model for the type of aggressive, take-no-prisoners students portrayed in the book *One L* by Scott Turow and the movie *The Paper Chase*. He had barely mellowed with age. He had clerked for Justice William J. Brennan, the leading liberal intellectual on the Supreme Court from the 1950s through the 1980s, and then served as a career federal prosecutor in New Jersey. He won a high-profile case against the mob and eventually became the U.S. Attorney for New Jersey. I met Chertoff when I served as Senator Hatch's general counsel on the Senate Judiciary Committee. He worked for Senator Al D'Amato as chief counsel of the special Senate committee investigating the Whitewater scandal. Chertoff is one of the most impressive lawyers I have ever met. He could operate at all levels of the law, from deposing witnesses to conducting a court-room trial to debating the niceties of high constitutional theory. His tongue was as sharp as his mind, either in asking questions or tagging someone playfully with his wit. With his obvious political skills and experience, Chertoff was supported by both of New Jersey's Democratic senators in 2003 when President Bush nominated him for a prized seat on the federal appellate court in the state. But after only two years, Chertoff could not sit still as a federal judge, and he accepted Bush's appointment to the cabinet as the secretary of the Homeland Security Department.

We didn't think we could hold Padilla for long. If Padilla knew he had to wait only a few months, he would never reveal his al Qaeda contacts. Over the next few weeks, lawyers at Justice, Defense, the CIA, and the White House worked quickly to develop an alternative to releasing him or charging him with a minor violation of law. After careful thought, we recommended to the President that an American could be taken into custody as an enemy combatant, but only if several agencies independently agreed. OLC reviewed the material on Padilla to determine whether he could qualify, legally, as an enemy combatant, and issued a legal opinion to that effect.[16] Chertoff's criminal division provided a "fact memo" with information on Padilla based on FBI and other sources of information. Based on its own intelligence, the CIA concluded that Padilla should, as a matter of policy, be transferred to military custody as a combatant. Rumsfeld's office conducted its own independent analysis, based on its own sources of information and on the CIA's work. Ashcroft relied on the OLC opinion that the military could legally take Padilla into custody, and also agreed with the CIA and DOD's recommendation that he be held as a combatant. Rumsfeld's office then sent a package of all these memos and findings to the White House, where it was reviewed by Gonzales and his lawyers. Gonzales briefed the President personally.

As the person who worked on the OLC document and had the proper clearances to read the intelligence reports, I not only wrote memos, but also assembled them and carried the growing pile of paper to its designated stops. I sometimes wondered what would happen if I were hit by a car while walking around Washington, D.C., with my beat-up, government-issue locked blue pouch of classified documents clutched in my arms. I was amazed at the level of paperwork and layers of review that the capture and detention of one enemy combatant generated in the middle of a war, but it signaled the importance placed on Padilla, and the care we all took, knowing both that an American's liberty was at stake and that this case would set a precedent for the future.

On June 9, 2002, President Bush ordered the Justice Department to transfer Padilla to the Defense Department pursuant to his authority as commander in chief and Congress's AUMF. In his order, Bush determined that Padilla "is closely associated with al Qaeda, an international terrorist organization with which the United States is at war;" that he "engaged in conduct that constituted hostile and war-like acts, including conduct in preparation for acts of international terrorism" against the United States; that he "possesses intelligence" about al Qaeda that "would aid U.S. efforts to prevent attacks by al Qaeda on the United States"; that he "represents a continuing, present and grave danger to the national security of the United States"; and that military detention "is necessary to prevent him from aiding al Qaeda in its efforts to attack the United States."[17] Defense transferred Padilla to the brig in Charleston, South Carolina. Ashcroft announced the decision to the American public in an ill-advised television address from Moscow, where he was on a diplomatic trip. His mention of the dirty bomb sent the stock market down several dozen points.

Two days later, Padilla's lawyer filed for a writ of habeas corpus in New York City, arguing that his detention by the military violated the Constitution. While Judge Mukasey agreed that the President had the authority to detain Padilla as an enemy combatant, he also decided that Secretary Rumsfeld was the proper defendant,[18] that Padilla could challenge disputed facts in a habeas proceeding, and that the standard to be used in reviewing the government's facts would be a relatively generous "some evidence" standard. A court of appeals panel reversed and ordered Padilla released, concluding that neither the President's commander-in-chief power nor the AUMF authorized detention of an American on American soil, even if he had associated himself with the enemy.[19] The Bush administration filed an appeal with the Supreme Court, which it granted.

Some civil libertarians believe that judges should supervise the military's detention of enemy combatants not only in the United States, but anywhere in the world. They contend that U.S. citizens like Hamdi and Padilla should be released or tried in civilian courts, and that courts ought to superintend captured enemy *aliens* held abroad, such as at Guantanamo Bay. In the weeks after 9/11, lawyers at State, Defense, the White House, and Justice formed an interagency task force to study the issues related to detention and trial of members of al Qaeda. The one thing we all agreed on was that any detention facility should be located outside the United States. Civilian criminal courts might not even be able to handle the numbers of captured terrorists—overwhelming an already heavily burdened system. We researched whether the courts would have jurisdiction over the facility, and concluded that if federal courts took jurisdiction over POW camps, they might start to run them by their own lights, substituting familiar peacetime prison standards for military needs and standards. We were also strongly concerned about creating a target for another terrorist operation.

No location was perfect, but the U.S. Naval Station at Guantanamo Bay, Cuba, seemed to fit the bill. Or, as Rumsfeld remarked at a press conference, Gitmo was "the least worst place" for the detention facility, a phrase the base personnel printed up on T-shirts. Gitmo was well-defended, militarily secure, and far from any civilians. The first Bush and the Clinton administrations had used Gitmo to hold Haitian refugees who sought to enter the United States illegally. One case from that period had concluded that by landing at Gitmo, Haitians did not obtain federal rights that might preclude their return. This suggested that the federal courts probably wouldn't consider Gitmo as falling within their habeas jurisdiction, which had in any event been understood to run only within the territorial United States or to American citizens abroad.

Civil liberties lawyers selected several enemy combatants at Guantanamo Bay to test the legality and conditions of detention through a writ of habeas corpus before a federal judge. They lost before a federal district judge in Washington, D.C., and a unanimous panel of the court of appeals upheld the decision. A federal appeals court in California, however, decided that Guantanamo Bay should be considered part of the territory of the United States, ignoring the fact that Guantanamo's lease, though perpetual, states that the base remains within Cuba's sovereignty. These cases moved forward to the Supreme Court to be decided along with *Padilla* and *Hamdi*.

The civil libertarians pushing the *Padilla* and *Hamdi* cases fervently believe that the courts need to check the executive branch and Congress to protect individual rights, especially in matters of war when the chances of abuse of executive power might be high. Their position is that the President cannot detain American al Qaeda members other than through the criminal justice system. Columbia law professor Louis Henkin, the nation's leading international law scholar, and Harold Koh, dean of the Yale Law School, filed a brief declaring: "The indefinite executive detention of U.S. citizen Jose Padilla on United States soil offends the rule of law and violates our constitutional traditions."[20] Their belief was that presidential policy should remain exactly as it was before 9/11. "The existence of war or other armed conflict does not alter the fundamental structure of the Constitution or the constraints it imposes on executive power," Henkin and Koh wrote. "The U.S. Constitution contains no wartime or emergency exception to the scope of the President's powers. Indeed, the word 'war' appears nowhere in Article II of the Constitution."[21]

They are mistaken. The taking of prisoners has been a basic feature of war throughout human history, and the United States has captured prisoners in every major war it has fought.[22] "Lawful combatants are subject to capture and detention as prisoners of war by opposing military forces," the Supreme Court observed during World War II, due to "universal agreement and practice."[23] We captured hundreds of thousands of prisoners in World War II and thousands in the Korean, Vietnam, and Persian Gulf wars, both lawful and unlawful combatants (those who obeyed the laws of war and those who did not). How we deal with enemy detainees affects other aspects of the war, such as morale, intelligence gathering, and the treatment of American POWs. Resources spent on detention reduce those available for other war needs. Throughout American history, control of prisoners captured in war has rested with military commanders, and ultimately the President. This power is implicitly part of the Constitution's grant of the commander-in-chief power to the executive branch, hardly an aggrandizing Bush power grab, as some like to claim. While Congress has the power to create the military and establish its rules of discipline, it has never sought to dictate a POW policy at odds with the President's.

There is no rule in law, or in history, that American citizens are constitutionally exempt from war. In the Civil War Confederate soldiers were all American citizens; when they were captured, they were held by the military, not the civilian courts. The Constitution has been consistently interpreted to permit our armed forces to detain American citizens as well as aliens fighting on behalf of our enemies. It is well-settled that the President, as commander in chief, has the power to determine how to defeat the enemy. This includes who to detain and how to detain them.[24]

Should a new President or Congress create a different rule for Americans who are captured fighting for al Qaeda? Some civil liberties lawyers want American citizens to be immune from military detention, even if they fight against us. Nothing in American history supports such a contention. Before 9/11, two cases, one from the Civil War, one from World War II, had reached the Supreme Court involving Americans captured while fighting against their nation. Both hold that Americans who join our enemies have no greater right to be free from detention when captured than alien enemy combatants.

In *Ex Parte Milligan*, Lamdin Milligan, a citizen of the Union and a resident of Indiana, was arrested on October 4, 1865, by the military commander for Indiana.[25] According to Union military authorities,

Milligan had joined a secret society known as the Order of American Knights to overthrow the government. Apparently Milligan's group planned to seize munitions stored at Army arsenals, liberate Confederate prisoners, kidnap the governor, and communicate with the enemy. He was tried by a military commission on October 21, and sentenced to hang. Nine days before the sentence was to be carried out, Milligan filed for a writ of habeas corpus, claiming that the military had no jurisdiction over him.

The Supreme Court granted the writ, releasing Milligan on two grounds. Milligan had been apprehended well away from the front, had never communicated with the enemy, and was only a partisan of the Confederate cause.[26] The Court concluded that Milligan "was not engaged in illegal acts of hostility against the government." Milligan, in other words, was not an enemy combatant; he was only a Confederate sympathizer. The Court also observed that Milligan was captured behind Union lines, not on the battlefield, where "the courts are open and their process unobstructed."[27]

Milligan, a 5–4 case with the Chief Justice in dissent, identifies when the military cannot detain citizens: when they have not joined the enemy and are located away from the battlefield, where the civil courts are open. *Milligan* contains much stirring language, often quoted by civil libertarians, about the rule of law and the excesses of wartime zeal. The Court observed that the "Constitution of the United States is a law for rulers and people, equally in war and in peace, and covers with the shield of its protection all classes of men, at all times, and under all circumstances. No doctrine involving more pernicious consequences was ever invented by the wit of man than that any of its provisions can be suspended during any of the great exigencies of government. Such a doctrine leads directly to anarchy or despotism."[28] All quite true. The Court recognized, however, that the Constitution grants the government the power to respond to attack, and that this includes the power to suspend habeas corpus or impose military rule in areas under attack.

Milligan's protections do not reach citizens who have actually joined enemy forces. Nor do they extend to detainees, citizen or not, at the front or on battlefields abroad. Otherwise, the Union could not have fought the Civil War, because the courts should have ordered President Lincoln to release thousands of Confederate POWs and spies. Obviously, this did not happen during the Civil War, nor afterward. The Court also decided *Milligan* on December 1, 1866, well after the end of hostilities, continuing the judicial practice of waiting until the end of a conflict to do anything that might interfere with ongoing military operations.

Almost eighty years later, the Supreme Court affirmed this understanding of the President's war power, in a case involving Nazi saboteurs. In June 1942, eight Nazi agents secretly landed on Long Island, New York, and in Florida, with plans to attack factories, transportation facilities, and utility plants. All had lived in the United States before the war, and two were American citizens.[29] One of the Nazis decided to turn informer. After initially dismissing his story, the FBI arrested the plotters, and their capture was revealed at the end of June. President Roosevelt established a military commission and the Supreme Court ultimately entertained a habeas petition in the case of *Ex Parte Quirin*.[30] The captured saboteurs argued that they should be released from military custody because, like Milligan, they were citizens, the civilian courts were open, and they were captured within the United States, far from any battlefield. The Court rejected these arguments and upheld FDR's decision to try them—even those who may have been born in the United States and were presumably American citizens—before a military court.

In doing so, the Court adopted the understanding of *Milligan* outlined above. What is important, the *Quirin* Court said, is not so much the time or place of the enemy combatant's capture, or the manner of capture, or even the combatant's citizenship, but whether in fact he is a member of the enemy's forces. In a unanimous holding, the Court held that individuals, regardless of citizenship, who "associate" themselves with the "military arm of the enemy" and "with its aid, guidance and direction enter this country bent on hostile acts are enemy belligerents within the meaning of the Hague Convention and the law of war."[31] *Quirin* flatly declared that the government could detain enemy combatants regardless of whether they were citizens or not: "Citizenship in the United States of an enemy belligerent does not relieve him of the consequences of a belligerency which is unlawful."[32] Milligan was not a belligerent because he had never associated with the enemy armed forces.[33]

Padilla and Hamdi's lawyers tried to argue that the American military can detain only uniformed members of regular armed forces captured on the battlefield.[34] This contention is blind to the realities of the post–9/11 world, tying our hands precisely because our enemy, in disguise, targets civilians on our own soil. This is nothing but an invitation to al Qaeda to stop trying to fight anything resembling a conventional battle. No more Tora Boras—just more World Trade Centers.

As if talking about al Qaeda itself, the *Quirin* Court said that "those who during time of war pass surreptitiously from enemy territory into our own, discarding their uniforms upon entry, for the commission of hostile acts involving destruction of life or property, have the status of unlawful combatants."[35] Legally, the Padilla case is virtually identical to that of the Nazi saboteurs.

Critics of the war also argue that military detention is illegal and unconstitutional because it is "indefinite."[36] Military detention is only indefinite because there is no criminal conviction and sentence. "Indefinite" does not mean "forever." The United States has released many Gitmo detainees who have been determined to no longer pose a threat. They have been mostly released to the governments of their countries of origin, once appropriate assurances have been obtained that they will not be released to renew their combat.[37]

Some critics contend that detention without knowledge of the release date amounts to cruel or inhuman treatment in itself. This claim flies in the face of centuries of wartime practice. Under the rules of war, nations have always held enemy combatants until "the cessation of active hostilities."[38] In war there is no requirement of a fixed time period like a criminal sentence to detain the enemy, nor any requirement of a "trial" to fix any such "sentence." At least there was none until the Supreme Court suggested it might create one, for the first time in history, in the *Hamdi* case. This has since been mooted by the

2005 Detainee Act. Combatants have historically been detained until the end of a conflict so they cannot rejoin the fighting. No POW has ever had any idea on what date he would be released. In this, al Qaeda and Taliban fighters detained at Guantanamo Bay are no different.

While the war with al Qaeda has been going on for five years, and while it's hard to imagine a peace treaty, hostilities will end at some point. American wars have been short by historical standards. But FDR did not know in 1942 that World War II would last only three years, nor could Lincoln have predicted in 1861 that the Civil War would last four years. There have been much longer wars, such as the Iran-Iraq war and American involvement in Vietnam, not to mention the Thirty Years' War or the Napoleonic Wars. Just because those wars were long did not mean that nations lost their right to detain captured enemy combatants. Just because the war on terrorism has proven longer and in some ways more difficult than previous American wars does not require that we release or try al Qaeda operatives.

Defeating al Qaeda will take longer than five years, but there is no reason to believe it will go on for a generation. Only those who imagine that the war against al Qaeda is a war against a persistent social problem, like the war on drugs or the war on crime, can honestly believe that the conflict will never end. Our current conflict is with al Qaeda, and we can declare hostilities over when it can no longer attack the United States in a meaningful way. Then the United States can transfer al Qaeda prisoners to the custody of their national governments.

Civil libertarians liken the case of Padilla or Hamdi to FDR's internment of Japanese-Americans.[39] There is no parallel with *Korematsu*, the 1944 case in which the Supreme Court upheld the detentions. The Japanese-Americans detained by FDR were American, not enemy, citizens, whose disloyalty was assumed solely because of their ethnicity. Today our military has detained no one because they were Arab or Muslim, but only those who have been caught on a battlefield or working with al Qaeda. Of the three Americans detained as enemy combatants, one was Hispanic, one Caucasian, and one Arab.

Critics also argue that the Anti-Detention Act of 1972, which prohibits the peacetime detention of Americans without criminal charge or other authorization by law, says that only Congress may authorize detentions.[40] Padilla's lawyers claimed it was enacted specifically to repudiate the Japanese-American internment and emergency detention laws against spies and saboteurs.[41] Thus, they say, if President Bush has the power as commander in chief to detain enemy combatants at war, which they do not concede, this power does not extend to suspects at home, who must be handled under rules set by Congress.

The lesson of September 11, reinforced by the AUMF, the logic of *Hamdi*, and the Patriot Act's removal of the artificial Wall between foreign and domestic intelligence, was that mere geography or even citizenship can no longer divide the powers of war from the powers of peace. Al Qaeda operatives had launched the attacks from within the United States by hijacking American airliners. They had succeeded where the Nazi saboteurs had failed. The Constitution would not have disabled the President and Congress from confronting a threat all the greater when waged by enemy operatives on American soil. Under *Quirin*, the President has clear authority to detain enemy combatants, even citizens, in wartime. But control over the federal criminal laws rests with Congress. Interpreting the law to prevent the President from military detentions merely because the enemy has been found in the United States would provoke a direct conflict between the constitutional authorities of the two branches. With the Anti-Detention Act, Congress hoped to prevent detentions of loyal citizens, not the enemy, in time of war.[42] Congress's AUMF implicitly included the power to detain enemy combatants.[43] Civil libertarians are arguing that Congress authorized the military to shoot to kill enemy combatants, but not to capture and detain them.[44]

Civil libertarians, not the Bush administration, seek a radical reordering of our system for making war. They demand a new role for Congress and the courts in overseeing basic military decisions. The most radical deny that the Constitution grants *any* role to the President in conducting war, foreign affairs, and national security policy. Congress, they say, should pass a law on every aspect of the use of

force, not in the AUMF's general terms, but only in declared specifics, such as the power to gather intelligence, to use force, to detain
the enemy, to accept surrender, to interrogate, to release detainees,
and so on.

As noted earlier, this is an ironic reversal on such critics' usual com-
plaints. When Congress delegates to the President in far less serious
matters, such as regulating industry and the environment, they argue
the opposite, that everything should be delegated to the agencies
within the executive branch.[45] If the Constitution gave Congress and
the President flexibility and discretion in anything, it was the conduct
of war. Put differently, Hamdi, Padilla, and their civil libertarian allies
want to all the laws and all the historical precedents of war to contain
a brand-new exception for everything that occurs on American soil or
involves Americans who join the enemy. After enemy combatants have
carried out the deadliest attack on American soil in history, an attack
the enemy is determined to repeat using covert means, this would
make no sense at all. This position takes "rights talk," as author and
legal scholar Mary Ann Glendon terms it, to an illogical extreme.

The law is not the same as policy. Whatever the government's legal
right or power to detain, it might, if it chose, use the criminal justice
system, much as it had prior to 9/11. Had it wanted to, it could have
reserved military detention only for members of the Taliban captured fighting in Afghanistan. These are policy decisions for our
elected decision-makers. So why did the President and Congress
choose otherwise?

Consider first the incentives. Al Qaeda would focus on recruiting
American citizens and on conducting covert operations on American
soil. The most dangerous covert operations against American civilians would become the easiest for our enemy to carry out. Osama
bin Laden offered John Walker Lindh the role of a suicide bomber
precisely to exploit his Western identity, cover, and access. Al Qaeda
recruited Jose Padilla for the same reasons. The last thing our government should do is give an advantage to operations on American
soil for spies and saboteurs to conduct terror attacks.

Al Qaeda members with American citizenship could easily refuse to disclose their secrets by pleading the Fifth. Proof sufficient to meet the probable cause standard would have to be collected before they could be arrested. Americans with no previous criminal record who have carefully refrained from communicating with al Qaeda once in the United States could, for all practical purposes, never be identified and confined, short of pure luck. Luck is not going to protect us from this determined adversary.

Military detention is also one of our most important sources of intelligence, which in turn is our most important tool in this war. We will need to know who they are, where they are, who is helping them, and what they are planning, which will require surveillance, interrogation of captured enemy combatants, captured computers and documents, and undercover agents. And we need to maintain secrecy about the means and details of these captures and what we learn from them.

Should enemy combatants have the right to a lawyer? The demand for access to counsel seems reasonable enough at first glance—it is certainly one of the bedrock rules of due process in the American criminal and civil justice systems, ingrained into the popular imagination by TV cop shows and crime movies. Our criminal justice system assumes that truth emerges from the clash between prosecution and defense. It tilts the playing field against the government and in favor of the suspect. All relevant witnesses and evidence must be publicly presented in court, and lawyers help their clients exercise their right to say nothing that might incriminate them.

Introducing a lawyer right after capture, as Judge Doumar ordered in *Hamdi*, would essentially stop the questioning of enemy combatants. The defense lawyer's first action would be to order his client to say nothing to the government. This is perfectly appropriate in the criminal justice system. Invoking one's right to remain silent and to have access to counsel is protected by the Bill of Rights, which represents society's decision that we want the government to prove with a high level of certainty that someone is guilty, without relying on evidence that comes unwillingly from the defendant. Our society has decided that it is strong enough to withstand the occasional individual criminal who is set free.

This is not the case in war. Even under the Geneva Conventions, which do not apply to al Qaeda, a POW has no right to an attorney unless he is being tried for violations of the laws of war. The rules of war have never required a standard of "proof beyond a reasonable doubt" for the detention of a suspected member of the enemy. Nor have they ever required a judicial hearing after capture.

The Fifth Amendment's right to remain silent (which we think of today as "Miranda" rights) applies only in the criminal justice system. It declares that no person "shall be compelled in any criminal case to be a witness against himself." Same goes for the Sixth Amendment's right to counsel: "[I]n all criminal prosecutions, the accused shall enjoy the right . . . to have the Assistance of Counsel for his defence." We impose less burdensome standards in war because the costs of a future enemy attack are far greater than simply allowing a crime that has already been committed to go unsolved. But this flexibility comes at a price. Intelligence obtained in military detention usually can't be used in any kind of criminal prosecution, since it would have been obtained without Miranda rights. We will obtain information that may prevent a future al Qaeda attack, but that information cannot be used to convict the detainee of a crime.

Suppose civil libertarians prevailed in court and enemy combatants each received a trial to test their detention. To prove that a detainee is a member of al Qaeda, the soldiers and officers who captured and processed the enemy combatant would have to be recalled from the field to appear in court, and subjected to direct and cross-examination. Detainees would want access to any information about them in the government's posession. They could cross-examine al Qaeda leaders in U.S. custody who identified them to test the credibility of the government intelligence. These are all standard rights in a criminal proceeding. Not only would these hearings consume a huge amount of resources and time, they would provide enemy combatants with a treasure trove of U.S. intelligence secrets. Al Qaeda could discover what communications were being intercepted, which parts of its network were compromised, and which plans had been discovered. An open proceeding makes sense when we want to place the burden on the prosecution to prove that a defendant is guilty of a crime beyond a reasonable doubt. It makes little sense when the objective is to preserve our intelligence advantages against an elusive and shadowy enemy.

The Bush administration naturally wanted the courts to provide as much deference as possible to the facts supplied by the intelligence agencies and the military. "Matters intimately related to foreign policy and national security are rarely proper subjects for judicial intervention," the justices have observed.[46] To avoid recalling active-duty American soldiers, commanding officers, and al Qaeda prisoners for trials, we argued that the government had to meet the "some evidence" standard. That is, so long as sufficient evidence existed in the record put forward by the government, a court should uphold the detention. Courts have used this same standard in far less sensitive situations, such as extradition or immigration deportation hearings, where much less is at stake.[47]

In their eagerness to attack the Bush administration, critics ignored the administration's efforts to protect combatant civil liberties. For instance, it never challenged the courts' jurisdiction to review writs of habeas corpus or any other claims involving American citizens; it created a system to annually review the evidence to hold detainees; and it built a fair, due process–rich military commission system to handle war crime trials.

Critics have exaggerated their arguments in the press, claiming that President Bush wants to throw anyone into jail at any time just on his say-so. Not so. The government must prove that the detainee is an enemy combatant by showing affiliation with al Qaeda and hostile activity against the United States. A government official must submit a signed affidavit describing the facts. Any misrepresentations would be punishable, and they would undermine the government's position in future cases. In the Padilla case, the Mobbs Declaration, in addition to a classified memo by Vice Admiral Lowell Jacoby, head of the Defense Intelligence Agency, explained the national security concerns raised by allowing counsel to interfere with efforts to obtain intelligence from enemy combatants. In future cases, the government must provide the court with evidence detailing a detainee's links to al Qaeda and his hostile actions against the United States.

Civil liberties absolutists say sworn statements by our national security and defense officials aren't enough. Instead, they are eager to use the detainee habeas corpus proceedings to conduct fishing expeditions into the government's intelligence and military operations—they want to grill captured al Qaeda leaders or American agents in the field on their knowledge. Padilla, for example, would demand that the CIA or the NSA explain just how they learned his travel schedule, whether the information was produced by informants or intercepted communications, and how and by whom it was done. All of this, of course, helps defense lawyers test the credibility or trustworthiness of witnesses in criminal cases. At the same time, producing such information in open court or in any way in which it might be transmitted to the enemy would compromise military secrecy and make the job of defeating al Qaeda far more difficult. This tactic is so standard—either give us this information and lose your intelligence advantage, or release our client—it is known in the legal trade as graymail. Prosecuted spies, such as an Aldrich Ames or a Robert Hanssen, regulary make such demands, and often win plea bargains as a result. It was this very bind that lawyers for John Walker Lindh hoped to create for the government when they demanded access to captured al Qaeda leaders.[48]

Our laws do not allow the government to detain Americans on fabricated evidence, but they also should not allow detainees to use our own legal system as a weapon against our war effort. Today, the good faith of our government's efforts against al Qaeda is not, or should not be, at issue. No one is using the war on terror as a façade to pursue innocent Americans. We need the right balance between protecting military secrets and ensuring that no innocent people are wrongly detained as enemy combatants.

The right policy would look something like this: Courts can review the detention of enemy combatants found within the United States and develop a definition of their status. The information disclosed in open court would be limited and closed hearings would protect classified information. An American detainee would receive a lawyer after interrogation by military and intelligence officers. Any information they obtain would be off-limits for any future criminal prosecution. Defense attorneys would have to hold security clearances. For now, both the Supreme Court and Congress seem content to leave the development of such a system up to the executive branch, the military, and the lower courts. They very well might strike the right balance between checks and balances and effectiveness in war, but if they cannot, Congress may have to enact a statute. So far Congress seems satisfied with staying silent and letting the President take the lead and bear the responsibility.

Congressional silence is hardly a warrant for full-blown judicial intervention. If Congress will not act to contain the imperial President, they say, the courts should step in to police our military and our intelligence agencies.[49] Despite claims to the contrary, no one has questioned the role that the judiciary plays. The administration has not claimed the military could hold Lindh, Hamdi, or Padilla without any recourse to the courts, even though such a claim might have been an option.[50] The question is how much information must be produced in court, and how much can be discussed in public.

Courts once regarded themselves as having no business reviewing the military detention of enemy aliens outside the United States at all. In *Johnson v. Eisentrager* (1950), the Supreme Court denied a habeas petition brought by German World War II prisoners, captured in China, who challenged their trial and conviction by military commission.[51] The Court declared that only American citizens (anywhere in the world) and aliens who enter American territory could enjoy "the privilege of litigation" in American courts because "their presence in the country implied protection."[52] The *Eisentrager* Court deferred to the decisions of the political branches because "trials would hamper the war effort and bring aid and comfort to the enemy."[53] Judicial proceedings would engender a "conflict between judicial and military opinion," interfere with military operations by recalling personnel to testify, and "diminish the prestige of" a field commander called "to account in his own civil courts" and "divert his efforts and attention from the military offensive abroad to the legal defensive at home."[54] While *Eisentrager* was over-ruled in 2004 by *Rasul,* which asserted jurisdiction over enemy detentions, Congress essentially restored *Eisentrager* last year in the Detainee Act of 2005.

The constitutional rights of Americans and aliens within the United States certainly require that we develop a process to ensure against mistaken or improper detentions. But the same does not apply to aliens fighting us abroad. In 1990, the Supreme Court found that aliens could not challenge alleged violations of the Bill of Rights occurring outside the country,[55] precisely because it would make fighting wars impossible. Every dropped bomb would be a taking of property for which compensation would be owed, every detention an unconstitutional arrest, every killing a deprivation of due process. Applying the Fourth Amendment to aliens abroad, Chief Justice Rehnquist wrote for the Court, "could significantly disrupt the ability of the political branches to respond to foreign situations involving our national interest."

This is not to say that the military can hold alien enemy combatants arbitrarily. Our armed forces have no desire to hold civilians, nor to hold enemy combatants any longer than necessary. Detention operations place a drain on soldiers and resources that could be better spent on taking the fight to al Qaeda. As Rumsfeld more colorfully put it, the military has no desire to be the world's jailer.

The military has released scores of captured enemy combatants to the custody of their governments. Detainees are screened and reviewed at multiple levels of military command. Only those with the highest threat profile or the most intelligence value are sent to Guantanamo Bay. In 2004, in response to the Supreme Court's decisions, the Defense Department created Combatant Status Review Tribunals (CSRTs). Headed by officers, the tribunals use all available information to review annually whether a detainee still qualifies as an enemy combatant. A detainee has a right to appear before the tribunals with the assistance of a military representative.[56] Those who still pose a threat of further terrorist activity or who might have valuable information will continue to be held. Determining whether a detainee is lying or is in fact a civilian takes time and should be done patiently. These concerns should not be understated. Several suspected al Qaeda and Taliban detainees who were released in 2003 and 2004 have since been recaptured in Afghanistan conducting attacks against coalition forces or engaging in efforts to destabilize the Karzai government.[57]

If the military were required to act like a police force, it would inevitably be at the expense of actual war-fighting, subordinating the fight with the enemy to worries about the litigation to follow. As *Eisentrager* observed, "[I]t would be difficult to devise a more effective fettering of a field commander than to allow the very enemies he is ordered to reduce to submission to call him to account in his own civil courts and divert his efforts and attention from the military offensive abroad to the legal defensive at home."[58] We cannot expect our soldiers in the field to worry about warrants, lawyers, Miranda, forensic evidence, and chains of custody if we want to win the war on terrorism.

Press reports might give the impression that the Supreme Court rejected all of this in 2004. Actually, the Court confirmed the administration's basic legal approach to the war on terrorism, while making clear, however, that it would no longer regard military detentions as outside its purview.

Concern for the new challenges of 9/11 might also have led the Court to adopt a "some evidence" standard narrowing judicial inquiry to the facts known to the government and subject to production in court.[59] But the Court did not choose this route. Rather, it issued a vague order to the lower courts to develop a fair process to review detentions for every detainee under the control of the United States anywhere in the world. It was an unprecedented intrusion into the traditional powers of the President and Congress over war and one that required it to overrule *Eisentrager*. The Court was asserting that judges could make factual and legal judgments, in the midst of war, far beyond what had once been considered their normal areas of expertise.

In 2004, the Supreme Court decided a trilogy of enemy combatant cases. Most Court observers thought that *Padilla* would be the centerpiece. As an American captured outside a traditional battlefield, he certainly seemed to be the toughest case. Instead, the Court dismissed it because the plaintiff had brought it in the wrong place.[60] Eventually, a court of appeals unanimously found in late 2005 that "[u]nder the facts as presented here, Padilla unquestionably qualifies as an 'enemy combatant'" as that term was defined in the Supreme Court's cases,[61] even though he had been detained in the United States, not in Afghanistan. While Padilla's case was on appeal to the Supreme Court, the Justice Department concluded it had enough evidence to prosecute Padilla for crimes. On November 22, 2005, a Miami grand jury indicted Padilla on charges of conspiracy to commit murder and to provide material support to al Qaeda as part of a North American terrorist support cell already under prosecution.[62] The Supreme Court dismissed the appeal as moot since he was now in criminal court.

Instead, *Hamdi v. Rumsfeld* became the central opinion on the war on terrorism. *Hamdi* rejected arguments that terrorism had to be understood solely as criminal activity and that war could only occur between nations. A four-justice plurality, composed of Chief Justice William Rehnquist and Justices Sandra Day O'Connor, Anthony Kennedy, and Stephen Breyer, agreed that the September 11 attacks had initiated a state of war, that the Afghanistan conflict was part of that war, and that enemy combatants could be detained without criminal charge.[63] The court plurality found that the September 18 AUMF provided sufficient authority to detain Hamdi and did not question its constitutionality. "There can be no doubt that individuals who fought against the United States in Afghanistan as part of the Taliban, an organization known to have supported the al Qaeda terrorist network responsible for those attacks, are individuals Congress sought to target in passing" the AUMF.[64]

The four justices agreed with the argument we had developed years earlier that detention was part of the executive's use of force.[65] The justices also reaffirmed that individuals, including U.S. citizens, who associate with enemy forces, are enemy combatants who may be detained, and observed that the purpose of detention in the military context is not to punish, but merely to prevent combatants from returning to the fight.[66] Its indefiniteness did not make the detention unconstitutional.[67] Rather, "the United States may detain, for the duration of these hostilities, individuals legitimately determined to be Taliban combatants who 'engaged in an armed conflict against the United States.'"[68]

Contrary to the much-publicized views of pundits and professors, the *Hamdi* Court upheld the core of the administration's approach to terrorism. Chicago's O'Hare Airport, New York Harbor, and the Mexican and Canadian borders will be the front lines of this war in the future. If the Court had prevented the government from detaining an American al Qaeda, it would have seriously handicapped this nation's ability to defend itself in the next chapter of this war.

Up to this point, the Court had remained well within the boundaries of tradition by which courts have usually deferred to the President and Congress in matters of war.[69] Despite the arguments of a coalition of law professors, members of the bar, and commentators, it would have been remarkable for the Court to have disregarded this framework developed over the nation's long history.[70] But victory for the administration was far from complete. While rejecting the positions of Hamdi and the government, the Court fashioned a compromise—that an enemy combatant must receive notice and "a fair opportunity to rebut the Government's factual assertions before a neutral decisionmaker."[71] The Court borrowed an amorphous standard from a case about the termination of welfare benefits, which balanced the private interest affected by government action, the government's interests, and the costs of providing greater process, to judge whether procedures provided to an enemy combatant comport with fair process.[72,73]

That the *Hamdi* Court had to resort to a case about procedural due process in a welfare case shows the extent to which it was improvising. On the one hand, Justice O'Connor wrote, an individual citizen's interest "to be free from involuntary confinement by his own government without due process of law" is fundamental.[74] On the other hand, the government has a "weighty and sensitive" interest in preventing enemy combatants from returning to fight against the United States.[75]

Requiring the government to reveal intelligence data in court could
be fatal. So, then, which is it? The Court gives no clue how courts
should balance these interests. Should a court gauge the government's
interest in protecting the national security by figuring out the number of lives potentially saved times the probability of an attack, using
the average value of a life as measured by the Environmental Protection Agency? And how to measure the individual liberty interest
against unwilling detention—in average amount of dollars per hour an
average citizen would pay to avoid detention? If effort to monetize
these values seem silly, it is because there is no systematic, rational
way to strike a balance between these competing values. The Supreme
Court punted to the lower courts to make the tough decisions about
specific procedures, such as how much evidence the government
should provide to a judge.

After the Court's decision Hamdi renounced his citizenship and was
released to the custody of Saudi Arabia.[76] But *Hamdi's* impact was still
wide—largely because of the Court's decision in *Rasul v. Bush.* Safiq
Rasul and Asif Iqbal were two British citizens captured in Afghanistan
and sent to Guantanamo Bay. Through relatives, they filed suits in
federal court in Washington, D.C., seeking their release on the ground
that they were not enemy combatants and had never fought against
the United States. The courts joined their case with those of two Aus-
tralians and twelve Kuwaitis held at Gitmo who demanded their release because they were not charged with a crime. Both the federal
trial courts and appeals court, following governing Supreme Court case
law in place since World War II, said they had no jurisdiction to hear
cases brought by aliens held abroad.

But the Supreme Court in *Rasul* ruled that Guantanamo Bay lay
within the jurisdiction of the federal courts, and that district judges can
review habeas corpus challenges regardless of a detainee's citizenship
or location. This is something previous Supreme Courts had always
avoided, for good reason.[77] Without saying so explicitly, *Rasul* seemed
to overrule, and certainly ignored, *Eisentrager's* concerns about judicial
interference with military operations. It was a wrongheaded decision

that posed the threat of judicial micromanagement of military operations as never before.

Worse, *Rasul* provided no guidance on how the courts were to shoulder this vast new responsibility. How soon should hearings be held? Where? Who could participate? How would classified intelligence remain protected?[78] What kinds of evidence or witnesses would the government have to produce? How long could it interrogate before giving the detainee access to an attorney? *Rasul* studiously avoided any discussion of what substantive rights enemy detainees might have, no doubt on purpose. But while the Court's ambiguous *Hamdi*'s balancing test might have left the other branches some flexibility on these questions, it also made a struggle between the federal judiciary and the other branches inevitable.

About the only thing it was safe to assume was that if *Hamdi* defined due process for citizens on U.S. soil, its standards ought to suffice for aliens held outside the country too. To avoid further judicial intervention, the Pentagon could adapt its existing review process for Guantanamo prisoners to meet the standards of *Hamdi* (as Justice O'Connor seemed to invite).[79] Military commissions could be altered to meet the Court's procedural requirements. The Court's ambiguous balancing test for fairness gives the executive branch little choice but to follow all of *Hamdi*'s suggestions in all cases, with further litigation inevitable and judges now charged with interpreting and applying the new vague law in unpredictable ways.

Civil libertarians make a reasonable-sounding argument defending the expansion of the judicial role. We trust courts to make decisions on many of our society's important issues, including abortion, affirmative action, the death penalty, police power, and the place of religion in the public square. It fulfills our Constitution's original design to allow the courts to check and balance the actions of the President and Congress. If the federal courts can potentially review the arrest and sentences of every criminal defendant in the country, should they not also provide a final check on wartime detentions by the President and Congress?

While this is a straightforward and appealing argument, it has no basis in our two-hundred-year history. Until 2004, our courts had never reviewed a single case of the military detention of an enemy alien held abroad during wartime.[80] Civil libertarian arguments appeal to our traditional American distrust of government power and of standing armies, attitudes recorded even by de Tocqueville. Courts play a significant role to ensure that the people's agents—the government—obey the limits on their delegated powers as expressed in the Constitution. In order to restrict the government and protect individual rights, judges must have as much independence and neutrality from the elected branches of government as possible.

But in the area of national security, the judiciary's strengths become weaknesses. In wartime, we want to expand, not limit, the powers of government against the enemy. But enemy aliens are not part of the American political community and do not have the same constitutional rights as its actual members. The avant-garde effort today is to enact a conception of human rights into law worldwide. While this is a noble goal, we have no workable or legitimate mechanism of world government to legitimize these efforts other than the old-fashioned method of treaties that are domestically ratified in whole or in part—though international lawyer-activists often proclaim otherwise.

In war, our courts should not stand (and historically have not stood) as neutral arbiters between our government and the enemy. Courts viewed their role as helping the other branches conduct the war effectively, which was why only American citizens or aliens on U.S. territory were entitled to the benefits of our Bill of Rights.

The federal judiciary has significant institutional disadvantages in making or carrying out national security policy. Judges are generalists. They are not appointed because of their expertise in any particular topic, but because of their careers as prominent litigators or public officials. With few exceptions, Congress has organized the federal courts into a decentralized system along geographic, not subject matter, lines. In contrast, foreign affairs requires expertise in matters such as international politics, regions, technologies, or intelligence, subjects in which few judges have experience.

Courts acquire information only through the course of litigation, they make decisions in a formalized way with an inner logic often unrelated to the matter at hand, and they are slow to correct their errors or to change policy in response to new circumstances, because of the years typically needed to complete a case.[81] The enemy combatant cases, in which the legal issues were clear, no discovery was needed, and detainees had significant interest in a swift resolution, still required roughly two to three years of litigation before any hearings could even be held. Appeals to correct errors usually take years to resolve. Judicial mistakes in peacetime will not cost society much in a specific case, and errors can often be fixed over time. By contrast, a judicial error (like any error) in wartime can have an immediate and dramatically higher cost that cannot be reversed.

Some welcomed the Court's intervention because it would prompt Congress to act. When Congress did act at the end of December 2005, it did the opposite of what civil libertarians expected. It overruled *Rasul.* Two months after the Court signaled that it would hear another detainee case from Guantanamo, Congress eliminated federal court jurisdiction over any case from the base. Several hundred cases that had been pending were suddenly moot.[82] Clearly, the Rehnquist Court had gone too far in expanding the habeas corpus statute, abandoning *Eisentrager,* and intruding into the prerogatives of the political branches in waging war.

A long list of law professors lobbied against the bill's passage. They argued that by overruling *Rasul* Congress had unconstitutionally interfered with the judicial power of the Supreme Court to hear cases under federal law.[83] They seriously exaggerated. *Rasul* upset the settled understanding that the right to habeas corpus did not extend to aliens held outside the territorial United States in wartime. Congress was merely restoring the previous interpretation, a kind of statutory error correction. Congress was not removing judicial review over habeas cases that had long been recognized and applied.[84]

However, Congress took the Court's advice in part and added a review process for enemy combatants that had not previously existed. Congress vested jurisdiction in the U.S. Court of Appeals for the D.C. Circuit to hear appeals of the determinations of the Defense Department's CSRTs. Review, however, would be narrow. The D.C. Circuit's review is limited only to whether the tribunals followed the Defense Department's own rules. In other words, the D.C. Circuit does not sit to try an enemy combatant, or to reach its own decision on whether he should be released. The D.C. Circuit may also decide whether those procedures are consistent with the Constitution or federal laws. It does not appear, however, that a finding that procedures are unconstitutional would require the release of an enemy combatant. Rather, the Defense Department would be required to revise the procedures.

While the Detainee Act grants more judicial review than the Bush administration, or indeed any administration, would have liked, it eliminated habeas corpus for alien enemy combatants held outside the sovereign territory of the United States as well as claims of action under other laws, such as the Alien Tort Statute. It said, in other words, that the Supreme Court had gotten it wrong in *Rasul*. It was a rare and extraordinary thing for Congress to checkmate the Supreme Court as it did, and it signals how far the Court had exceeded the traditional practice of the judiciary in wartime. Whether the Detainee Act will serve as a sufficient warning to the courts not to meddle in the business of the political branches remains to be seen.

7

INTERROGATION

On March 28, 2002, it has been reported, American and Pakistan intelligence agents assaulted a two-story apartment building in Faisalabad, an industrial city in northeastern Pakistan. American agents threw stun grenades and swarmed an apartment where a dozen suspected al Qaeda operatives were sleeping. Four tried to escape by jumping to the roof of another building, and in the scuffle their leader was shot in the groin and thigh.[1]

Almost completely unfurnished, according to press reports, the apartment in the Shahbaz Cottage building held a trove of computer equipment, storage drives, and CDs. Occupants had told neighbors they were Arab traders selling T-shirts and sheets, but the apartment in reality had become a "provisional headquarters" for the al Qaeda terrorist network.[2] Soon American intelligence agents realized that their biggest catch wasn't computers, but al Qaeda's number three leader, Abu Zubaydah. With the death of Mohammed Atef in the American invasion of Afghanistan in November 2001, Zubaydah had assumed the role of chief military planner for al Qaeda, ranking in importance only behind Osama bin Laden and Ayman al Zawahiri.

It is difficult to understate the importance of the capture. Zubaydah had long been an integral part of al Qaeda plans to attack the West. One of the planners of the failed 2000 millennium attacks, he ran a foiled plot to bomb American and Israeli tourists in Jordan in 1999 and had directed frustrated attacks on the American embassies in France and the former Yugoslavia. Before 9/11, he had spent several years screening al Qaeda recruits. He chose several of the 9/11 hijackers, briefed shoe bomber Richard Reid, and met with Jose Padilla and approved his plans to explode a dirty bomb in the United States.

With his new promotion, Zubaydah headed the organization and planning of al Qaeda's operations. With al Qaeda reeling from American success in Afghanistan, and bin Laden and Zawahiri in hiding, Zubaydah took on the role of building and managing al Qaeda's network of covert cells throughout the world. More than anyone else, he knew the identities of hundreds of terrorists and their plans. In confirming the capture a few days later, Rumsfeld said, "We are asking for a good deal of information and intend to keep doing it."[3] If anyone had "actionable intelligence" that could be put to use straightaway to kill or capture al Qaeda operatives and frustrate their plans of attack, it was Zubaydah. It was as if a foreign enemy had captured Rumsfeld or Tenet.

Zubaydah was of a different generation than men like bin Laden and Zawahiri. According to press reports, he was young, comfortable with the communications tools of the twenty-first century, and skilled at the craft of intelligence operations. Responsible for training recruits, Zubaydah was an expert at resisting regular interrogation methods. He was said to be in charge of training materials for al Qaeda cells.[4] It was safe to assume that simple questioning and standard mind games (good cop–bad cop) wouldn't work on him. These would be ineffective with those who are willing to die for their cause and who have undergone extensive training to resist questioning.

In the months after Zubaydah's capture, the United States found several other al Qaeda leaders. A year to the day of the September 11 attacks, as the press has reported, Pakistani authorities captured Ramzi bin al Shibh after a fierce three-hour gunfight in Karachi,

Pakistan. Bin al Shibh was the right-hand man to Khalid Sheikh Mohammed, referred to by American intelligence and law enforcement as "KSM." A thirty-year-old Yemeni, bin al Shibh had journeyed to Hamburg, Germany, where he became close friends and a fellow al Qaeda member with Mohammed Atta, the tactical commander of the 9/11 attacks.[5] Handpicked by Osama bin Laden to join the 9/11 attackers, bin al Shibh's American visa applications had been repeatedly rejected. He continued to serve as a conduit for money and instructions between al Qaeda leaders and the hijackers. In interrogations, bin al Shibh described himself as the coordinator of the attacks.

Six months later, according to reports, American and Pakistani intelligence landed a bigger fish, KSM himself. Labeled by the 9/11 Commission Report as the "principal architect" of the 9/11 attacks and a "terrorist entrepreneur," KSM was captured on March 1, 2003, in Rawalpindi, Pakistan.[6] The uncle of Ramzi Yousef, who had carried out the first bombing of the World Trade Center, KSM had worked on the foiled plan to bomb twelve American airliners over the Pacific. It was KSM who met with bin Laden in 1996 and proposed the idea of crashing planes into American targets. He helped select the operatives, provided the financing and preparation for their trip to the United States, and continued to stay in close contact with them in the months leading up to 9/11. After the U.S. invasion of Afghanistan and the capture of Zubaydah, KSM became the most important leader after bin Laden and Zawahiri. If catching Zubaydah was like capturing al Qaeda's defense secretary, finding KSM was like netting al Qaeda's chairman of the Joint Chiefs of Staff.

These three seasoned al Qaeda commanders, as the 9/11 Commission Report makes clear, provided useful information to the United States.[7] As the press has reported, one arrest followed the other—information from Zubaydah allowed the United States to capture bin al Shibh, which finally led to KSM.[8] Not only did their captures take significant parts of the al Qaeda leadership out of action, they led to the recovery of much information that prevented future terrorist attacks and helped American intelligence more fully understand the operation of the terrorist network. As the government has publicly acknowledged, all three were involved in approving, training, and preparing Jose Padilla for his mission to the United States.[9] Both Porter Goss, the past director of the CIA, and Vice President Cheney, who know far more than they can reveal publicly, have said that such operations, are vital to protect the United States from attack.[10]

Law

If administration critics had their way, however, it is likely that none of this information would ever have come into our hands. They want us to question al Qaeda leaders only verbally, no matter how much information they might have or what attacks might be planned in the future. Further, they argue that any effort to coerce a detainee, even an Abu Zubaydah or Ramzi bin al Shibh or KSM, constitutes prohibited "torture."

Critics tell a "torture narrative," which goes like this: The Bush administration used torture to extract information from al Qaeda leaders, and decided to use the same methods on the detainees at Guantanamo Bay, whom it deprived of Geneva Conventions protections precisely for this purpose.[11] Harsh interrogation methods became part of military culture and "migrated" to Iraq, where they produced the horrible abuses at Abu Ghraib.

This argument is an exercise in hyperbole and partisan smear. The Bush administration researched and debated the Geneva issue three months after the 9/11 attacks. Iraq presented a different situation entirely because Iraq clearly *was* a war covered under the Geneva Conventions. Iraq was never once mentioned by anyone during the debates within the administration in December 2001 and January 2002. American forces were still in Afghanistan and President Bush would not launch his political offensive on Iraq until the fall of 2002. The invasion of Iraq was more than a year in the future.

There is a clear legal difference between the war against al Qaeda and the war in Iraq. Iraq is a party to the Geneva Conventions. Its troops have fought in accordance with the requirements for POW status (as they did in the first Persian Gulf War in 1991). At the outset of the invasion, President Bush and the Pentagon declared that the Geneva Conventions applied. Nonetheless, the pictures of the appalling abuses at Abu Ghraib, which emerged in the summer of 2004, allowed some to jump to a conclusion—one that was utterly false—that the Pentagon had ordered the torture of Iraqis. Believers of the narrative refuse to trust a word of the bipartisan investigations that have demolished the link between the decisions about Guantanamo Bay and Abu Ghraib, or between decisions in Washington and the prison abuses.

The Abu Ghraib photos sparked extensive leaking inside the Beltway. Classified memos prepared by OLC analyzing how the Geneva Conventions, the Convention Against Torture (CAT), and a federal law banning torture applied to captured al Qaeda and Taliban fighters were handed to the press. After administration opponents had finished scouring them for juicy passages for popular consumption, the charges that the Bush administration had sought to undermine or evade the law flew fast and furious. Senator Dianne Feinstein claimed that the analyses appeared "to be an effort to redefine torture and narrow prohibitions against it."

In August 2002, Bybee signed an opinion that concluded, after a thorough review of the law, that "physical pain amounting to torture must be equivalent in intensity to the pain accompanying serious physical injury, such as organ failure, impairment of bodily function, or even death. For purely mental pain or suffering to amount to torture (under U.S. law), it must result in significant psychological harm of significant duration, e.g., lasting for months or even years." While the advice was entirely accurate, conspiracy theories have since grown up around our work. One has it that it was really Vice President Dick Cheney's office, led by David Addington, which wrote parts of the memorandum to promote Cheney's drive to expand the powers of the executive branch.[12] Others claim that OLC had allied with "neo-cons" in other agencies, such as the Defense Department's civilian leadership and Cheney's office, to promote the violation of international and federal law without proper controls by other offices in the Justice Department and other agencies.

Bandied about as they may be, these theories are utterly without foundation in the truth. The subject matter was certainly extraordinary and demanded unusually tight controls because of its sensitivity. Justice Department officials have prohibited any specific discussion of the process that produced the 2002 memo, out of concern about revealing confidential information. But I can describe the standard process for opinions involving intelligence matters. Normally, the general counsel of one of the intelligence agencies would identify a legal issue involving a proposed operation or program. The NSC's legal adviser would formally ask OLC for the opinion. He would set the classification level of the work and would dictate, in consultation with the White House counsel, which agencies and personnel would have access to it. Sometimes neither State nor Defense lawyers would know about the opinion. We regularly notified the offices of the attorney general and the deputy attorney general about all pending opinions, and gave them periodic updates on our progress. Within OLC, career attorneys handle the initial research and drafting of opinions, with editing and review by two political appointees at my level, and then final rewriting and editing by the head of the office. Any opinion would circulate to the NSC legal advisor, the White House counsel's office, and the intelligence agencies for their comments. OLC always welcomed comments, suggested edits, and questions. But in no case was a single word of any opinion every written by anyone outside the Justice Department.

Some in the media have speculated that the opinion somehow did not move through the proper channels within the Justice Department. That too is wrong. Aside from the restricted circle of personnel who could work on it, the opinion went through the normal process of review. No one urged us to make any significant changes in the opinion, and I do not recall anyone disagreeing with the basic conclusions of the opinion. That is not to say that anyone thought it was an easy question to answer; everyone understood that the opinion addressed difficult questions fraught with serious consequences.

Controversy has surrounded OLC's opinion ever since. In December 2004, just a few days before Alberto Gonzales's confirmation hearings to become attorney general, DOJ replaced the memo with a super-seding legal opinion in an effort to satisfy the administration critics, who were having a field day attributing the Abu Ghraib photos to the 2002 legal memos. I felt it was a disservice to the personnel, especially those in the field, who had to rely on the Justice Department's advice to take risks in fighting the war on terrorism. Since the legal conclusions in the new memo were basically the same, this exercise in political image-making may have seemed worth it simply to ease Gonzales's confirmation (though not by much, as it turned out). But it was a misguided politicization of the Justice Department's job of giving legal advice. The second opinion not only retracted the bright lines the 2002 memo attempted to draw, replacing them with vague language that gave less offense, it provided much less guidance or clarity. The men and women risking their lives in the field to protect the country would now not be allowed to know specifically what they could and could not do.

Because the federal antitorture law used words rare in the federal code, no prosecutions had been brought under it, and it had never been interpreted by a federal court. We wrote the memo to give the executive branch guidance on these specifics. The 2002 memo was, in effect, rewritten in 2004 to take out language about what torture was or wasn't, to placate the sensibilities of those who didn't like seeing the law of torture and harsh interrogation even discussed. Nothing of substance about the law had changed.

The harder question was what interrogation methods fell short of the torture ban and could be used against al Qaeda leaders. Federal law commands that al Qaeda and Taliban operatives not be tortured. The President had gone much farther than that, ordering from the outset that they be treated *humanely*. In its antitorture law in force at the time of the 2002 memos, Congress made clear that the United States could not use interrogation methods that caused "severe physical or mental pain or suffering," and no one in the government questioned that ban, or suggested methods to violate it. But would limiting a captured terrorist to six hours' sleep, isolating him, interrogating him for several hours, or requiring him to exercise constitute "severe physical or mental pain or suffering"? Are these actions inhuman or cruel? Could these methods be used if our government had intelligence that al Qaeda was seeking to carry out another attack on the United States? The legal meaning of "torture" is not as all-inclusive as some people would like it to be. Legally, we are not required to treat captured terrorists engaged in war against us as if they were suspects held at an American police station. Limiting our intelligence and military officials to polite questioning, and demanding that terrorists receive lawyers, Miranda warnings, and a court trial, would only hurt our ability to stop future attacks. Unpleasant as it is, our government has a responsibility to eliminate the al Qaeda threat and to do what is reasonably necessary in self-defense.

So far we have prevented another successful attack on the United States, but some forget how hard that is to accomplish. The point of the 2002 memo was to give clear guidance on the state of the law, not to give the administration political cover, much less paint a pretty picture for a broad range of sensibilities.

It should be clearly understood that neither the August 2002 memo nor the Justice Department advocated or recommended torture or any other interrogation tactics. Rather, OLC addressed this question: What is the meaning of "torture" under the federal criminal laws? What the law forbids and what policy makers choose to do are entirely different things, and analyzing the laws is what the Department of Justice and the OLC exist to do.

What if, as the popular Fox television program *24* recently portrayed, a high-level terrorist leader is caught who knows the location of a nuclear weapon in an American city. Should it be illegal for the President to use harsh interrogation short of torture to elicit this information? In 2004 Senate hearings, even Senator Charles Schumer acknowledged that "very few people in this room or in America . . . would say that torture should never, ever be used, particularly if thousands of lives are at stake." Senator John McCain, himself the victim of terrible abuses at the hands of the North Vietnamese, in late 2005 sponsored a law extending Congress's prohibition of torture to the much broader category of "cruel, inhuman, and degrading treatment." But even

McCain concedes that the President ought to violate his own law if al Qaeda has hidden a nuclear bomb in New York and American intelligence captures one of the plotters. "You do what you have to do," McCain said in the fall of 2005. "But you take responsibility for it. Abraham Lincoln suspended habeas corpus in the Civil War, and FDR violated the Neutrality Acts before World War II."[13]

Unfortunately, these are no longer hypothetical questions. We do face an enemy that is intent on carrying out surprise attacks on innocent civilians, with WMDs if possible, by using covert cells of operatives hidden within the United States.

Critical moral and policy concerns surround interrogation policy, but first we have to clarify the legal framework, which has been much exaggerated and mistaken. A good example is the opinion of the International Committee for the Red Cross (ICRC), which has not lived up to its responsibilities as a neutral intermediary in wartime, but instead has pushed a political agenda. An ICRC report on Guantanamo Bay criticized interrogation as a "system devised to break the will of the prisoners [and] make them wholly dependent on their interrogators."[14] It said that "the construction of such a system, whose stated purpose is the production of intelligence, cannot be considered other than an intentional system of cruel, unusual, and degrading treatment and a form of torture." It did not say that any particular interrogation method constituted torture, but instead that the whole system of gaining intelligence was cruel, unusual, degrading treatment that amounted to torture. If attempting to gain intelligence by breaking the "will of the prisoners" and making them "wholly dependent on their interrogators" constitutes torture, then virtually all interrogation is torture and illegal, including what goes on in U.S. police stations every day.

A politicized UN followed in the ICRC's footsteps. Its Committee Against Torture (CAT) issued a May 2006 report demanding that the Guantanamo Bay facility be closed.[15] This committee, established to monitor compliance with CAT, was "concerned that detainees are held for protracted periods" and lack "legal safeguards" and "judicial assessment of the justification of their detention." It also claimed that detaining al Qaeda without access by the ICRC was a violation of the antitorture treaty. The CAT does not cover the detention of enemy combatants—the laws of war do, and they have long allowed for detention without judicial review. The UN presented the spectacle of some of the world's worst human rights abusers, including China and Russia, advising the American delegation that their treaty interpretations would reign supreme over United States law.

American law prohibits torture. But not all forms of interrogation that go beyond questioning are torture. Physical or mental coercion that does not constitute torture include threats of poor treatment or promises of better treatment or nonharmful physical contact. Solitary confinement is not torture. Marine instructors don't commit torture in boot camp.

In 1994, the United States ratified the CAT, which required the criminalization of torture.[16] It also declares that parties "undertake to prevent . . . other acts of cruel, inhuman, or degrading treatment or punishment which do not amount to torture."[17] Thus, the central international treaty on the subject makes a clear distinction between torture on the one hand, and harsh measures characterized as "cruel, inhuman, or degrading treatment" on the other. CAT required states to criminalize only the former—not the latter.[18] The Reagan administration made clear that the treaty did not regulate all forms of mistreatment, which, below the level of torture, would remain the domain of American law. It reported to the Senate: "Rough treatment as generally falls into the category of 'police brutality,' while deplorable, does not amount to 'torture.'"[19] And Congress completely agreed.

Congress maintained this distinction in a 1994 law criminalizing torture outside the United States. It defined torture as an "an act committed by a person acting under the color of law specifically intended to inflict severe physical or mental pain or suffering (other than pain or suffering incidental to lawful sanctions) upon another person within his custody or physical control."[20] Congress unquestionably intended its prohibition on torture to be narrow, much narrower than many popular understandings of the word. The alleged torturer must have acted with "specific intent," the highest level of criminal intent known to the law—

the difference between premeditated, first-degree murder, and manslaughter.[21] If severe physical or mental pain or suffering results, but was unintentional, or unanticipated, or resulted from negligent or perhaps even reckless action, it would not be torture. Further, if someone acts under the good faith belief that his actions do not violate the law, they do not meet the level for specific intent.

Critics scoff that this definition would allow a government agent to get away with torture if he claims to be doing so for good reasons. Perhaps so. However, this has nothing to do with the definition of specific intent. "Good reasons" are defenses to a charge of wrongful action.[22] Killing in self-defense is a *defense* to the charge of murder; it does not eliminate the requirement of an intent to kill. Congress chose to prohibit torture only when the perpetrators intended to do so, not to call everyone who in any way might inflict severe mental or physical pain a torturer.

Congress also only prohibited "*severe* physical or mental pain or suffering." The ban on torture does not prohibit *any* pain or suffering, whether physical or mental, only severe acts. Congress did not define "severe." Standard dictionaries define "severe" in the context of pain as something that is "grievous," "extreme," "sharp," and "hard to endure."[23] OLC interpreted "severe" as a level of pain "equivalent in intensity to the pain accompanying serious physical injury, such as death, organ failure, or serious impairment of body functions."[24] Many critics don't like this definition, preferring that it encompass more.

OLC's first 2002 opinion did not make up this definition out of thin air. It applied a standard technique used to interpret ambiguous phrases in a law. When Congress does not define its terms, courts commonly look in the United States Code for the use of similar language. The only other place where similar words appear is in a law defining health benefits for emergency medical conditions, which are defined as severe symptoms, including "severe pain" where an individual's health is placed "in serious jeopardy," "serious impairment to bodily functions," or "serious dysfunction of any bodily organ or part."[25] Obviously, Congress's terminology here was not exactly on point, but it was the closest Congress had come to defining severe pain. It was an illustration of severe pain, not an effort to limit its definition. Assertions in the media that the Bush administration defined torture *only* as serious organ failure or death are misrepresentations.

By focusing only on this phrase, administration critics imply that the Justice Department limited torture to direct physical abuse. They have claimed that the Justice Department would allow the denial of medical care, or the use of psychotropic drugs, or the playing of Russian roulette, or the threatening of a detainee or their family members with death. This claim was made by partisans who either did not read the 2002 legal opinion or the text of the 1994 antitorture law itself, or are ignoring them both. The law prohibits the infliction of severe mental pain or suffering in so many words, which it more precisely defined as "the prolonged mental harm" caused by four specific acts: (a) the threat or administration of actual physical pain and suffering, (b) the threat or administration of "mind-altering substances or other procedures calculated to disrupt profoundly the senses or the personality," (c) the "threat of imminent death," or (d) the threat of inflicting these harms on a third person.[26] This definition prohibited certain things, but allowed others. That is the nature of drawing a line. By requiring that the mental harm be "prolonged," Congress prohibited the causing of posttraumatic stress disorder or chronic depression but not the temporary strain of a police interrogation. No Russian roulette—this clearly violates (c)—but threats such as "If you do not cooperate, you will be tried and sentenced to death" or "If you do not talk, you will stay in this prison so long, you will die here" were permissible.[27] No psychotropic drugs—this clearly violates (b)—but a much-fabled truth serum that did not cause pain, or even getting an al Qaeda leader mildly drunk, might be legal. These would not "disrupt profoundly" the senses or personality, which we took to mean something more serious in its effects.

Human rights advocates claim that such aggressive interrogation methods violate the ban on torture. Perhaps they have succeeded in convincing public opinion that anything beyond shouted questions is torture, but that isn't the law. Congress made this clear by what it didn't do as much as by what it did. Before the McCain Amendment,

Congress opted not to prohibit the broader category of "cruel, inhuman, or degrading treatment or punishment," on the grounds that these words were too vague.[28] A European court had suggested that German officials had violated this standard by refusing to recognize a prisoner's sex change.[29]

Executive branch officials wanted to make sure that the United States did not adopt any international legal obligations that went beyond what American law already required. They suggested, and the Senate adopted, a definition that "cruel, inhuman, or degrading" meant conduct which the Constitution's Fifth, Eighth, or Fourteenth Amendments already prohibited.[30] This followed American practice of ratifying human rights treaties so as to require no change in domestic law. Cruel, inhuman, or degrading treatment was prohibited only to the extent it was already prohibited by the Constitution.

Domestic law remained unchanged by the 1994 antitorture law. Within the United States, federal and state law already regulated interrogation, and outside the United States, Congress banned torture, but not interrogation techniques short of it.[31] It would have been remarkable for the United States, without much discussion, to have accepted an enormous extension of rights to all foreign citizens in wartime whenever detained by the U.S. government. Even if this were so, this would not have barred coercive interrogation. The Eighth Amendment's ban on cruel and unusual punishments covers everyone, citizen or alien, being dealt with within our criminal justice system, but our law does not extend its privileges (or those of the rest of our Bill of Rights) to enemy aliens *outside* the United States.[32]

In all of the critics' claims that the administration sought to redefine torture to permit it, they almost never define torture themselves, much less accurately state the existing law on the books. And they never say how they might choose to apply it to captured al Qaeda leaders. Looking back now, I realize that we did not explain ourselves as clearly as we could have in 2002. I failed to anticipate that the memo would leak and that it would become susceptible to quotations out of context. The definition of severe physical pain or suffering as similar in level to that accompanying organ failure, loss of a limb, or death did not do justice to the more complete definition in the memo itself. The environment of war did not give us the luxury to worry about future perceptions of our work.

But like it or not, the antitorture statute narrowly defined torture as the infliction of *severe* physical or mental pain or suffering. Congress could easily have chosen to broaden this to "all" or "any" physical or mental pain or suffering, or the like. It did not. Plenty of bad acts are illegal under the definition of torture that Congress adopted, but not all forms of coercive interrogation are. Methods that are manipulative but do not cause severe pain or suffering are permitted.

In order to provide the White House better guidance, we compiled numerous examples from actual cases. We reviewed American and international literature. American judicial decisions on the Torture Victims Protection Act create a civil remedy for victims of torture and give a definition very similar to the criminal statute.[33] Those cases speak of torture as severe beatings, mock executions, threats to cut off body parts, burning, electric shocks, sexual assaults, or torturing a third person within view.[34] They illustrate what torture has been considered to be, mostly in the context of truly brutal authoritarian regimes. They are not meant to comprise an exclusive list or to define any line below which all else can be considered lawful.

It is often said that the United States has defied the opinion of the rest of the world with its antiterrorism tactics. That is absurd. Counterterrorism agents in the United Kingdom and Israel first developed methods to break the will of terrorists without inflicting severe physical harm. In the U.K., the British forced certain IRA members to stand against a wall, placed hoods on their heads during questioning, played loud noises, or reduced their sleep or rations. The European Court of Human Rights (ECHR) found the British methods to be inhumane and degrading treatment, but also found that Britain's interrogation methods "did not occasion suffering of the particular intensity and cruelty implied by the word torture."[35] Reagan administration officials had, in transmitting the CAT to the Senate, specifically pointed to the British methods as an example of conduct that would not violate the torture ban.[36]

Israeli experience held the same lesson. In response to the Palestinian intifada and a campaign of suicide bombings, Israel's General Security Service (GSS) employed a combination of stress-inducing methods to interrogate terrorist suspects—forcing detainees to withstand uncomfortable positions, forceful shaking, excessively tight handcuffs, and sleep deprivation. Israel's Supreme Court heard a challenge to GSS procedures in 1999 and reached a similar conclusion to the British case. It found that legislative authorization was needed for the methods because they were inhumane and degrading—but that they were not torture.[37] Obviously, the judicial decisions of other countries don't bind the United States legally. But they are examples of other democratic nations with legal traditions not unlike our own dealing with an ongoing terrorist problem. Both Britain and Israel adopted a ban on torture, and their courts and commissions found that it did not prohibit coercive interrogation. Critics could argue that coercive interrogations did nothing to solve the ultimate terrorism problems in either Ireland or Israel, and that neither country became safer. No one in the government, however, argued that aggressively interrogating al Qaeda leaders would end the threat of al Qaeda. It could produce information that might prevent attacks and save American lives. Both the Israeli and British experiences are examples of democracies with legal traditions similar to our own making the difficult decisions required by terrorism.

So, even for al Qaeda leaders, our rules prohibited severe physical pain or suffering. Limited stress—by forcing detainees to assume uncomfortable physical positions, or limiting their sleeping patterns or food—was not barred under this standard. This is not a police or prison brutality standard, as the critics have alleged. It is more like basic training or boot camp in the Army or Marines, where the purpose is to break down trainee resistance. These are measures, it should be emphasized, that no one should be happy to think about. Ideally, everyone would prefer a system in which a detainee was read his rights and then allowed to remain silent, if he so chose. But it was al Qaeda's attacks that made the costs of silence and inaction so great. After 9/11 our government had to make tragic choices between saving American lives from future terrorist attacks and observing the rights of suspected al Qaeda leaders. Not using such measures is just as much a choice as using them.

Commentator Anthony Lewis likened the 2002 memo's legal discussion to that of "a mob lawyer to a mafia don on how to skirt the law and stay out of prison."[38] Critics of the war on terrorism seem to believe it is wrong or immoral for our elected leaders even to ask about the legal limits of their powers, or for government lawyers to answer their questions. President Bush and his advisers should not have asked about the meaning of the antitorture law, according to New York University law professor Jeremy Waldron, because doing so suggested that they wanted to act up to its limit. As Waldron puts it, "[T]here are some scales one really should not be on, and with respect to which one really does not have a legitimate interest in knowing precisely how far along the scale one is permitted to go."[39] According to the critics, Justice Department lawyers should have refused to answer the White House's question, out of moral outrage. This is wrong. A President would be derelict in his duty if he did not review the full legal extent of his options in deciding policy, especially when confronted by the challenges of this new kind of war.

Our political system holds its leaders accountable for their decisions. If the electorate disagrees with those choices, they can press Congress to change the law or they can seek to remove the official responsible for the policy through the electoral process. Our nation had a presidential and congressional election after Abu Ghraib and the leaking of the OLC memos. If the people had disagreed with administration policies, they could have made a change. The complaint of the critics was, in essence, that government lawyers should impose specific policies upon the President, following their personal policy views on what the law ought to be. The critics sought to use litigation to move wartime policy in their preferred directions rather than working through our elected representatives.

The critics' desire to impose their own policy concepts, by misreading the law, comes through on the question of defenses to possible violations of the antitorture law. Before 9/11, legal thinking had focused on whether necessity or self-defense could justify or excuse torture.[40] Necessity—or the "choice of evils," as it is known—is the most discussed justification for violations of criminal law. Defendants raise it whenever they feel they have to violate a law to avoid even greater harm or evil to themselves or others.[41] The well-known "ticking bomb" scenario is often cited in discussions of the necessity defense: What kind of force should be used with a terrorist who knows the location of a ticking time bomb that will take many civilian lives? Legal thinkers love to wrestle with the probabilities, ethics, and costs and benefits of this problem. Is it justifiable to kill an innocent person to save two other lives? What if, post–9/11, we found an al Qaeda member involved in a plot to blow up a nuclear weapon in Los Angeles? After all, "any harm that might occur during an interrogation would pale to insignificance compared to the harm avoided by preventing such an attack, which could take hundreds of thousands of lives."[42]

Self-defense is another possible defense for an intelligence agent.[43] Congress expressly refused to rule it out when it passed the anti-torture law. A defendant can use "reasonable force" when he reasonably believes he or another person is in imminent danger of bodily harm.[44] As with necessity, whether a claim of self-defense will be upheld will depend on the facts.[45] It is also possible that a nation's overall right to defend itself from terror supports an individual agent's claim in his use of force against a terror suspect.[46] If self-defense is a standard defense to homicide, it is difficult to see why it would not be a defense to torture as well.

Administration critics strongly disagreed with the discussion of defenses. A group of law professors and lawyers attacked the notion of a defense as "contrived" and "distorted,"[47] wrongly and unjustifiably implying that there is no such thing as a defense against a law. Congress considered eliminating common law defenses for government officials engaged in harsh interrogation, but decided against it. It intentionally left out of the statute CAT provisions that eliminated defenses based on war or public emergency.[48] American law thus presumes self-defense and necessity defenses to exist for violations of any criminal law. Unless Congress changes the law, these defenses will apply.[49]

Columnist Anthony Lewis replies that discussing available legal defenses shows a criminal desire on the part of the administration to violate the law and get away with it. We work to send our police officers onto the streets with a full understanding of the rules on the use of force, including the rules on firing their weapon in self-defense. Our intelligence officers deserve the same clarity. Otherwise, those who risk their own lives to keep other Americans safe will be forced to struggle with broad, vague prohibitions, behind which lurk massive liabilities. I think that our agents in the field deserve better.

In the summer of 2004, as the Abu Ghraib controversy hit the front pages, the Justice Department bowed to administration critics and withdrew the leaked 2002 opinion. I thought this a terrible precedent. It showed that Justice Department judgments on the law had become just one more political target open to partisan attack and political negotiation. The implication was that if one put enough pressure on the Justice Department it, like any other part of the government, would bend. It also suggested to me that the leadership of the Justice Department that had replaced the team there on 9/11 was too worried about the public perceptions of its work.

At the end of 2004, the Justice Department issued a revised opinion. The biggest change was that it withdrew the 2002 discussion of defenses on the grounds that "[c]onsideration of the bounds of any such authority would be inconsistent with the President's unequivocal directive that United States personnel not engage in torture."[50] In 2002, we thought that the opinion interpreting the federal antitorture law ought not be tailored to any single interrogation method. Two years later, DOJ officials looked back with the benefit of 20/20 hindsight to second-guess us. To say that this was unnecessary was akin to a situation in which a passenger, having arrived at his destination, tells the driver there is no need to read the map to find the best route. Obviously, once policy makers have made their choices, other possibilities become irrelevant, but not before.

The 2004 memo's other significant change was to replace the 2002 definition of torture. It said that torture might be broader than "excruciating or agonizing pain or suffering," using words not much different from those of the antitorture statute itself. It then proceeded to list acts that everyone would agree were torture. The 2004 opinion studiously avoided providing a precise definition of the law. In essence, the Justice Department in 2004 said we had made a mistake two years earlier by trying to interpret the law with any clarity.

Though it criticized our earlier work, the 2004 opinion included a footnote to say that all interrogation methods that earlier opinions had found legal *were still legal.* In other words, the differences in the opinions were for appearances' sake. In the real world of interrogation policy nothing had changed. The new opinion just reread the statute to deliberately blur the interpretation of torture as a short-term political maneuver in response to public criticism.

For some new officials at Justice, who came onto the job years after 9/11, withdrawing the 2002 opinion wasn't enough. It was as if, sensing the 2004 opinion's ambivalence and its decision to muddy the legal waters, these individuals decided they needed to go to extraordinary lengths to discredit the first opinion. They ordered the opening of an investigation into all those who worked on it, from the career attorneys to the head of the office, to determine whether we had violated our professional responsibilities in providing legal advice.

Investigators decided to rely on criticism in the press as the grounds of their inquiry. One section of the 2002 opinion argued that the antitorture statute's general prohibitions should not be interpreted to apply to military and intelligence operations in wartime.[51] Congress had included no language specifically regarding national security affairs, and if it had, that might conflict with the President's commander-in-chief power to defend the nation from attack. This section of the memo provided a legal framework for the White House and the CIA. What might happen if someone stepped over the line was a question we would have been derelict not to address. The antitorture law's vague terminology and the scarcity of authoritative decisions also elevated the chance of a conflict between the branches arising at some point in the future.

A collection of law professors, human rights activists, and former American Bar Association presidents, among others, declared that the idea that the President can refuse to obey an unconstitutional law is "an unprecedented and under-analyzed claim that the Executive Branch is a law unto itself," which is "incompatible with the rule of law and the principle that no one is above the law."[52] They argued that the idea that the commander-in-chief power could override the anti-torture statute violated professional ethics because we did not discuss Justice Robert Jackson's individual opinion in a famous separation-of-powers case, *Youngstown Sheet & Tube Co. v. Sawyer*.[53] Democrat senators turned *Youngstown* into a rallying cry during Gonzales' confirmation hearings as attorney general.

Youngstown addressed President Truman's effort to seize steel mills shut down by a labor strike during the Korean War. Truman claimed that maintaining steel production was necessary to supply munitions and material to American troops in combat. *Youngstown* held that the regulation of labor-management relations constituted lawmaking that could only be performed by Congress. Because Congress had rejected any delegation of authority to the President, the steel mills were beyond Truman's control. Justice Jackson penned a well-known opinion, representing his views alone, with a three-part framework: Presidential power supported by congressional approval would be at its greatest height, presidential power in the face of silence would be in a "zone of twilight," and presidential power faced by disapproval would be "at its lowest ebb."[54] Based on Jackson's approach, critics of the executive branch claim that the President cannot act against the wishes of Congress, even in wartime.

We did not cite Justice Jackson's individual views in *Youngstown* because earlier OLC opinions, reaching across several administrations, had concluded that it had no application to the President's conduct of foreign affairs and national security. *Youngstown* reached the outcome it did because the Constitution clearly gives Congress, not the President, the exclusive power to make law concerning labor disputes.[55] It does not address the scope of the commander-in-chief power involving military strategy or intelligence tactics in war. If anything, *Youngstown* supports the proposition that one branch cannot intrude on the clear constitutional turf of another. Even Justice Jackson recognized that, at its lowest ebb, the President would prevail if "he can rely only upon his own constitutional powers minus any constitutional powers of Congress over the matter." Detention and interrogation policy are at the heart of the President's commander-in-chief power to wage war, and long constitutional history supports the President's leading role on such matters.[56] This is why all administrations have refused to acknowledge the legality of the War Powers Resolution, and have regularly started and continued military conflicts without congressional approval.

The Justice Department officials who launched the ethics investigation either ignored the department's long tradition in defending the President's commander-in-chief power or responded reflexively to political controversy. They certainly did not check the bona fides of the critics who first made the accusation that not citing *Youngstown* amounted to a failure of professional responsibility. Many of the leading critics were former Clinton officials who overlooked their administration's own legal views, which, on the matter of executive authority in war and national security, were nearly identical to ours. In 1994, Janet Reno's OLC, headed by Duke law professor Walter Dellinger, opined that the President could "decline to enforce a statute that he views as unconstitutional."[57] This is especially true, OLC observed, "of provisions limiting the President's authority as commander in chief." His office later found unconstitutional a congressional proposal to prohibit American troops from serving under foreign or international commands.[58] Dellinger's opinion cited *Youngstown* only once—in support of the proposition that the President has the right to *refuse* to execute a law. A second opinion never mentioned *Youngstown*. Far from inventing some novel interpretation of the Constitution, OLC was really doing little more than following in the footsteps of the Clinton Justice Department and all prior Justice Departments.

I cannot help but think that Justice Department officials panicked when the Abu Ghraib scandal erupted, and then were misled by the charges about ethics. Claims about "ethics" always emerge as a weapon, both on the left and the right, when the party in power cannot be budged on policy specifics. Justice officials surely did not consider the long-run implications of what they were doing. The Justice Department and specifically OLC serve in part as the lawyers for the executive branch. If they were to accept that *Youngstown* controlled the executive branch in war, the President's powers would be crippled. If the President had no independent constitutional powers, Congress could pass laws preventing a President from firing cabinet members, signing international agreements, or directing foreign policy or military strategy without getting approval from Congress first. No President's administration wants that, Republican or Democrat.

In the rush to distance themselves from the 2002 opinion, the Justice Department leaders forgot to think about incentives. In the war on terrorism, we will need officials at all levels, from career civil servants to cabinet members, to innovate and take risks. An ethics investigation only signals that those who try to work through the difficult issues of this war, and work aggressively to defeat al Qaeda, may wind up under fire if political controversy erupts.

The administration sought to "move on" and appease its critics. The effect was predictable. The critics were not appeased. They were only emboldened by their success at making administration members look for all the world like confessed torturers. So this purely political gambit did not allow the administration to "move on." Instead, it paid a high price. By refusing to defend its own logic, and pretending to distance itself from it, the administration only succeeded in eroding public support for the war against al Qaeda.

Attorney General Ashcroft made that political decision, and I think it has become fairly clear that it was a mistake. I can understand the pressures he and others were under. I believe that he worked as hard as anyone in his department to get up to speed on terrorism issues. Admirably, in other cases he did not flinch when he and his department became the subject of critics' ire.

But his office pretended during the summer of 2004 that the attorney general had been out of the loop in 2002. It was a transparent effort to avoid responsibility by pleading ignorance of the activities of his own department. No opinion of that significance could ever issue from the Justice Department without the review of the attorney general's staff, in particular that of his counselor, or without the attorney general's personal approval. I wish Ashcroft had stood up and defended the work of the dedicated men and women in his department. Instead an investigation was launched into so-called "ethics." It is fair to disagree with our conclusions on the merits. But to claim ethical violations is unfounded and unfair.

The purpose of all OLC opinions is to make sure the government operates within the boundaries set by law. The 2004 OLC opinion withdrew the discussion of defenses and the Commander-in-Chief Clause, and intentionally blurred the definition of torture. But it still found that all the interrogation methods approved under the 2002 opinion were legal.[59] In 2002, we believed that legal clarity could help win the war on terrorism. In 2004, justice put politics first.

Policy

American law prohibits torture but not coercive interrogation. Once a classic law school hypothetical, it is now up to our elected leaders to decide what kind of coercive interrogation *is* allowed. If they had ignored this task, they would have cast the burden on our troops and intelligence officers to guess just what is permitted and what not, at their own peril.

Some believe that coercive interrogation is never justified in a moral society that respects human rights and rejects barbarism, even if the consequences are another 9/11 or worse. NYU law professor Jeremy Waldron, perhaps the leading legal philosopher of his generation (and a former Berkeley colleague of mine), when confronted with the hypothetical of using "excruciating pain" to learn the location of a nuclear bomb in an American city, says, "My own answer to this question is a simple No."[60] Under this absolutist view, the ban on coercive interrogation overrides any other consideration of policy or costs and benefits; the number of lives that could be saved, even if in the millions, is irrelevant.

Such arguments, of course, turn us away from the actual choices we face. Many legal philosophers will say they reject torture or other forms of physical pressure, but shy away from Waldron's inflexible position. My Berkeley colleague Sandy Kadish writes, "[T]he use of torture is so profound a violation of a human right that almost nothing can redeem it—almost, because one can not rule out a case in which the lives of many innocent persons will surely be saved by its use against a single person."[61]

I think most Americans, and certainly anyone of either political party who must actually run a government, would find Kadish's position reasonable. We remain horrified by the idea of using physical or mental pressure to elicit information, but we cannot rule it out in all cases. A leader can also be morally wrong to choose to allow the deaths of thousands of citizens rather than consider coercive interrogation of a single terrorist leader. Civil libertarians often claim that this is not a realistic choice, but just an artificial hypothetical. That is simply wrong. We continue today to face an enemy that murdered three thousand citizens on September 11. It has attempted to acquire biological and nuclear weapons, and will use them against us if possible. Unfortunately, these are hypotheticals no more.

Waving away these new realities also denies a more basic reality of modern politics. Our government makes cost-benefit decisions all the time, sometimes in cases where human life or safety is at stake. The death penalty is only one example;[62] some criminal offenses are so heinous that we end the lives of those who commit them. Take the use of force by soldiers or police. We allow the military to shoot to kill members of the enemy and to destroy property so as to protect the country and pursue the national interest. We ask soldiers to launch attacks in which some will lose their lives for military objectives. We permit cops to resort to deadly force to protect their lives or the lives of others. We ask firemen and police to risk their lives for the public safety. Our government makes hard, tragic choices in less obvious ways every day. It sets pollution levels for the air or water knowing that it will produce some level of sickness and disease, but that it must balance economic growth against environmental protection. It must decide how fast to bring drugs to market, understanding that some will suffer serious or even life-threatening side effects, while others will die while approval is pending. The government makes these trade-offs in many areas of regulation almost every day.[63]

Most of the arguments against coercive interrogation are not about moral absolutes, but about whether the costs outweigh the benefits. Critics of the Bush administration raise a number of claims, I believe, which understate the benefits and overstate the costs. One common claim is that torture does not work and produces only unreliable information or lies from terrorists,[64] and so therefore, by extension, coercive interrogation won't work either. This argument is implausible. FBI agents prefer to build a rapport with detainees, while military lawyers believe that "the use of force is a poor technique, as it yields unreliable results, may damage subsequent collection efforts, and can induce the source to say whatever he thinks the interrogator wants to hear."[65] But there is substantial current, and historical, evidence that coercive interrogation can produce important information, or "actionable intelligence."

The most extensive up-to-date evidence is from Israel. The Landau Commission, an Israeli investigation into allegations of torture against its security services (the GSS), found that effectively preventing some terrorist bombings would have been "impossible" without the use of coercive interrogation methods. In a 1997 report to the United Nations, Israel said that because of these methods, "some 90 planned terrorist attacks have been foiled. Among these planned attacks are some 10 suicide bombings, 7 car-bombings, 15 kidnappings of soldiers and civilians, and some 60 attacks of different types."[66] In its 1999 opinion, the Israeli Supreme Court accepted that coercive interrogation had forced a terrorist to reveal the location of a powerful bomb similar to one that had destroyed a Tel Aviv café, killed three civilians, and wounded more than forty others in 1997.[67] Israel's security services appear to have continued their use of coercive interrogation methods.[68] And in the last few years, Israel has succeeded in substantially reducing the number of terrorist attacks against its people. While no doubt a large part of this reduction is due to the construction of the security barrier between Israel and the West Bank, the creation of the Palestinian Authority, the withdrawal from some of the occupied territories, and other antiterrorism policies, some of it is no doubt due to information learned through coercive interrogations.

The most convincing evidence that coercive interrogation works in certain circumstances comes from the fight against al Qaeda. In 1995, Filipino authorities captured an al Qaeda operative who had accidentally exploded bomb-making materials in a Manila apartment. Under terrible physical abuse (which does not bear any resemblance to the British, Israeli, or American methods), he divulged information that allowed intelligence agencies to disrupt a plan to simultaneously destroy twelve American airliners flying across the Pacific.[69] His testimony in federal court eventually helped convict Ramzi Yousef, the mastermind and leader of the 1993 World Trade Center bombing.

Coercive interrogation of Abu Zubaydah, Ramzi bin al Shibh, and KSM, all captured in the space of about one year, netted American interrogators a great deal of information—as a careful reading of the text and footnotes of the 9/11 Commission report reveals. Interrogating these men revealed not only how 9/11 was carried out, but the entire command structure of al Qaeda, its processes and organization, and how operations are planned, approved, and executed. These leaders discussed the gaps that allowed them to penetrate American security, and the types of attacks they sought to carry out. Interrogation also yielded the names of other al Qaeda agents diverted from 9/11 to future operations.[70] Interrogation of KSM produced the names of two al Qaeda pilots in addition to Moussaoui slated for a second wave of attacks in the United States,[71] and led to Jose Padilla. This is invaluable information.

A last example, made public by the White House and the Defense Department in June 2004, is that of Mohamed al Kahtani.[72] Kahtani is a Saudi national thought to have been the "twentieth hijacker."[73] The 9/11 hijackers had hijacked four planes, with three teams of five and one team of four, for a total of nineteen. American intelligence believed a twentieth hijacker had failed to join his compatriots in time for the attacks. American forces picked up Kahtani on the border between Afghanistan and Pakistan in December 2001. During initial questioning, he told military interrogators that he was in Afghanistan to buy falcons. Investigation showed that he had flown from Canada to Orlando on August 4, 2001, but was denied entry by an alert customs official who found his answers to questions suspicious. Telephone records show that Mohammed Atta was waiting in the Orlando airport on that very day and at that very time.

Following techniques designed to counter standard interrogation, Kahtani initially refused to tell investigators anything of value. Based on the evidence, there was good reason to believe that he had been sent to the United States to meet Atta. Kahtani therefore could have possessed very important information about any other al Qaeda operatives still in the United States, providing support for terrorists or, worse, waiting for future attacks.

It was Kahtani's case that set in motion the military's consideration of coercive interrogation. Officials in the fall of 2002 were concerned that al Qaeda would try another attack to commemorate the September 11 anniversary, and intelligence reports were spiking. In October 2002, Gitmo's commander sent a request forward, which Rumsfeld approved on December 2, to use coercive interrogation methods on Kahtani.[74] Rumsfeld approved stress positions, such as standing for up to four hours, isolation for up to thirty days, deprivation of light and sound in his cell, removal of clothing, changing rations, shaving of facial hair, and use of phobias to induce stress. In his usual candid way, Rumsfeld approved, but asked in a handwritten note: "However, I stand for 8–10 hours a day. Why is standing limited to 4 hours?"

Gitmo's commander requested even more aggressive measures, but only one—mild physical contact that does not injure, such as poking or grabbing—was approved. After unspecified concerns were raised at Guantanamo Bay about the use of these methods, Jim Haynes, DOD general counsel, went to Rumsfeld to ask him to suspend his approval until a broader review could be done. Rumsfeld did so on January 15, 2003. There have been unverified media reports based on Army logs that some interrogators went beyond their orders and made Kahtani wear women's underwear, put him on a leash and made him bark like a dog, and put him on an IV when he went on a hunger strike.

But what were the results of this use of coercive interrogation? Kahtani admitted that his cover story was false. He confessed that he was an al Qaeda operative who had met with Osama bin Laden several times. He acknowledged that he was sent to the United States by KSM. He provided detailed information on Reid and Padilla, whom he had met in al Qaeda training camps. Most important, he provided information on an al Qaeda operative, Saudi citizen Adnan el Shukrijumah, who is still on the loose and was believed to be in the United States in 2003 and 2004 to carry out another 9/11–style attack. KSM had apparently told interrogators earlier that El Shukrijumah was a high-level operational commander, on a par with Mohammed Atta, whose job was to organize a cell of operatives and oversee their execution of a surprise attack in the United States. Some reports also indicate that El Shukrijumah was to have worked with Padilla on the dirty bomb plot. El Shukrijumah would have little difficulty blending into American society, as he had lived in the United States for several years. His parents still live in south Florida, and he had been seen there in 2003. In May 2004, Ashcroft issued a warning that al Qaeda planned to attack the United States that summer, and launched an urgent manhunt for El Shukrijumah, along with six other al Qaeda suspects. The attacks never happened; perhaps the intensive scrutiny caused El Shukrijumah and his cell to scuttle their plans. Kahtani not only confirmed that he was the twentieth hijacker, but he also gave up information that helped our law enforcement and intelligence piece together an undiscovered plot within the United States.

This evidence, however, should not be overstated. It is not meant to prove that coercive interrogation should be used in every case, or even that it always works. It is only offered to show that coercive interrogation works in some circumstances, and therefore should not be ruled out across the board. We must carefully weigh the costs of coercive interrogations, but we must also be careful not to exaggerate them. Critics commonly make a number of claims about the costs of coercive interrogation based on highly speculative and empirically unsupported assumptions, such as that relaxing a prohibition on physical pressure will lead to a "standard operating procedure" where torture will become the norm.[75] Or that it will prove to be an added incentive for the enemy to fight all the harder.[76] Or that the information could be acquired another way. Or that it will undermine the advancement of international human rights, or the symbolism of Western law as a rejection of barbarism.[77] Or that it will cause allies to reject cooperation with the United States or cause us to lose the moral high ground in the war against terrorism.

These objections are pragmatic considerations based on hunches—albeit perhaps perfectly legitimate ones—about the way the world works. Coercive interrogation in an individual case might even make sense, a critic might concede, but because we cannot rationally balance costs and benefits under the pressure of war, or we only think of the short term, following a prohibition in all cases would still make for better policy overall. The problem, however, is that this hypothesis is often stated as fact, without any convincing evidence. Take the most commonly heard claim, that if we allow the use of coercive interrogation with terrorists it will undermine the ban on physical pressure in other situations.[78] This is the familiar "slippery slope" argument.[79] Soon, these civil libertarians worry, the use of coercive interrogation will create a constituency in the intelligence and military agencies that will support the expansion of its use against legal POWs and even criminal suspects.[80]

This argument is plausible, but it is anything but clear that coercive interrogation forces us inevitably onto a slippery slope. Other democracies, such as Israel and Great Britain, that have employed coercive interrogation do not seem to have allowed the practice to spread to their broader military or law enforcement activities. France's use of torture against Algerian terrorists does not seem to have infected its investigation of garden-variety crimes in metropolitan France.[81] We have laws that permit the police to use force, even deadly force, against suspects to protect themselves or the lives of others. The slippery slope argument would predict that this would lead to a weakening of respect for the rights of suspects by the police and create a "constituency" in the law enforcement community in favor of ever more brutal physical methods against crime. But this does not seem to be the case. We also have many cases of police brutality and prison abuse in the United States every year, but this does not mean that the rules promote or facilitate police or prison brutality.

The critics usually point to the mistreatment of Iraqi prisoners, speculating, as journalists Seymour Hersh and Michael Isikoff do, that the use of coercive interrogation methods against al Qaeda leaders must have led to their use at Guantanamo Bay, and that this culture must have then migrated to Iraq and inspired Abu Ghraib. Articles have appeared claiming abuses at Guantanamo such as long-term isolation, stress positions, and exposure to extreme heat or cold or noise. At this writing we cannot know if such reports are false, or isolated examples. They are currently unverified and the subject of continuing investigations. But slippery slopes produced by policy choices are one thing, and simple violations of rules another. If you look at the facts, instead of speculation and conspiracy theories, abuses at Abu Ghraib were found by multiple commissions and investigations to be solely the acts of individuals—in no way authorized as a matter of policy, law, or "atmosphere." Abu Ghraib operated under the Geneva Conventions from the start, as it should have under our laws. Several Pentagon investigations, most notably a bipartisan panel chaired by two former secretaries of defense, James Schlesinger and Harold Brown, have found the charges of a secret policy to engage in coercive interrogation to be false.[82] They report that the abuses at Abu Ghraib resulted not from orders out of Washington, but from flagrant disregard of interrogation in Iraq and detention rules by the guards. Schlesinger described conditions at the prison "as a kind of *Animal House* on the night shift" and blamed a lack of resources, training, and leadership.[83] A separate investigation by the naval inspector general, Vice Admiral Albert Church, who was charged with conducting an overall review of detainee policy, affirmed this conclusion. In the unclassified portion of his report, Church concluded, "It is clear that none of the pictured abuses at Abu Ghraib bear any resemblance to approved policies at any level, in any theater."[84]

While the Brown-Schlesinger report admitted that some migration of interrogation techniques from Guantanamo Bay to Iraq was possible, it found that whether they had migrated or not, this hadn't caused the Abu Ghraib abuses. It also found that the rate of abuse of detainees was actually lower in the war on terrorism than in previous American wars. The military has conducted literally tens of thousands of interrogations in the war on terrorism. Admiral Church's investigation found (as of September 2004) 71 cases of detainee abuse and 6 deaths, with only 20 of those cases involving interrogation, and 130 cases still under investigation. This included cases not just at detention facilities, but those that occurred at the point of capture, when soldiers are under much greater stress. He found no pattern to the abuses; they were committed in different theaters, by different personnel and units. Given that the United States had detained by that time approximately 50,000 individuals, this is an extremely low error rate. As Senator Joseph Lieberman observed at a Senate Armed Services Committee hearing on the Church report, this amounted to abuse of one tenth of one percent of all detainees. While each case of abuse is regrettable, it is not possible for a large organization charged with protecting the national security, under extraordinary pressure, to perform its mission error-free. A few high-profile, graphic cases do not reflect the actual overall performance of the military.

The "culture of abuse" theory has no reliable evidence to support it. Has the death penalty, or abortion, created a "culture of death" in the United States? That many say so does not make it true. Compare the Defense Department's interrogation methods at Guantanamo Bay with what happened at Abu Ghraib. Abu Ghraib featured terrible examples of physical and sexual abuse, imposed not in any interrogation context, but as sadistic entertainment when higher officers were not present.[85]

Interrogation methods at Guantanamo Bay, by contrast, were the result of a careful vetting process through a Defense Department–wide working group.[86] In January 2003, Rumsfeld asked Haynes to establish a group to consider the policy, operation, and legal issues involved in the interrogation of detainees in the war on terrorism. OLC advised the group, composed of both military officers and Defense Department civilians, on constitutional and other legal issues.

I have conducted many briefings in my time, for senators, judges, White House staff, and cabinet members. And of course I have taught many hundreds of Berkeley students—no easy job, that. The toughest reception I ever received was from that working group, which took no legal conclusion for granted and challenged every assumption and step in reasoning. Anyone who thinks the working group was there to rubber-stamp Rumsfeld's decisions does not know the military and its tough officers, nor the hardworking Defense Department staff.

The media has made a civilian named Alberto Mora, then the Navy's general counsel, into a minor celebrity (complete with a spread in the *New Yorker*) by claiming he protested the use of coercive interrogation and attempted to stand in the way of the working group's conclusions. This claim is usually made without reference to what the working group actually approved, which bears no resemblance to actual examples of torture. Mora, who has gone on to work in the general counsel's office at Wal-Mart, claims that I met with him and told him that the President could order the torture of the Gitmo detainees. I would not have said any such thing; no interrogation methods of anything like torture were under consideration. Mora seems to buy the standard position of human rights advocates that anything more than oral questioning would be torture, a view that lets him assert whatever he wants for media purposes.

That April, the working group issued a report approving interrogation methods for use at Guantanamo Bay. The group recommended twenty-six techniques for general use at Guantanamo Bay, of which twenty-two were strategies for purely verbal questioning, such as "Pride/Ego Up" or "Pride/Ego Down."[87] Most of these were already authorized for use against all enemy combatants, whether covered by the Geneva Conventions or not, by the U.S. Army field manual on interrogation.[88] Only two involved any physical contact. One allowed an interrogation to occur with the detainee wearing a blindfold, a second authorized only "lightly touching a detainee or lightly poking the detainee in a completely non-injurious manner."[89] Nine other "exceptional" methods were requested by interrogators at Guantanamo Bay: isolation, prolonged interrogation, forced shaving of hair or beard, prolonged standing, sleep deprivation, exercise, a sudden face or stomach slap to cause surprise, and removal of clothing. Only the ninth—creating a sense of anxiety by playing on a detainee's aversions—could be said to be similar to what happened at Abu Ghraib, because the example given was of the "simple presence of a dog without directly threatening action."[90]

Conspiracy theorists say this last proves their "culture of abuse" point. But they have no facts other than mention of the word "dog." Abu Ghraib *violated* these rules. The rule in place about dogs was that they could be used in a nonthreatening posture, only by specially trained interrogators who had received "senior level approval" for the interrogation, only as an exceptional measure, only at special facilities, and only on healthy detainees with vital intelligence.[91] And it could not be used if it would produce physical or mental injury to the detainee.

Hardly the call to take the gloves off. The working group, after carefully considering all the issues, approved a set of twenty-two oral interrogation methods while reserving anything more aggressive for use only on specific detainees with important information subject to senior commander approval. It reiterated President Bush's 2002 executive order that all prisoners be treated humanely, consistent with the principles of the Geneva Conventions—even though al Qaeda and Taliban fighters were not legally entitled to those protections. The group also outlined the potential costs of exceptional interrogation methods—loss of support among allies, weakened protections for captured U.S. personnel, confusion among interrogators about approved methods, and weakening of standards of conduct and morale among U.S. troops.

Perhaps the most important fact ignored in all the press was that *Rumsfeld specifically refused to authorize these exceptional interrogation methods for Guantanamo Bay, but for one.*[92] Concerned about the possibility of physical mistreatment, Rumsfeld struck the use of blindfolds and even mild, noninjurious physical contact from the list of conventional interrogation techniques. Of the exceptional methods, Rumsfeld authorized only isolation, and only if it would last no longer than thirty days. That was it. Rumsfeld did not approve use of dogs, physical contact, slapping, sleep deprivation, stress positions, or required calisthenics.

All this strongly indicates that the Abu Ghraib abuses would have occurred regardless of anything Rumsfeld decided. They would likely have happened no matter what the CIA had done. The CIA's interrogations were carefully cordoned off from other departments. The Pentagon had approved no physical pressure for use at Guantanamo Bay, much less Iraq. The guards responsible for the Abu Ghraib abuses were not reading OLC legal opinions, nor were they parsing Rumsfeld's orders to Southern Command.

No one is denying the abuses of Abu Ghraib or attempting to understate their terrible nature. But multiple investigations have shown that they occurred because of a lack of sufficient resources and personnel at the prison. Defense Department officials had not devoted sufficient troops to the task of rebuilding Iraq in general, and to detention operations in particular. Iraqi counterinsurgency operations produced large numbers of detainees that clearly overwhelmed the limited resources of the prison guard units sent to Iraq. Abu Ghraib was not secure, and often subject to attack, which produced enormous stress on the units there. These circumstances do not represent a conspiracy to abuse Iraqi detainees. Furthermore, the abuses at Abu Ghraib first came to the attention of military investigators and disciplinary proceedings had already begun long before any media revelations occurred. Since the leaking of the Abu Ghraib photographs, the process of military justice has continued, and several enlisted personnel and officers have been tried and convicted, while others are currently under investigation.

Abu Ghraib has been a propaganda bonanza for America's enemies and critics, undermining America's claims to be a force for good in the world and fanning anti-American conspiracy theories. Yet one could equally argue that America's response to the abuses of Abu Ghraib have put the strength and openness of our democracy on display. Despite all the remonstrations, the United States openly investigated abuses, corrected them, and openly debated interrogation policy. No one could responsibly mistake America for a Middle Eastern autocracy.

Efforts by China, Russia, and some European nations to contain America's military and economic power are probably far more important in the long term than the negative publicity from Abu Ghraib.

These costs must be balanced against the benefits. Unpopularity abroad, taken alone, cannot be a veto on American policy. President Reagan's decision to base intermediate nuclear missiles in Europe in the mid-1980s, as part of a general buildup in nuclear and conventional forces and pursuit of an antimissile defense, was deeply unpopular, leading to mass protests and accusations that the United States was risking nuclear war with the Soviet Union. Reagan went ahead anyway, because his administration judged that the gains from restoring American military strength and bankrupting the Soviet Union outweighed the political costs. Reagan was proved right. Today our elected leaders must decide if rejecting coercive interrogation of al Qaeda outweighs the lives that might be saved from a possible future attack. In 2002, the Bush administration decided that the intelligence gained through coercive interrogation was needed to prevent another attack on the United States, and that this priority outweighed the costs.

What if we had chosen inaction? Suppose a second attack in the United States, equal to or greater than 9/11, had occurred in the intervening period? Al Qaeda has a record of follow-up attacks, has sent more operatives to the United States since 9/11, and has actively sought weapons of mass destruction—nuclear, chemical, and biological. Is a second attack an acceptable price to pay for rejecting coercive interrogation? I doubt any responsible American political leader would take any such position. John Kerry criticized Bush for allowing the Abu Ghraib abuses to occur, but did not declare that he would ban coercive interrogation with good reason.

Limits

Abu Ghraib, no doubt, has harmed America's efforts in the war on terrorism, not just the scandal itself but because a law passed at the end of last year now prohibits certain coercive interrogation measures.

Known as the McCain Amendment, after its chief sponsor, Arizona Republican Senator John McCain, the legislation prohibits cruel, inhuman, and degrading treatment by both the military and intelligence agencies. It limits interrogation methods to those specified in the military field manual (a new edition is under development to replace the 1987 version).

As a downed pilot tortured for years by the North Vietnamese, Senator McCain speaks with an unmatched moral authority on the issue of torture. But I believe his law is unwise. Such flat prohibitions leave little discretion for unforeseen or catastrophic circumstances. If the text of the McCain Amendment were to be enforced as is, we could not coercively interrogate a terrorist, even if he were involved in a plot to detonate a WMD on an American city. Realizing this, Senator McCain himself acknowledged that the legislation should not prevent the President "from doing what he would have to do" in a ticking-bomb scenario. McCain's amendment did not explicitly prohibit necessity or self-defense as common law defenses. Thus, under the law, these defenses will continue to exist, as they did in the earlier 1994 antitorture law.

The McCain Amendment was one way of regulating coercive interrogation. Several others have been proposed. The Israeli Supreme Court recognizes a ban plus an express necessity defense. Law professor and pundit Alan Dershowitz proposes a system of warrants issued by judges, like FISA, but that replicates FISA's faults. Law professors Eric Posner and Adrian Vermeule argue that our legal system should handle coercive interrogation as it does police use of deadly force: with training, special rules, and immunity for those who follow the rules.[93]

All of these proposals have their points of common sense, their advantages and disadvantages. A stated rule like the McCain Amendment may seem clear, but no rule clarifies or foresees everything about the future. Rules in this area unduly restrict the flexibility of the people who must make good decisions among shifting complexities, particularly in the areas of foreign affairs, national security, and

war. Proposals like Dershowitz's require judges to approve events beforehand, which will not often be possible. Judges are good at focusing on what has happened in the past. Whether an attack might occur
in the future, its magnitude, and how to stop it is beyond their usual
expertise.

Posner's and Vermeule's approach is preferable, in that it judges
whether a standard has been broken after the fact. But they propose
in essence a large, costly regulatory apparatus that could suffer from
20/20 hindsight and politicization as much as other judging bodies. For
judging if someone has done something truly wrong, we already have
several large bureaucracies, and the legal system.

The McCain Amendment gave future presidents, CIA directors,
national security advisers, secretaries of defense, and generals less
room for discretion, telling the executive that some forms of interrogation are never worth the benefits, no matter what, and that the letter of the rule must trump the good faith judgment of those actually
dealing with ticking time bombs. Like Miranda, it ties the hands of
the government with a rule. But Miranda is less costly to society. It is
easy to follow, and the harm any individual ordinary criminal can inflict, if wrongly freed, is limited. The potential harm an al Qaeda operative can inflict is potentially enormous.

There are ways that the legal system could develop effective approaches toward coercive interrogation. A President could decline to
prosecute an officer whom he believed properly acted in self-defense,
or in an emergency, or out of necessity. A President could pardon those
involved. Even if a prosecution occurs, a jury must still find that the
defense is not met, and convict the agent and his superiors of violating federal law. It would require only one juror to agree that it was
reasonable for the defendants to believe the coercive interrogation
would yield information that would save many lives, and that it was
necessary under the circumstances, to prevent a conviction. This approach, as the Israeli Supreme Court pointed out, maintains society's
moral condemnation of harsh interrogation, but also recognizes an
exception for emergencies. Defenses are an appropriate escape hatch

for rules that will at some point need some exceptions to be drawn, even exceptions that prove the rule.

I cannot help but wonder, though, if critics will descend upon even this modest explanation of how legal defenses might work, outraged by the mere suggestion that sometimes exoneration of a government interrogator might be the right outcome.

Prosecution enforces the criminal law. Judges ultimately would decide what interrogation is too harsh. We have all the problems of courts: 20/20 hindsight, courtroom posturing, media circuses, lack of secrecy, exposure of sources and methods of intelligence-gathering, and uninformed, unpredictable juries. At root is the judicial branch's basic, structural lack of executive, managerial, and policy expertise.

The executive branch should continue to bear primary responsibility for deciding when to use coercive interrogation, training special operations teams, and developing guidelines for its use, while keeping the House and Senate intelligence committees informed. Covert actions developed by the President and his staff and briefed to the intelligence committees have included targeted killings and paramilitary operations against foreign nations. Judicial review has not intervened, nor has it been necessary. These institutional arrangements could also be up to supervising interrogations.

In the world of intelligence, the executive branch agencies have understood for many years now that congressional support is essential for the long-term success of their missions. They have been and will increasingly be reluctant to carry out any debatable action without both the approval of the President and the political support of Congress. Whether this is a good development, only time will tell.

People have different values and principles, and they will balance the costs and benefits of coercive interrogation differently. But the war we face is anything but ordinary.

September 11 requires us to make difficult choices. The law does not give us all the answers. The law requires our elected leaders to make policy judgments. That is how it should be. Coercive interrogation can produce information from al Qaeda leaders and operatives that helps our military, intelligence, and law enforcement personnel prevent future attacks. It will have costs on the world stage and in the changing moods of the public. But we should also not lose sight of the benefits—for it is much more than luck that has allowed our government, to date, to frustrate and disrupt terrorist efforts to carry out another 9/11.

8

MILITARY
COMMISSIONS

President Bush announced his most practical, yet least success-ful, antiterrorism initiative—an executive order establishing military commissions—shortly after September 11.[1] Military com-missions are a specialized form of military court that presidents and generals have used in most American wars. They are meant to bal-ance two competing goals: providing a fair trial for enemies who commit war crimes, and protecting the nation's military and intelli-gence interests.

Military commissions had been dormant for many years, but OLC staff knew all about them. A bronze plaque on the wall of our fifth-floor offices commemorated the 1942 trial by military commission of nine German Nazi saboteurs. On September 12, 2001, a Justice De-partment veteran reminded me about the plaque, growling that any terrorists we caught ought to be tried in the same way. The Justice Department under George H. W. Bush had considered a military com-mission to try the bombers of the Pan Am flight over Lockerbie, Scot-land, too, he told me.

An OLC colleague and I were asked to review President Bush's military order in the weeks after 9/11. We didn't think it ran afoul of the Constitution. In fact, it read just like the order issued by President Franklin Roosevelt in 1942, the constitutionality of which the Supreme Court had upheld in *Ex Parte Quirin*. Military commissions seemed a good choice for bringing terrorists to justice. Trial in open federal court posed obvious national security and secrecy issues. International war crime tribunals for the former Yugoslavia and Rwanda had been slow, costly, and, in Slobodan Milosevic's case, susceptible to being used as a platform for grandstanding by the accused. Even with full international sanction, these tribunals had been widely criticized on a number of grounds. Meanwhile, military commissions to try enemy combatants enjoyed a long pedigree in American history.

Yet as soon as the order left the White House, civil libertarian lobbies, the media, and the academy screamed "foul." The editorial page of the *New York Times* thundered, "In his effort to defend America from terrorists, Mr. Bush is eroding the very values and principles he seeks to protect, including the rule of law."[2] The *Times* was of the opinion that military commissions "do an end run around the Constitution" and were "an insult to the exquisite balancing of executive, legislative and judicial powers that the Framers incorporated into the Constitution." A group of law professors sent a letter to the Senate Judiciary Committee claiming that President Bush's decision "undermines the tradition of the Separation of Powers" and confidently asserted, "No court has upheld unilateral action by the Executive that provided for as dramatic a departure from constitutional norms as does this Order."[3] Harvard law professor Laurence Tribe, the nation's leading liberal constitutional law professor, and Neal Katyal, a Georgetown professor who has gone on to litigate challenges to the military commissions, announced that such tribunals were unconstitutional without a declaration of war or a new congressional statute.[4] Senator Patrick Leahy, then chairman of the Senate Judiciary Committee, complained that President Bush had "cut out Congress in determining the appropriate tribunal and procedures to try terrorists."[5]

The truth is that military commissions rest on centuries of American practice, Supreme Court precedent, and, not least, the Constitution's text and structure. The administration had made no secret about them. In November 2001, President Bush issued a skeletal order, under his authority as commander in chief and the power given to him by Congress in the AUMF, that military commissions would be used to try only non–U.S. citizens involved with al Qaeda or other terror groups that threatened the United States. The September 11 attacks, the order said, had created "a state of armed conflict that requires the use of the United States Armed Forces." Military commissions to try enemy combatants would be established to "protect the United States and its citizens, and for the effective conduct of military operations and prevention of terrorist attacks." The commissions would provide a "full and fair trial," but could use more relaxed rules of evidence, and could convict on a vote of two thirds of the commission. Authority was delegated to the Department of Defense to fill out this framework.

To put our initial approval on paper, OLC issued a lengthy legal opinion on the constitutionality of military commissions. Press reports also describe a struggle between the White House, the Defense Department, and Attorney General Ashcroft over who would decide when military commissions ought to be used. Defense wanted to decide, but Ashcroft, ever a defender of his bureaucratic turf, wanted a veto. After a contentious White House meeting, President Bush broke the deadlock by deciding that only he would decide when an al Qaeda detainee would be sent before a military court—which was the right outcome, placing the responsibility where it ought to rest.

In the fall of 2001, some Senate Democrats decided that military commissions would be their point of attack to paint the Bush administration as a threat to civil liberties. We helped Chertoff and Ashcroft prepare for public hearings before the then-Democrat-run Senate Judiciary Committee, where Leahy was eager to spearhead the opposition. He fumed that the administration's antiterrorism policies as a whole disregarded "the checks and balances that make up our constitutional framework."[6] This was just two months after September 11, while our troops were on the ground in Afghanistan and our agents were searching feverishly for sleeper cells in the United States. Civil libertarians were pursuing the most extreme of positions and were putting everyone on notice that they would use the Judiciary Committee hearings to come after the administration full bore.

Chertoff and Ashcroft were a study in contrasts. While Chertoff liked to pore through the briefing books and come up with his own perfectly turned phrase, Ashcroft prepared by talking the issue through over and over with staff. After several days of briefings, explanations, and trial runs, Chertoff and Ashcroft were ready.

Chertoff went first. In a hearing before the Senate Judiciary Committee on November, 28, 2001, Senate Democrats accused the Bush administration of inventing a bizarre military court system free of any congressional or judicial oversight. Chertoff was a predator ready to spring. He shot back that military trials fell within the President's power as commander in chief, that they had been used in wars going back to the Revolution, and that they fell within carefully established constitutional limits.[7] Chertoff's ability to understand law at the highest constitutional levels while maintaining a command of the details was masterful. Senators showed no desire to engage him in a debate over constitutional theory or historical practice. Their confidence renewed, Senate Republicans worked hard to support tough measures in the war against terrorists. With their help, Chertoff had successfully defused the growing momentum in the Senate to harass the administration with hearings and investigations at the very start of a war. After Chertoff's performance, it was clear that no one had the stomach for that fight, at least not yet.

Chertoff was like a fullback, clearing the field for Ashcroft. A week later, Ashcroft appeared before the Judiciary Committee and went over the same legal theory about executive authority to establish military commissions. Polls showed large majorities favored military tribunals for terrorists. Ashcroft commented wryly that "charges of kangaroo courts and shredding the Constitution give new meaning to the term 'the fog of war.'"[8] Going too far, he chided his critics as those "who scare peace-loving people with phantoms of lost liberty," and charged that "your tactics only aid terrorists" and "erode our national unity and diminish our resolve." After that, no one on the committee had the heart for the fight anymore. Most of the hearing turned to the use of federal background checks on gun buyers to check for terrorists. Nevertheless, Ashcroft's rhetoric against the civil libertarian critics and their allies in Congress became the lead story of the hearings.

Chertoff and Ashcroft succeeded in defusing any congressional effort to regulate military commissions. While Senate critics introduced a few bills, none ever made it out of commitee. Congress took a wait-and-see approach. If military commissions fouled up down the road, Congress could blame the administration and pass a new law. But just months after 9/11, most congressmen, like their constituents, supported the use of military tribunals for terrorists, and Senator Leahy and his civil libertarian allies were the outliers.

Nearly five years later, the Defense Department still hasn't tried a single terrorist. Military commissions have been the Bush administration's most conspicuous policy failure in the war against al Qaeda. The delay has been due to the sheer multitude of issues involved in building a working court system from scratch. There were no off-the-shelf procedures or lists of war crimes to use. The Defense Department wanted a showcase of military justice at its finest, with rules of substance and procedures that would withstand any scrutiny, both at home and abroad. It was a laudable goal, but it inevitably led to long bureaucratic delays among all the involved agencies. Some military lawyers also resisted creating the commissions. They had trained only for the court-martial system, not this. Military commissions, they argued, would "taint" the court-martial process. Military commissions became another flash point in the struggle pitting the military establishment against Rumsfeld and his civilian advisers in his effort to transform the military in order to address twenty-first-century challenges.

The Defense Department ultimately issued rules giving unprecedented rights to the accused. In late March 2002, DOD provided for a defendant's presumption of innocence, the right to counsel, conviction by proof beyond a reasonable doubt, the right to present evidence and defense witnesses, and the requirement of unanimity for the imposition of a death penalty.[9] DOD followed up with regulations defining the crimes that could be charged, such as killing protected persons, attacking civilian targets, and pillage, which were mostly consistent with the customary practice of international law. But they did not issue until April 30, 2003—about a year and a half after President Bush's original order.[10] The rules took so long to emerge from the machinery of government that any advantage in using military commissions was lost.

It was good to show the world that the tribunals were hardly some sort of kangaroo court and would provide as fair a trial as the world has known in a war context. Their procedures provided more due process than those of the International Criminal Court, from which the United States had withdrawn in the early years of the Bush administration.[11] The main criticism was that they did not provide for review of any conviction by a civilian court, but neither had the World War II commissions. The detail in construction caused the commissions to lose an important advantage. Commissions now seem to work best for approving plea bargains with cooperating enemy combatants at Guantanamo Bay.

This delay was compounded when lawyers for the detainees were permitted to challenge the constitutionality of the military commissions themselves in the federal courts. To be sure, these JAG lawyers were only doing their job by providing their clients with the most vigorous defense possible. But the constitutionality of the military commissions had long been settled. Their appeals asked the Supreme Court to overrule its practice of allowing the President and Congress a free hand to win wars while fighting was ongoing. This gambit succeeded in delaying military commissions another three years, and it might yet pull down military commissions altogether. A judge for whom I once worked gave a well-known speech in the 1970s asking whether too much lawyering "was strangling capitalism."[12] Lawyering is beginning to strangle our government's ability to fight and win the wars of the twenty-first century.

Policy

Before discussing why military commissions, far from being some radical innovation in our judicial system, rest well within American constitutional and historical traditions, we should first ask why we need them at all. And for that, it is helpful to have a close look at the case of Zacarias Moussaoui, the only 9/11 plotter captured and put on trial.

In May 2006, a Virginia jury sentenced Moussaoui to life in prison. The end of the trial came almost five years after his arrest. As the jury delivered its verdict of life rather than the death penalty, Moussaoui yelled out, "America you lost! I won." Later in the proceedings he hissed to the judge: "God curse America, and God save Osama bin Laden! You will never get him!"[13] A life sentence frustrated Moussaoui's wish to become a martyr. Instead he will spend the rest of his days in the "Alcatraz of the Rockies," the federal government's most secure prison in Colorado, in a small concrete cell for all but one hour a day, where his only contact will be with prison guards and the occasional visitor.[14]

The story of Moussaoui's trial and conviction shows why the civilian criminal justice system is inadequate to the task of fighting al Qaeda and the threat of mass attacks on American cities. Moussaoui's avoidance of the death penalty probably sparked the most outrage. Members of the Virginia jury believed that his desire to kill three thousand Americans and to inflict billions of dollars in damage on September 11 was "mitigated" by his difficult childhood with an abusive father in a hostile French society. In the framework of the criminal justice system, which is designed to draw every ambiguity in favor of the criminal, the jurors could not come to grips with the unremitting hatred of someone who still, even after his trial had ended, wanted to kill thousands of Americans.

Interrogation of al Qaeda leaders confirmed that Moussaoui came to the United States to be either a backup pilot for the 9/11 plot or a pilot in a second wave of attacks (or both).[15] Attorney General Ashcroft pressed hard to have Moussaoui tried in civilian court; he thought it important in the weeks after 9/11 to show the American public that the criminal justice system could respond to terrorism. Some wanted to preserve the option of using military tribunals to try Moussaoui as an illegal enemy combatant, but no one really pushed hard for that position and the commissions were still under development. Ashcroft prevailed in the interagency debate without much of a fight. The Justice Department indicted Moussaoui in December 2001 for conspiring to commit terrorist attacks, and he was sent to Alexandria, Virginia, only minutes from the Pentagon, for trial.

Moussaoui took the opportunity to grandstand in the proceedings before Judge Leonie Brinkema. At his April 2006 plea hearing, he called a defense attorney a "Judas."[16] He was often removed from the courtroom for interrupting the proceedings. Pointing to his defense counsel during jury selection, Moussaoui yelled, "I'm al Qaeda. They are American. They are my enemies. This trial is a circus."[17] He fired his public defense counsel, refused to meet with them for years, and instead attempted to defend himself. The judge appointed them to assist him anyway to guarantee a fair trial. Moussaoui responded with more outbursts and long handwritten motions insulting his lawyers and Judge Brinkema. He also wrote a letter to Richard Reid, the shoe bomber, who had been a member of the same mosque as he in London.

Moussaoui openly admitted that he was a member of al Qaeda and that he wanted to kill Americans in a second wave of attacks. At times, he also said that he was involved with the 9/11 plot and wanted to plead guilty to conspiring with al Qaeda leaders and operatives to carry out the attacks. In 2002, he pled guilty but then changed his mind a week later. Defense lawyers filed motions questioning his sanity, and only after three years and a personal meeting with Moussaoui did Judge Brinkema find him competent.

His trial would have gone on years longer had Moussaoui not cooperated by pleading guilty on April 22, 2005, more than three and a half years after the 9/11 attacks. The government hadn't yet presented a single piece of evidence or put a single witness on the stand. Using legitimate means available in any criminal case to tie the government in knots, Moussaoui and his "standby" defense counsel had sent the case up on appeal twice in hopes of forcing the release of reams of classified information on al Qaeda.[18]

Moussaoui had pressed his rights under the Constitution's Sixth Amendment "to have compulsory process for obtaining witnesses in his favor." This is an essential right to guarantee a fair trial in garden-variety crimes. A routine and fair request in peacetime—but in war a serious problem, because it required that Moussaoui receive access to Khalid Sheikh Mohammed and other captured al Qaeda leaders, and that they potentially testify in open court.

In an ongoing war, the costs of openly disclosing information can be very high. Such costs do not exist in the normal criminal situation. Disclosure in court, or in the media, of sensitive information will help al Qaeda gain insight into our intelligence methods and sources, which will lead it to shut down leaking parts of its organization and expand operations we know nothing about. For example, just hours after information leaked in the 1990s that U.S. intelligence could intercept calls on bin Laden's cell phone, he stopped using it. An individual who is giving us information may shut down if his identity might have to be disclosed in court. The enemy might become alert to spies, who would then be rendered useless or become targets for murder. Imagine the glee of defense counsel demanding that the government identify its informants or meticulously describe its interception technology and how it verified its information.

This is not a mere classroom hypothetical. Andrew McCarthy, a former federal prosecutor, tried Omar Abdel Rahman, known as the "blind sheikh," for participation in the 1993 World Trade Center bombing. He complied with standard criminal discovery procedures and turned over to the defense a list of two hundred possible unindicted coconspirators.[19] In essence, it was a sketch of American intelligence on al Qaeda, and it was delivered to bin Laden in Sudan within days of its production in court. It was later found during the investigation into the African embassy bombings. Bin Laden, who was on the list, could now see who was compromised and who was not, and could figure out how American intelligence had learned its information and what our future moves were likely to be.

Moussaoui and his on-again, off-again defense counsel followed this litigation game plan precisely. Moussaoui maintained that he was not involved in September 11. To disprove the charge, he demanded access to Khalid Sheikh Mohammed, Ramzi bin al Shibh, and other al Qaeda leaders in the government's custody, who, he claimed, would testify that he was not part of the original 9/11 attacks, but of a second wave. Judge Brinkema agreed that Moussaoui's constitutional right to a fair trial required access to other enemy combatants, and when the government refused to produce them, she sanctioned them by ruling out the death penalty.[20]

OLC worked closely with a special group headed by Olson and Chertoff to handle the appeal. It was clear to me that winning the war came first, and I could not imagine that enemy combatants would be made available for Moussaoui. We argued that a district court had no constitutional authority to order production of a witness who would interfere with the government's ability to wage war—and that since the witnesses were outside the reach of the court and unavailable, the criminal trial should go on without them. I was dubious that this argument would prevail, although it had some good authority behind it. The easy answer was simply that the government had a choice of producing witnesses or dropping its prosecution. Courts would be unwilling, I thought, to force a compromise between Moussaoui's right to present an effective defense with live witnesses and the nation's security interests.

My pessimism found its source in Watergate.[21] Independent counsel Archibald Cox had placed the burglars and the conspirators John Ehrlichman, H. R. Haldeman, and John Mitchell on trial for fraud and obstruction of justice. The prosecutor subpoenaed President Nixon for secret tapes of conversations in the Oval Office, but Nixon refused on the ground of executive privilege, claiming the President had a constitutional right to confidential communications with his senior aides. In *United States v. Nixon*, the Court unanimously ordered Nixon to turn over the tapes. It held that the defendants' Sixth Amendment rights to seek information for their defense outweighed the President's interest in confidential advice. "A President's acknowledged need for confidentiality in the communications of his office is general in nature, whereas the constitutional need for production of relevant evidence in a criminal proceeding is specific and central to the fair adjudication of a particular criminal case in the administration of justice. Without access to specific facts a criminal prosecution may be totally frustrated."[22] While the *Nixon* Court had cautioned that presidential privilege would be greater if foreign policy or national security secrets were involved, it also gave the executive branch a choice. If presidents believed the secrets were important enough to protect, they should drop the prosecution. There, the Court had been unwilling to compromise over the constitutional right to call witnesses in a criminal trial.

We developed a fallback argument. Not every witness a defendant wants to appear at trial is available. Some might be dead, others might be overseas and outside the jurisdiction of the courts. In such situations, a jury might receive "substitutions": written summaries describing what the missing witness would have said.[23] If the government were not to agree to a written summary that satisfied the trial judge, the court could dismiss the prosecution.

Much to the angst of our federal prosecutors in Alexandria, who had the unenviable chore of trying Moussaoui, we had no intention of granting access to al Qaeda informants in the middle of a war. Allowing Moussaoui to interview them and haul them into court could have seriously undermined our ongoing efforts to gain intelligence from them. "Their value as intelligence sources can hardly be overstated," the Court of Appeals in the Moussaoui case recognized.[24] It found reasonable that "interruption [of their interrogation] could result in the loss of information that might prevent future terrorist attacks." If he could interview al Qaeda leaders, grilling our intelligence agents or FBI and DOJ officials about the whys and wherefores of their decisions would have been the inevitable next step.

If it came down to choosing between trying Moussaoui or preserving the intelligence needed to defeat al Qaeda, I had little doubt that the prosecution would be dropped and Moussaoui would go to a military tribunal. Pursuing a criminal case consistent with the Bill of

Rights, without interfering with the conduct of the war, is an incredibly delicate balancing act. Moussaoui served as a test case to square the requirements of a civilian criminal trial with the needs of operational secrecy in future cases involving American citizens, for whom the military tribunal route was not open.

As feared, the appeals court didn't buy our argument that al Qaeda witnesses could be withheld completely. In April 2004, it upheld Judge Brinkema's decision that they could provide material testimony in support of Moussaoui's defense, but also ordered that written summaries could substitute for live testimony. Judge, defense counsel, and prosecution had to work together to develop statements that adequately represented what the al Qaeda witnesses would say in Moussaoui's defense.[25] That gave the prosecutors enough of a lifeline to continue their work, or at least postponed the day of reckoning.

Courtroom maneuvering went on for another year, as Moussaoui's lawyers appealed yet again to the full appeals court and then to the Supreme Court, which declined to review the case. The trial could not resume until March 2005, more than three years after Moussaoui was indicted. He made important, legitimate constitutional arguments. No criminal trial can go forward until basic issues of access to witnesses and classified material are resolved. It was not even clear that the issues were finally concluded, because others might well have cropped up once Moussaoui began to seek access to other al Qaeda members and more classified materials. The time and effort this process took testify to the generous protections of our criminal justice system, and the potential for misuse.

Luckily, Moussaoui himself relieved the government of its quandary between protecting national security secrets and prosecution. About a month after the Supreme Court turned down his appeal, Moussaoui bizarrely changed his mind again and returned to his original guilty plea. Moussaoui handed the Justice Department its victory on a silver platter. If he had continued to maintain his innocence, as any responsible defense attorney would have insisted, the trial and appeals would have continued for years longer. He might have forced the government into dropping the prosecution, or been acquitted by

the jury. Even if a way could be found between this Scylla and
Charybdis, the trial's demands for information would already have the
effect of changing the nature of the interrogation of al Qaeda operatives, or by encouraging other al Qaeda defendants in the future not
to cooperate.

Moussaoui said that bin Laden had personally ordered him to fly a
plane into the White House.[26] A special jury trial was then held on the
death penalty. This consumed yet another year of proceedings in which
the prosecution rehashed the devastating losses of September 11. The
defense dramatized Moussaoui's personal background (he was said to
have been an abused child and alienated youth) and tried to put the
government on trial by showing that it did little to prevent the 9/11 attacks. The defense, in other words, was that Moussaoui's decision to
join al Qaeda's jihad was the product of a tough childhood, rather than
his own choice, and that the United States was really to blame for 9/11.

Moussaoui had to be ejected several times during the death penalty phase for interrupting the proceedings. He began by execrating
President Bush for his "new campaign, a revenge against terrorists."
Then, he castigated his lawyers, calling them a "KKK lawyer" and a
"geisha."[27] As the prosecution described the events of 9/11, he smiled
and then pumped his fists and shouted, "God curse America!"[28] On
the stand, Moussaoui proclaimed proudly, "I was supposed to pilot a
plane to hit the White House," and said he'd known in advance about
the plans to strike the World Trade Center. He described his great
pleasure upon learning of the casualties on September 11, called the
collapse of the twin towers "gorgeous," and predicted that "three
thousand miscreants" will burn in "hellfire." In clear and calm tones,
he announced, "I consider every American to be my enemy," adding,
"Every American is going to want my death because I want their
death."[29] After listening to testimony about the deaths in New York,
the Pentagon, and on United flight 93, Moussaoui testified that the
September 11 survivors and family members were "pathetic" and "dis-
gusting." He admitted again to joining al Qaeda and the 9/11 plot, told
the prosecutor that the death toll was too low, and proudly declared
he would join a suicide mission again if he could.[30]

After lengthy deliberations in which a single juror blocked the death penalty, the jury sentenced Moussaoui to life in prison. Nine of the twelve jurors found that his difficult childhood mitigated his responsibility. More than four years after he was first indicted, the trial ended, though not before giving Moussaoui a platform to air his anti-American speeches and insult those who died on 9/11 and their families. He also used the generosity of the American criminal justice system as a tool to force the government to reveal important secrets in the war against al Qaeda.[31] Yet, our criminal justice system spared his life, based on psychological excuses that Moussaoui himself found insulting. As President Bush remarked after the verdict, "Mr. Moussaoui got a fair trial" and his life was spared, which "is something that he evidently wasn't willing to do for innocent American citizens."[32]

Those who believe the Moussaoui case shows that the criminal justice system can try terrorists have not paid close attention to the proceedings. If Moussaoui had chosen to fight on, as would be standard operating procedure with a competent defense counsel, his case would still be going on today. Then, in your mind, multiply that by hundreds or thousands of other terrorists.

II.

If Justice Department officials could do it all over again, they certainly would have sent Moussaoui to a military commission. Military commissions are the historic compromise between protecting a nation's secrets and its ability to conduct war, on the one hand, and due process for the accused on the other. They are flexible enough to respect the needs of wartime, and bring more expertise than a civilian court.

Unlike regular courts, military commissions can close portions of proceedings when classified material is involved or an enemy leader might testify. A fair trial is still guaranteed, because the defendant's defense attorneys are present. The defense attorneys must have appropriate security clearances. Assurances are obtained that neither they nor the defendant will leak any classified information.

A military commission can also use more flexible rules of evidence. Our criminal trials impose a very high standard on the information that reaches a jury. Witnesses generally must testify in person, hearsay evidence typically must be excluded, and the reliability of evidence must meet high procedural hurdles. This is because the jury is supposed to be kept ignorant of certain types of evidence that might be assumed to sway the novice. Juries are not trusted to make difficult judgments about the reliability of broad, contextual information. Military commissions, however, are staffed by professionals versed in the reliability of hearsay evidence, or in whether an item of evidence is more probative than prejudicial. Rules of courtroom procedure, like the exclusionary rule's bar on evidence that was obtained without a warrant, seek to regulate police conduct and have less to do with the relevance or credibility of evidence. These rules do not apply to war, because courtroom outcomes do not "regulate" how the military does its job on the battlefield.

Our military does not play the same role in our society that the police do. Police must follow the exclusionary rule and the Miranda warnings, or courts can let the suspect go free. Courts use these rules to encourage the police and prosecutors to respect the defendant's rights and because the costs to society of the occasional error in a criminal's favor are deemed low. These rules do not make sense in war, where the primary purpose of the armed forces is to defeat the enemy. If the military had to abide by a host of legal rules, it would interfere drastically with its ability to fight effectively. As one military analyst has put it, the job of the 82nd Airborne is to vaporize, not Mirandize.

Civilian courts would not allow into evidence important military evidence in at least two cases.[33] Suppose Osama bin Laden called his mother to warn her of the 9/11 attacks and she told a friend. A civilian court would exclude this as hearsay testimony. But a military commission could allow it. A *Wall Street Journal* reporter found a hard drive filled with al Qaeda documents in a Kabul market. This information would likely not be admitted in civilian court, because its chain of custody from al Qaeda to the Kabul market couldn't be verified. A military commission could review the information if it thought it was reasonably reliable. Another example is information gained through interrogations, intelligence intercepts, and informants. None of this information complies with the Fourth Amendment's warrant requirement or Miranda, but if it is reasonably relevant, the military will act upon it.

In fact, thoughtful civil libertarians ought to welcome military commissions. Military commissions have the benefit of limiting any compromises between national security and civil liberties. Civil libertarians, most recently Geoffrey Stone in his *Perilous Times*, warn that courts historically bend too far to accommodate the needs of national security in wartime.[34] Such patterns drawn from the past don't necessarily describe the present or predict the future, particularly in the face of unprecedented change. The main worry ought to be that compromises that favor national security will permanently affect our domestic criminal law in times of peace. Military commissions in fact have a civil libertarian function, by confining the more flexible rules for national security cases so they will not seep over to civilian cases. Trying enemy combatants in civilian courts could have the opposite effect, particularly in periods just after a major enemy assault like 9/11.

Military commissions are also more secure. Civil trials of terrorists in the United States make an inviting target for al Qaeda. Even before 9/11, our government recognized the threat to judicial personnel by placing heavy security in the New York City federal court building and putting federal judges who tried the al Qaeda cases of the 1990s under constant protection.[35] Civilian trials tend to be in major cities, such as New York City or Washington, D.C., compounding potential loss of life if they were targeted for attack. In this war military tribunals are conducted at Guantanamo Bay, a well-defended military facility far from any American population centers.

Some critics believe the military can't run fair trials. They claim that they are secretive, unfair because they operate without juries, and presume the guilt of the defendant. The title of a recent book by a civil liberties lawyer says it all: *Secret Trials and Executions: Military Tribunals and the Threat to Democracy*.[36] Civil libertarians think military

officers can't be effective defense attorneys because they are susceptible to "command influence"—being swayed by their superior officers' desire to convict. In short, they argue that military commissions
are inherently flawed because their rules and procedures are just too
different from those of the standard criminal trial system.

This viewpoint displays a serious lack of understanding of the military justice system. Millions of American servicemen and women serve
today under the Uniform Code of Military Justice (UCMJ). That system has developed over many decades, and it provides a fair and open
trial. Unlike our criminal trials, in which jurors are selected for their
ignorance, military tribunals are populated by officers who are college
graduates with extensive professional knowledge. The system requires
defense attorneys to do their best to represent their clients free from
command influence. Indeed, President Bush did not order the military to convict whomever he wanted to, but to provide each defendant a "full and fair trial." And the military is bound to carry out his
orders.

Civil libertarians, members of the media, and academics portray
military commissions as some Frankenstein creation of the Bush administration. According to the *New York Times*, "in the place of fair trials and due process," President Bush "has substituted a crude and
unaccountable system that any dictator would admire."[37] It is anything
but. Only pundits with little knowledge of American history or no
contact with the military and its legal system would voice such a view.

Military commissions are the customary form of justice for enemy
prisoners who violate the laws of war. They have also served as courts
of justice during occupations and in times of martial law. American
generals have used military commissions in virtually every significant
war from the Revolutionary War through World War II.[38] As commander of the revolutionary armies, George Washington put John
Andre on trial for spying in 1780 before a military commission.[39]
Major Andre had been found, out of uniform, carrying the plans for West
Point, which he had received from Benedict Arnold. Washington's military "Court of Inquiry" convicted Andre and sentenced him to hanging.
During the War of 1812, General Andrew Jackson employed military

commissions in the areas under his command, and then used them again in an 1818 Indian War. These special military courts did not assume the name "commissions" until the Mexican-American War, when General Winfield Scott established two types, one to help maintain law and order in the occupied parts of Mexico, the other to try violations of the laws of war, such as guerrilla warfare.

Military commissions witnessed their heaviest use in the Civil War. Union generals established military commissions in early 1862 to try suspected Confederate operatives behind Union lines, to prosecute violations of the laws of war, and to administer justice in occupied areas. Later that year, President Lincoln proclaimed that "all rebels and insurgents, their aiders and abettors within the United States," and anyone "guilty of any disloyal practice affording aid and comfort to rebels" would be subject to martial law, "and liable to trial and punishment by court martial or military commissions."[40] Congress gave them jurisdiction over several other violations of law in the following year. After the North prevailed, Congress authorized their use as courts of occupation in the military districts of the conquered South. They were used most notably to try Lincoln's assassins and the commander of the Andersonville prisoner of war camp. According to a definitive study of military law, military commissions tried about two thousand cases during the Civil War, and about two hundred during Reconstruction.[41]

Several cases involving military commissions made their way to the Supreme Court during the Civil War. In *Ex Parte Vallandigham*, the Supreme Court held that it did not have the jurisdiction to hear a challenge to a sentence imposed by a military commission, and the Court did not hear another such challenge during the war.[42] In *Ex Parte Milligan*, the Court held that the government could not try civilians on loyal Union territory by military commission, if the civil courts were open and if the civilians had not associated with the enemy. Implicit in this was that if Milligan had been an enemy combatant, not a civilian, a military commission *could* have tried him for war crimes. Lincoln's assassins were tried by a military commission convened by President Andrew Johnson and approved by an opinion of the attorney general. A federal court rejected a challenge to the use of the commission.[43] The attorney general's opinion stated that long practice under the rules of warfare permitted assassins to be tried and executed by military commission.[44]

With the end of Reconstruction, military commissions disappeared, though they were used sporadically in the Spanish-American War and World War I. World War II, however, witnessed the use of military commissions on an unprecedented scale, both to try war criminals and to administer justice in occupied Germany and Japan. Military commissions administering law and order in occupied Germany heard hundreds of thousands of cases.[45] They were also extensively used to try enemy combatants for violating the laws of war, the most famous examples being the Nuremberg Tribunal that tried Nazi leaders after the war, and the International Military Tribunal for the Far East that tried Japanese leaders for war crimes. American military commissions tried three thousand defendants in Germany and a thousand defendants in Japan for "terrorism, subversive activity, and violation of the laws of war."[46]

World War II military commissions operated both abroad and in the United States. FDR's commission order sparked a lawsuit, and the resulting Supreme Court opinion supported the legality of the Bush military commissions. Indeed, FDR took far more liberties with the constitutional law of the day than the current administration does.

In the 1942 case of the Nazi saboteurs, eight Nazi agents with plans to sabotage factories, transportation facilities, and utility plants landed on Long Island, New York, and in Florida.[47] All had lived in the United States before the war, and two were American citizens. When their capture was revealed, members of Congress and the media demanded the death penalty, even though no law authorized capital punishment for their crime. FDR decided to try them by military commission. On June 30 he explained to Attorney General Francis Biddle: "[T]he death penalty is called for by usage and by the extreme gravity of the war aim and the very existence of our American government."[48] Roosevelt was determined to execute the saboteurs. "Surely they are just as guilty as it is possible to be . . . and it seems to me that the death penalty is almost obligatory."

Biddle and Secretary of War Henry Stimson were of the opinion that the plot was too undeveloped to warrant more than a two-year sentence for the plotters in an ordinary criminal court. Stimson was surprised to find that Biddle was "quite ready to turn them over to a military court." Over dinner with Justice Felix Frankfurter, he was equally surprised to learn that Frankfurter felt the same way.

Biddle summarized the advantages of a military commission for Roosevelt: speed, easier standards of proof, and the availability of the death penalty. Plus, he thought the defendants would be disabled from appealing to the civilian courts: "All the prisoners can thus be denied access to our courts."[49] Biddle did not commit to writing another important consideration, secrecy, but he did confide it to Stimson. He wanted to keep quiet both the identity of the informant and the ease with which the Nazis had infiltrated U.S. lines. Biddle recommended that FDR issue executive orders establishing the commission, appointing its members, defining the crimes, and excluding federal judicial review. Roosevelt did so on July 2. The first executive order created the commission and defined its jurisdiction over aliens or foreign residents "who give obedience to or act under the direction of" an enemy nation, and attempt to enter the United States "preparing to commit sabotage, espionage, hostile or warlike acts, or violations of the law of war." He also ordered that the Nazis be barred from any other court.[50] FDR's second order established the procedures for the military commissions. Only one paragraph long, they guaranteed "a full and fair trial," allowed the admission of evidence that would "have probative value to a reasonable man," and required a two-thirds vote for conviction and sentence.

Because the Bush administration patterned its order on FDR's, the critics of military commissions have only FDR to blame. But in truth, FDR's handiwork intruded more on civil liberties than Bush's, and under the law of the time was of more questionable constitutionality. In 1942, the governing case on the books was *Ex Parte Milligan*, requiring the government to use federal courts if the defendant has not associated with the enemy and the civilian courts are open. Military counsel for the Nazi saboteurs challenged the commissions on just this ground—that the military commission could not exercise jurisdiction because courts were open, the defendants were not in a war zone, and a military commission violated the Articles of War enacted by Congress.

FDR intervened in the case in unprecedented ways, undeterred by the news that the Supreme Court had agreed to hear the case. Before oral argument, the Supreme Court Justices gathered in conference. Justice Owen Roberts said Biddle told him FDR might order the execution of the saboteurs, whatever the Court might decide.[51] Chief Justice Harlan Stone, whose son was working on the defense team, commented, "That would be a dreadful thing." Stone did not recuse himself, nor did Justice James Byrnes, who had been serving as an informal adviser to the administration. Justice Frank Murphy, who was at the conference in uniform as a member of the Army Reserve, did. Biddle himself argued the case and urged the Court to overrule *Milligan*. After two days of oral argument, the justices decided to uphold the trial of the prisoners by military commission. The great pressure on the Court was reflected in its decision to deliver a unanimous opinion on July 31, the day after oral argument, even though its judgment would not appear publicly until weeks later. The military commission began its trial the next day. Three days later it convicted the defendants and sentenced them to death. Five days later, FDR approved the verdict, though he commuted two sentences.

FDR's commissions operated under his two executive orders alone. There were no regulations such as those developed by the Defense Department to define the elements of the crimes that a commission can hear. A second Defense Department regulation established rules on the admissibility of evidence, the right of cross-examination, the right against self-incrimination, proof beyond a reasonable doubt as the standard for conviction, and the right of defense counsel to examine any exculpatory evidence in the prosecution's possession. Under the Bush commissions, unlike FDR's, a unanimous vote is required to impose the death penalty.[52]

What concerns today's civil libertarians is that military commissions do not afford as much due process as domestic criminal trials. But the truth is that the rules of military commissions under the Bush administration are far closer to the standards governing courts-martial of American soldiers than those set out by FDR, and they recognize many more procedural rights. Current Defense Department regulations specifically detail the crimes that can be tried. FDR stated only the general prohibition of "sabotage, espionage, hostile or warlike acts, or violations of the law of war," which could be interpreted to mean a lot of things. Convictions for spying today, for instance, require four different elements—that the defendant in wartime sought to "collect certain information," convey it to the enemy, and was "lurking or acting clandestinely, while acting under false pretenses." Extensive comments explain different terms and situations that might arise, closely resembling the Model Penal Code for civilian criminal law. Civil libertarians might cavil about the details, but the Bush administration's effort goes much further than FDR's orders to protect defendants' rights.

When the Court issued its unanimous opinion in *Ex Parte Quirin*, it narrowed *Milligan* and upheld FDR's use of military commissions. Unlike Milligan, the saboteurs clearly had joined the Nazi armed forces. Chief Justice Stone's opinion found that Congress's creation of the existing courts-martial system, and the lack of any legal code specifying the laws of war, did not preclude the use of military commissions. He read the Articles of War—the precursor to today's Uniform Code of Military Justice (UCMJ)—as authorization for military commissions, but didn't reach the question of whether FDR could have created them on his own.[53]

In later World War II cases, the Supreme Court continued to approve of military commissions. In *Ex Parte Yamashita*, General MacArthur ordered a military commission to try the commanding Japanese general in the Philippines for failing to prevent his troops from committing brutal atrocities and war crimes.[54] Appealing his conviction, General Yamashita sought a writ of habeas corpus from the Supreme Court, which he could because the trial was held on American territory in the Philippines. In 1946, Chief Justice Stone again rejected the challenge and found military commissions authorized by Congress in the

Articles of War. In two other cases, the Supreme Court refused to step in to review the convictions of Japanese leaders by an international war crimes tribunal run by MacArthur or to review the sentences of Germans captured in China after the end of hostilities.[55]

The claims of senators and academics that Bush's military commissions violate the Constitution because Congress hasn't approved them have little merit. It is true that Congress has not passed a law specifically authorizing military commissions in the war on terrorism, but it never enacted one in World War II either. Instead, the Supreme Court relied on Article 15 of the Articles of War, which Congress enacted in a 1916 overhaul of the rules of military justice. Article 15 is still on the books today, and continues to authorize military commissions.[56] Now part of the UCMJ, Article 15 declared that the creation of courts-martial for the trial of American servicemen for violating military rules of discipline did not "deprive military commissions . . . of concurrent jurisdiction with respect to offenders or offenses that . . . by the law of war may be tried by military commissions."[57] Congress here recognized that military commissions continue to be the President's prerogative. The Supreme Court in *Quirin* read it as direct congressional authorization of commissions. Congress chose not to disturb *Quirin* when it reenacted Article 15 as part of the UCMJ.

Congress supplemented this source of approval with the AUMF— if it authorizes the detention of enemy combatants, it should also permit their trial—and with the 2005 Detainee Act, which allows an appeal to the federal appeals court in D.C. of the verdict of a military commission. If Congress never approved of commissions in the first place, why would it create a review process for them?

Even if Congress hadn't authorized military commissions in the UCMJ, President Bush would still have authority to establish them under his constitutional authority as commander in chief. Congress, of course, has its own authority to establish military courts under its constitutional authority to "define and punish . . . offenses against the Law of Nations" and to "make Rules for the Government and Regulation of the land and naval Forces." Article II of the Constitution grants the President "executive power" and the power of commander in chief.

While Congress has sometimes authorized military commissions itself, American history affords many examples of presidents and military commanders creating them on their own.

The purpose of military commissions makes clear that they should remain within the discretion of the commander in chief. Waging war isn't limited to ordering which enemy formations to strike and which targets to bomb. It also involves setting policy on how to fight, how to detain enemy combatants, and how to sanction the enemy if it violates the rules of civilized warfare. Allowing military commanders to try and punish violators creates incentives for the enemy to follow the rules in the future and assures our own troops that war crimes will not be tolerated. As the Supreme Court recognized in *Yamashita*, "An important incident to the conduct of war is the adoption of measures by the military commander, not only to repel and defeat the enemy, but to seize and subject to disciplinary measures those enemies who, in their attempt to thwart or impede our military effort, have violated the law of war."[58] Military commissions help commanders properly restore order in the aftermath of a conflict. This can be an important way of making sure fighting does not flare up again.

Using a military commission does more than just maintain discipline. It also allows plea bargaining with enemy combatants who have valuable information. Al Qaeda members might prove more willing to talk with our intelligence officers if they can get lower sentences in exchange. Rules that guarantee a full and fair trial will make them even more willing to cooperate, and the transparent fairness of American military commission practice is extremely high by world standards, those of the enemy. One need only contrast the extensive due process in our military commissions with al Qaeda's practice of kidnapping Americans such as Daniel Pearl and beheading them on videotape.

Some critics respond that the President cannot use military commissions in the absence of a declaration of war. That claim runs counter to American history and practice. As it had in many previous wars, most recently the 1991 Persian Gulf War, Congress chose in the week after 9/11 not to declare war but instead to enact a statute authorizing the President to use "all necessary and appropriate force" against those connected to the 9/11 attacks. Congress's authorization serves the same function as a declaration of war. No court or serious war-powers scholar today believes that Congress must instead issue a declaration of war to authorize hostilities. Presidents have used military commissions in conflicts without any declaration of war, the Civil War being the most obvious example, and the Indian wars another. The declaration-of-war issue is a red herring. It ignores the fact that presidents have long used military force abroad without congressional approval of any kind.

This isn't to license an anything-goes attitude, by any means. Important limitations restrict the scope of military commissions. For one thing, their jurisdiction is limited only to war crimes. Military commissions have no constitutional authority to try Americans or non-Americans for garden-variety crimes, civil wrongs, or any other offense unrelated to war. They can hear prosecutions only for violations of the laws of war. President Bush also exempted American citizens, whereas previous military commissions tried *everyone* who violated the laws of war. In *Quirin*, at least one of the Nazi saboteurs was an American citizen, and recall that the Supreme Court concluded that "[c]itizenship in the United States of an enemy belligerent does not relieve him of the consequences of a belligerency which is unlawful."[59]

Some critics suggest that al Qaeda members cannot be subject to the jurisdiction of military commissions. Al Qaeda is not a nation, goes the logic, therefore it is not regulated by the laws of war and its members cannot commit war crimes. This is a mistaken return to the idea that only states can wage war. It would be absurd for the law to exempt al Qaeda, which has the destructive capabilities of a nation, because it is not a state. In civil wars, insurgent groups and other actors are held accountable to the rules of civilized warfare.[60] If a nation commits war crimes by intentionally targeting civilians, then al Qaeda should be subject to the same rules.

Critics also claim that the procedures are fundamentally flawed because there is no provision for federal judicial review of verdicts. But an appeals process does exist. It travels up from the commission, to an appeals panel, to Defense Secretary Rumsfeld, and ultimately to the President. Military commissions have long been run entirely by the armed forces, without any civilian judicial review. The small number of military commission cases that have successfully reached the federal courts involved American citizens or took place on American soil. Bush's order authorized only military commissions that fell outside those exceptions.

The landscape changed, to some extent, when *Rasul v. Bush* reversed *Eisentrager*.[61] But the 2005 Detainee Treatment Act overruled *Rasul* and created only a limited right to appeal a military commission verdict to the appeals court in Washington, D.C.[62] It allows reversal only if military commissions disobey Defense Department regulations.

The final argument of opponents of military commissions is that they violate international law, specifically the Geneva Conventions, which require that prisoners of war must be tried "by the same courts according to the same procedure as in the case of members of the armed forces of the Detaining Power."[63] Some law professors regard the use of military commissions as itself a war crime.[64] But the Geneva Conventions do not apply to al Qaeda or the Taliban, who are illegal enemy combatants.[65]

Commissions balance fair and open justice with the need to fight war successfully. Critics object that they are closed to the public and that one can choose only U.S. citizens with special security clearances as lawyers.[66] Any aspect of military commissions that deviates from the classic criminal trial of American citizens in peacetime, the critics find objectionable. Their solution? More Moussaoui trials.

Moussaoui's trial showed clearly that civilian courts with juries, maximum civil rights protections, and the luxury of time cannot handle enemy combatants in wartime. America's traditional method—military commissions—can. Military commissions have deep roots in American history and constitutional practice. The President has ordered them and Congress has recognized them. Their main problems have been bureaucratic delay in setting them up and interference from the federal judges who have blocked them. Until the federal courts step out of the picture, many detainees will still lack the definite sentences that the administration's critics want them to have, and the United States will have to continue to hold them—and this may prove to be for a very long time.

EPILOGUE

Five years ago, al Qaeda struck the United States an unexpected, devastating blow. This book tells the story of the policy and legal decisions made in response. The public mostly became aware of government actions piecemeal, often after unauthorized leaks to the press. To an outside observer, the strategies and tactics in America's war on terrorism can sometimes seem ad hoc, even made up on the fly.

To those who served in the government through 9/11 and its aftermath, these were the right decisions. We are at war. After September 11, the American people understood this quite well. We responded with all the diplomatic and military tools we had at our disposal. I think the costs were worth the greater security these policies brought us.

In a sense, the success of the administration's policies has proved its worst enemy. We have crippled al Qaeda, with dozens of its leaders and hundreds of operatives captured or killed, financial and communications networks disrupted, and new attacks averted. To some, we have achieved victory. Five years without a terrorist attack has critics questioning whether the United States needs preventive detention, targeted killing, the Patriot Act, coercive interrogation, and military commissions. The public only sees the after effects: the crater in Yemen from the missile strike, or the numbers of FISA wire-taps, or the allegations of harshness at Guantanamo Bay. Naysayers can always claim we would have been just as safe without taking these precautionary actions. We never see the deaths that were prevented.

Because of our aggressive policies, al Qaeda is no longer the threat it once was. Thousands of its operatives have been killed, about two-thirds of its pre-9/11 leadership has been eliminated, and it no longer has safe havens in Afghanistan where it can plan and train for attacks. But al Qaeda is still dangerous. It is resilient, ideologically driven, and draws comfort from the well of Arab discontent and anti-Americanism that exists in the Middle East.

The war against al Qaeda has been jarring at times because the rules of war are unfamiliar. The criminal justice system is more widely understood, and it provides more certainties, but it is not suitable to the realities of this new kind of war. At some point, the threat from al Qaeda will recede. We will kill or capture sufficient numbers of al Qaeda's leaders and operatives so that they can no longer leverage their organization to carry out significant attacks on the United States. Any violence committed by remaining al Qaeda members will be sporadic, posing limited threats to American lives, and we will be safe to use the criminal justice system once again. Are we at that point now? Perhaps the debate sparked by the Supreme Court's recent decisions on due process for enemy detainees will provide further clarity at this stage, from Congress.

What is the way forward? Though some of the policies discussed in this book have recently been blocked by the courts, many remain in place today. That doesn't mean they couldn't use reform or adjustment, particularly as time goes on and we gain confidence that we have eliminated specific threats. Unfortunately, the major proposals for policy change do not come to grips with the fundamental challenges posed by terrorism. Some urge a return to the criminal justice system, or the creation of a war-crime hybrid system, while others focus on changing the organization of the government agencies involved with security and terrorism—"moving the boxes in the org chart around," as Michael Chertoff has put it.

Some commentators and academics suggest that military methods have become unnecessary because the criminal justice system can be modified to handle terrorism. So long as defense lawyers are American citizens with security clearances, classified evidence is held in closed session, and captured enemy combatants are withheld as live witnesses, we could probably modify our criminal courts to accommodate national security matters. Should we? If we do, then the civilian courts may start to look the same as the military commission system. Instead of insisting on using our criminal system for terrorism, civil libertarians might think long and hard about what this might do to the civilian courts.

Even if we could modify the criminal justice system to meet the challenges of fighting terrorism, important differences would still remain between law enforcement and the military. This is most clear with the use of force. Our peacetime legal system does not permit the use of force in any situation other than against an imminent threat to life or public safety. Outside of war, we would be required to wait until an al Qaeda attack was imminent before we could resort to deadly force in self-defense.

Critics usually look to Congress as the main engine for the development of terrorism policy. Critics claim that Bush has violated the law, or acted as if he were above the law. They place all of their hopes in Congress. If only Congress would pass a law regulating terrorism policy, all would be right with the world. There are reasons to doubt whether any new laws would make a difference. Within a week of September 11, Congress enacted into law the broadest authorization possible for the use of force against anyone connected with the attacks, or anyone who supported or harbored those responsible. Congress's virtually unanimous support for military action did not stop human rights lawyers or activists from challenging every aspect of the war on terrorism. When Congress overruled the Supreme Court's *Rasul* decision, and supported the administration, the media and academics virtually ignored it. Opposition to the administration's policies would have occurred whether Congress had voted to approve the war on terrorism or not.

Congressional support for the war is a fact of life. There may be no grand statute that defines an enemy combatant and every step of the Defense Department's review process, but neither the detention facility at Guantanamo Bay nor military commissions could exist without congressional funding. No statute defines assassinations or sets out standards for targeted killings, but only Congress can authorize and pay for the CIA and armed forces' use of unmanned drones fitted with Hellfire missiles. Congress conducts oversight of the administration's activities in the war on terrorism, and the intelligence committees are regularly briefed on covert activities. Congress is on the job, and it has spoken. There has been no monarchic seizure of power by the President.

Wartime naturally enhances presidential power. Presidential initiative and direction of policy in war runs counter to popular notions of ordinary peacetime patterns of governance. We are used to a peacetime system in which Congress enacts laws, the President enforces them, and the courts interpret them. In wartime, the gravity shifts to the executive branch. Our constitution's framers designed the executive branch to respond swiftly to events, carry out policies with unity and energy, and gather and make use of expertise and intelligence. Congress's size, disorganization, and unwillingness to take political risks naturally keep it in a secondary role in foreign affairs and national security.

In addition, the executive branch is always in operation, indeed with much the same personnel from administration to administration regardless of party. It can better react with flexibility to unforeseen events. It is difficult for anyone, Congress or the agencies, to write laws that can anticipate every future emergency, especially events like 9/11 that were beyond the American experience. FISA or the Geneva Conventions were not written with terrorist groups wielding the destructive power of a nation-state in mind. As in any crisis, the administration had to act in the moment, and could not wait for Congress to prescribe detailed rules. Seeking a change in the laws might even tip off al Qaeda to our intelligence sources and methods. Only the executive branch has the ability to adapt quickly to new emergencies and unforeseen circumstances like 9/11.

In June 2006, in *Hamdan v. Rumsfeld*, a 5–3 majority of the Supreme Court held that Bush's military commissions did not meet the standards set out in the Uniform Code of Military Justice (UCMJ).[1] In effect, the Court tossed back to Congress the question of precisely how and whether to conduct military commissions, with some general instructions on issues of procedure that the Court found troubling and in need of further congressional authorization. In contrast to *Quirin*, the justices found that Bush had failed to explain why the normal courts-martial procedures used for American soldiers were impractical to use in war crimes trials. This, the Court said, seemed to be required by the laws establishing courts-martial. The Court also held that the UCMJ requires military commissions to follow common article 3 of the Geneva Conventions. Both the UCMJ and common article 3, the justices suggested, were violated by the very benefit, from the military perspective, provided by the commissions: preventing the defendant's access to evidence and witnesses critical to national security. The government had failed, the Court said, to show that such departures from regular courts-martial procedures were necessary.

Hamdan itself is certainly not the broad defeat for the Bush administration's terrorism policies that many in the media have claimed in its immediate aftermath. If the President and Congress wish, they can correct defects in military commission procedures, for instance, by making a good showing of the necessity for the differences in procedure and evidentiary standards between courts-martial and commissions. Or they might devise independent appeal or review mechanisms for any secrecy measures that might affect fairness to the accused. Or they might eliminate any possibility that procedural rules are changed unfairly in the middle of a trial, another lacuna pinpointed by the majority. Or it could pass a one-sentence amendment to the UCMJ supporting the Bush administration's military commissions and making clear that the Geneva Conventions, not even common article 3, do not apply to the war on terrorism.

The Court only addressed the use of military commissions. It did not hold them unconstitutional, nor did it revisit its *Hamdi* decision of two years ago which allows the government to hold terrorists until the end of fighting. Even if no military commissions were held, no al Qaeda terrorists at Guantanamo Bay would be back on the street. Justice Stevens' majority opinion carefully did not address the President's inherent constitutional authority. It limited itself to interpreting two provisions of the UCMJ, one which declared that passage of the UCMJ was not meant to deprive military commissions of their usual jurisdiction, and another requiring the use of courts-martial procedures except where not practical.

I think the Court's decision was mistaken on a number of grounds. It misread the 2005 Detainee Treatment Act, which had ordered federal courts not to take up habeas cases brought by enemy combatants, like *Hamdan*, from Guantanamo Bay. It narrowed the very same authorization to use military force that it had read broadly just two years ago, and ignored the literally centuries of practice by presidents and Congress on military commissions. The Court essentially overruled *Quirin*, which had found a law identical to the UCMJ provision to be solid authorization for FDR's 1942 military commission. Perhaps most troubling, the justices rejected the President's judgment that military necessity demanded commission procedures to protect classified information. Instead, it substituted its own view that the rights of an al Qaeda terrorist suspected of war crimes should come first. That view, while worthy of respect, was not informed by any of the nonjudicial considerations in the case, in particular, the nation's very serious *military* considerations. The Court admitted exactly this when it said that it had not been presented with any evidence about the need for any differences in trial procedure between courts-martial and military commissions. It was only for this reason that it struck down military commissions as not in compliance with the UCMJ.

The five justices in *Hamdan* rejected out of hand the usual judicial deference to presidential interpretation of treaties, particularly a law-of-war treaty while fighting was ongoing. Its analysis of the Conventions here was weak, selective, and ahistorical, never coming to grips with the fact that the background to the 1949 Conventions, the substantial commentary saying that the Geneva Conventions did not apply to international terrorist groups, and President Reagan's decision to reject the 1977 additional protocols to the Conventions, made it clear that neither the President nor Congress believed or anticipated that Geneva would bind the U.S. in conflicts with international terrorists such as al Qaeda who had never signed the treaties. Instead, the Court chose to reinvent this area of law out of whole cloth.

Johnson v. Eisentrager and other cases from World War II had found that Congress never intended the Geneva Conventions (in an earlier form) to provide benefits to enemy combatants in our own courts. The Court once believed that this was a question for the President and Congress, not the courts, to decide. The five justices in the *Hamdan* majority evaded its earlier precedents by imagining that Congress overruled *Eisentrager* in 1950. Why? That year, Congress passed the UCMJ. When it did so, it reenacted Section 821's recognition of military commissions unchanged from its text at the time of *Quirin* and before. The Court provided no historical evidence at all to think that Congress believed it was overruling *Eisentrager* and applying Geneva's common article 3 to non–state actors. In fact, this would have been impossible, because *Eisentrager* was decided after Congress had passed the UCMJ. The United States did not even ratify the 1949 Geneva Conventions until 1955. This glaring mistake shows how far the five justices in *Hamdan* were willing to go to impose their preferred policies on the war on terrorism.

But *Hamdan* portends much more than whether the administration can subject ten or twenty al Qaeda suspects to trial by military commission. The *Hamdan* Court displayed a lack of judicial restraint that would have shocked its predecessors. This signals a dangerous judicial intention to intervene in wartime policy. American practice has long recognized that the President, as commander in chief, plays the leading role in war. Presidents have started wars without congressional authorization, and they have exercised complete control over military strategy and tactics. Presidents can act with a speed, flexibility, and secrecy that the other branches of government cannot match. By contrast, legislatures are large, diffuse, and slow. Their collective design may make them better for deliberating over policy, but at the cost of delay, lack of resolve, and difficulty in adapting flexibly to unforeseen circumstances.

The September 11 attacks succeeded in part because our government was mired in a terrorism-as-crime approach. In the pre-September 11 world, we worried less about preventing terrorist attacks and more about protecting against presidential abuse of civil liberties typified by Watergate—hence the Wall that prevented our law enforcement and intelligence agencies from sharing information. Our laws considered war as conflict only between nations, and failed to anticipate the rise of a non-state terrorist organization that could kill 3,000 Americans, destroy the World Trade Center, and damage the Pentagon in a single day.

President Bush invoked his authority as commander in chief to fight this new, shadowy enemy that does not wear uniforms, targets civilians for surprise attack, and refuses to obey any of the rules of civilized warfare. Like Washington, Jackson, Lincoln, and FDR before him, Bush established military commissions to try enemy combatants for war crimes. If Bush's commander in chief authority does not extend to something so tied up in strategy and tactics as punishing and deterring war crimes by the enemy, then we have accepted a system where the slaves would have remained confederate property during the Civil War, and where FDR could not have brought the United States to the aid of Great Britain as it was reeling from the German onslaught.

What makes this war fundamentally different is not that President Bush acted and Congress watched, but that the Supreme Court has decided to interfere with warfare still continuing. With its seizure of control over some of our nation's most controversial issues, like abortion, affirmative action, and public aid to religion, maybe the justices' intervention should come as no surprise. But its effort to impose the Geneva Conventions on American conduct in the war on terrorism threatens judicial micromanagement not just of the trial of enemy combatants, but of the way the United States detains, interrogates, and even targets them for attack. This is something entirely new in American history. The Supreme Court has never sought to impose policies governing warfare on the President while fighting was ongoing.

Here, unlike with the issues of abortion or religion, the Supreme Court does not have the last word. Congress and the President can enact a simple law putting the Court back in its traditional place, and our war effort will probably go forward with its usual combination of presidential initiative and general congressional support. The Supreme Court may believe it is protecting the Constitution by requiring Congress to pass a law authorizing Bush's antiterrorism policies, but all it has done is interfered with the working arrangement that the President and Congress had already reached. As with the 2005 Detainee Treatment Act, the justices will merely have forced the President and Congress to expend significant political time and energy to overrule them—time and energy better spent on taking the fight to al Qaeda.

It should come as no surprise that Congress has not enacted a grand statue regulating all facets of terrorism policy. There wouldn't be much political upside and, if they choose rules that turn out to be mistaken, it might come back to haunt them at the ballot box. Instead, Congress has focused its attention on the far less risky enterprise of reorganizing the government. Reform of intelligence and national security has now consumed a great deal of time and energy. Two national commissions, the 9/11 Commission and the Silberman-Robb Commission, held extensive hearings and issued detailed reports. Congress issued two broad pieces of legislation, one establishing the Department of Homeland Security, the other creating the Director of National Intelligence. Investigating and studying, populating and funding these new agencies, developing new lines of management, and fighting all the resulting battles over turf and power has required resources that might have been better spent on tracking and destroying parts of the terrorist network.

Creating a Homeland Security Department or a National Intelligence Director creates the appearance of reform, but whether it leads to improvements in security or more capable offensive operations against terrorists is questionable. Centralization has created yet another layer of bureaucracy between the President and the agencies in charge of handling intelligence and national security—the secretary of homeland security first, and now the director of national intelligence. Firing the incompetent or the ineffective doesn't happen very often in government because civil servants are protected by the equivalent of tenure, so reforms are inherently limited to reshufflings of the deck. Judge Posner has recently argued that our intelligence agencies prior to the current reform initiatives were probably more efficiently organized than the ones we have today.[2] I tend to agree.

Reshuffling among agencies is relatively cheap, and it deflects attention away from hard challenges on terrorism. One difficult truth is that surprise attacks have succeeded against the United States in the past and are difficult to stop. Attacks in the future will take unexpected forms that will be difficult for us to imagine beforehand—which is why they sometimes succeed. A well-oiled intelligence system cannot stop everything. Improving intelligence, tightening border searches, and increasing security at vulnerable domestic targets may help to keep us safer, but some proposals will be expensive and demand more personnel than we currently devote to security.

Whether to overhaul the FBI is one of the most difficult questions we have yet to address. The FBI, which is the closest thing we have to a national police force, combines both domestic law enforcement and counterintelligence functions. As this book has shown, the crime and national security approaches to terrorism are very different. Arguably the FBI's failings contributed to our inability to stop the 9/11 attacks. The FBI, which follows a plan of decentralization centered around its 56 field offices—it has stumbled badly in attempting to install a modern computer network that will allow better information-sharing and has not successfully integrated its national security responsibilities.[3] The FBI's culture is fundamentally that of law enforcement, which is not surprising given its primary duties, but this inevitably shapes the way its agents approach national security and intelligence. When criminal investigators want to assemble a case that can be brought in court, they look retrospectively at the evidence, and they ultimately seek to imprison the guilty as a deterrent to others. Intelligence officers focus prospectively—on preventing a future attack—and they are less interested in winning high-profile convictions than they are in infiltrating and eliminating enemy networks. Great Britain recognizes the incompatibility of law enforcement and national security and has divided its domestic intelligence agency, known as MI5, from the traditional domestic policing functions of Scotland Yard, and from foreign intelligence (MI6).

If Congress is going to continue its fetish for reorganization, it should turn to the most important and difficult question, whether the FBI's efforts at reform are succeeding, or whether it is time to establish a new domestic intelligence agency separate from crime fighting. A hard truth about terrorism is that even if we devote more resources to domestic security, great uncertainty will still surround our ability to defeat the terrorists.

The fairness and transparency of our laws—and America's solicitude for human rights, both before and after the detainee cases—takes a backseat to no nation. The many men and women of the DOD and the DOJ and many other agencies who spent three years studying and setting up our military commissions to be both fair *and* protect this nation's security did an excellent job under radically new, difficult circumstances. They deserve our gratitude. The threats we face today are new, but our laws are old. Many of these old laws contain core principles with hard-won wisdom it would be foolish to try to reinvent. The future of the American war against terrorism will probably not come in a comprehensive statute that "reforms" policy and anticipates every future contingency. The future of the American war against terrorism, like it or not, is being and will continue to be fought by the men and women of the executive branch of this nation. If 9/11 taught us anything, it was that al Qaeda is unpredictable, resourceful, dogged, and on the move in their jihad against our country. New laws could bring political certainties and consensus, but they will come at the price of flexibility and adaptability. In their brevity and relative simplicity, and because they are rooted in history honed by experience, the rules of war give our armed forces and intelligence agencies the flexibility to respond aggressively and creatively to new threats in a realm in which individual judgment and initiative are central, and not every problem can be solved by a rule book. Because of the nature of the President and the Congress, built into their DNA by the Constitution, we will continue to see initiative from the executive branch and relative passivity from the legislature.

We can't know how the courts of the future will respond to inevitable future litigation, but *Hamdan* shows that they are not shy about asserting new powers. I predict that we will not find the answers to terrorism in new government reorganizations, new job descriptions, and new judicial rulings. The best we can do to prevent another terrorist attack is to spend less energy reengineering government and overturning settled practice, and to devote more resources to taking the offensive against al Qaeda abroad and defending ourselves at home.

ACKNOWLEDGMENTS

A number of people in government have helped me think about the questions in this book. Some of them are mentioned in it, some of them are not. All of them, especially those I worked with in the Justice Department, have my deepest thanks. We are fortunate to have a government staffed by such selfless, devoted public servants. I have benefited greatly by the comments of my friends and colleagues Jesse Choper, Robert Delahunty, Sandy Kadish, Laurent Mayali, Eric Posner, Sai Prakash, Ricki Silberman, and Adrian Vermeule, who have read parts or all of the manuscript. I have benefited from the superb help of outstanding research assistants, including Peter Brachman, Sean Callagy, Patrick Hein, Keenan Kmiec, Galit Raguan, and Will Trachman. Boalt Hall's dean, Chris Edley, has generously supported my research and writing, and the head of the American Enterprise Institute, Chris DeMuth, has given me the opportunity to develop some of these ideas in the Washington, D.C., policy world. I am grateful to them both; they are model academic administrators and gracious leaders.

My agent, Lynn Chu, was an amazing translator of sometimes soporific academic prose. She coached this book from the first glimmer of an idea to the last stroke on the keyboard. Jamison Stoltz at

Grove/Atlantic, Inc., in addition to being a much-needed editor, gave this book its focus and immediacy.

My parents, John Hyun Soo Yoo and Sook Hee Lee Yoo, have been a constant encouragement and source of support over the last years. Their courage in leaving the land of their birth to come to America to make new lives for themselves and their children has always served as an example to me. My brother, Chris, has always been the very definition of the good brother: loyal, giving, and cheerful. Much of my thinking on these questions has been shaped, in part, by his good common sense. Without my wife, Elsa, this book, and anything else I have managed to do, would have been impossible. During some very difficult and challenging times, she has been more understanding, helpful, and supportive than I could ever deserve. I could not have survived my time in government, and the years after it—and could not have written this book—without her. This book is for her.

NOTES

Introduction

1. Letter from Thomas Jefferson to James Madison, Sept. 21, 1795, in 16 *The Papers of James Madison* 88–89 (J. C. A. Stagg et al. eds. 1989).

Chapter 1

1. Philip B. Heymann, *Terrorism, Freedom, and Security: Winning Without War* 20 (2003).

2. Joyce Appleby & Gary Hart, "Bush Power Grab Must Be Stopped by U.S. Citizenry," *San Jose Mercury News*, March 29, 2006.

3. Bruce Ackerman, *Before the Next Attack: Preserving Civil Liberties in an Age of Terrorism* 13 (2006).

4. See Brief for Respondent, *Rumsfeld v. Padilla*, No. 03–1027 (Apr. 12, 2004), at 2004 WL 812830.

5. Brief of Janet Reno, et al., Amici Curiae in Support of Respondents, *Rumsfeld v. Padilla*, No. 03–1027 (Apr. 12, 2004), at 2004 WL 782374.

6. See, e.g., *United States v. bin Laden*, 132 F. Supp. 2d 168 (S.D.N.Y. 2001).

7. Jean Bethke Elshtain, *Just War Against Terror: The Burden of American Power in a Violent World* (2003).

8. They are inspired by the thinking of Sayyid Qutb, a leading thinker in the Muslim Brotherhood movement. *The 9/11 Commission Report: Final Report of*

the National Commission on Terrorist Attacks Upon the United States 51 (W.W. Norton, 2004) (hereinafter *9/11 Commission Report*).

9. Id.

10. Id.

11. Id. at 54.

12. Id. at 47.

13. Id. at 51.

14. U.S. Dep't of State, Fact Sheet: "The Charges Against International Terrorist Osama bin Laden" (Dec. 15, 1999), available at http://usinfo.state .gov/topical/pol/terror/99129502.htm.

15. An enemy's conscious political object also distinguishes war from an emergency, which can arise from an act of God, such as Hurricane Katrina or a pandemic, or impersonal market forces, such as the Great Depression. Ackerman, *supra* note 4, believes 9/11 was neither crime nor war, but an emergency. This could be a simple problem of categorization. If an emergency because of terrorist attack allows the government to exercise the same powers as in wartime, then labeling the post-9/11 world an emergency rather than a war is of no real difference.

16. The 1996 Amended Protocol II to the 1980 UN Convention on Prohibitions or Restrictions on the Use of Certain Conventional Weapons art. 1(2), S. Treaty Doc. No. 105–1, at 39 (1997).

17. See 3 "U.S. Practice in International Law" § 2, at 3443 (1995). See also G. I. A. D. Draper, The Red Cross Conventions 15–16 (1958).

18. Posse Comitatus Act, 18 U.S.C. § 1382.

19. Memorandum for the Deputy Counsel to the President, From: John Yoo, Deputy Assistant Attorney General, Re: The President's Constitutional Authority to Conduct Military Operations Against Terrorists and Nations Supporting Them (Sept. 25, 2001).

20. John Yoo, "The Continuation of Politics by Other Means: The Original Understanding of War Powers," 84 Cal. L. Rev. 167–305 (1996); John Yoo, "Clio at War: The Use and Misuse of History in the War Powers Debate," 70 U. Colo. L. Rev. 1169–1222 (1999); John Yoo, "Kosovo, War Powers, and the Multilateral Future," 148 U. Pa. L. Rev. 1673–1731 (2000); John Yoo, "Why Were International Legal Scholars MIA on Kosovo?," 1 Chi. J. Int'l L 149–57 (2000); John Yoo, U.N. Wars, U.S. War Powers, 1 Chi. J. Int'l L. 355–73 (2000). Parts of these articles later appeared in John Yoo, *The Powers of War and Peace* (2005).

21. Address to a Joint Session of Congress and to the American People, Sept. 20, 2001, available at: http://www.whitehouse.gov/news/releases/2001/09/ 20010920-8.html.

22. Detention, Treatment, and Trial of Certain Non-Citizens in the War Against Terrorism, 66 Fed. Reg. 57833 (Nov. 13, 2001).

23. Authorization for Use of Military Force, Pub. L. No. 107–40, 115 Stat. 224 (2001).

24. Uniting and Strengthening America by Providing Appropriate Tools Required to Intercept and Obstruct Terrorism (USA Patriot Act) Act of 2001, Pub. L. No. 107–56, 115 Stat. 272.

25. Homeland Security Act of 2002, Pub. L. No. 107–296, 116 Stat 2135.

26. Describing September 11 as "mass murder," as President Bush did in one speech, also suggests crime fighting rather than war. Statement by the President in his Address to the Nation, Sept. 11, 2001, http://www.whitehouse.gov/news/releases/2001/09/20010911-16.html.

27. 124 S. Ct. 2686 (2004).

28. 124 S. Ct. 2633 (2004).

29. *Hamdi*, 124 S. Ct. at 2640.

30. U.N. Security Council Res. 1368, S/RES/1369 (2001).

31. International Court of Justice (hereinafter ICJ) (July 9, 2004), para. 139. This result traces its origins back to another controversial ICJ decision, *Nicaragua v. United States*, 1996 ICJ 14 para. 195, which found that the United States had attacked Nicaragua by supporting the Contras. The United States withdrew from the ICJ's jurisdiction and refused to comply with the decision.

32. See, e.g., *Mapp v. Ohio*, 367 U.S. 643 (1961). The exclusionary rule has been effectively criticized by Akhil Reed Amar, *The Constitution and Criminal Procedure: First Principles* 20–31 (1997).

33. *People v. Defore*, 150 N.E. 585, 587 (N.Y. 1926).

34. *Hamdi*, 124 S. Ct. at 2640 [quoting *Ex Parte Quirin*, 317 U.S. 1, 20 (1942)].

35. See, e.g., *Tennessee v. Garner*, 471 U.S. 1 (1971) (use of force against suspect must be reasonable).

36. *9/11 Commission Report, supra* note 8, at 47.

Chapter 2

1. See, e.g., Phillippe Sands, *Lawless World: American and the Making and Breaking of Rules—From FDR's Atlantic Charter to George W. Bush's Illegal War* 205 (2005); Kenneth Roth, "Getting Away With Torture," 11 Global Governance 389 (2005).

2. Marc Sandalow (quoting William Schulz, executive director of Amnesty International USA), "American Treatment of Prisoners Assailed," *S.F. Chron.*, May 26, 2005.

3. Geneva Convention (Third) Relative to the Treatment of Prisoners of War, Aug. 12, 1949, 6 U.S.T. 3316, 75 U.N.T.S. 135 (entered into force Oct. 21, 1950) (hereinafter GPW).

4. 18 U.S.C. § 2441.

5. Memorandum for Alberto R. Gonzales, Counsel to the President, and William J. Haynes II, General Counsel, Department of Defense, From: Jay S. Bybee Assistant Attorney General, Office of Legal Counsel, U.S. Department of Justice (Jan. 22, 2002).

6. GPW, *supra* note 3, art. 120.

7. Id. at art. 2.

8. Id. at art. 3.

9. See, e.g., Joyce Gutteridge, "The Geneva Conventions of 1949," 26 Brit. Y.B. Int'l L. 294, 300 (1949); Commentary on the Additional Protocols of 8 June 1977 to the Geneva Conventions of 12 August 1949, at 4399 (Yves Sandoz et al. eds., 1987); Irving Draper, *Reflections on Law and Armed Conflicts* 108 (1998).

10. See, e.g., Jeremy Waldron, "Torture and Positive Law: Jurisprudence for the White House," 105 Colum. L. Rev. 1681, 1691–95 (2005).

11. See, e.g., *The Prosecutor v. Dusko Tadic* (Jurisdiction of the Tribunal), (Appeals Chamber of the International Criminal Tribunal for the Former Yugoslavia 1995), 105 I.L.R. 453 (1997); Military and Paramilitary Activities In and Against Nicaragua (*Nicaragua v. United States*), ICJ (1986), 76 I.L.R. 218 (1988).

12. Message to the Senate Transmitting a Protocol to the 1949 Geneva Conventions, Jan. 29, 1987, available at http://www.reagan.utexas.edu/archives/speeches/1987/012987B.htm.

13. *United States v. Curtiss-Wright Export Corp.*, 299 U.S. 304, (1936).

14. *Clark v. Allen*, 331 U.S. 503 (1947).

15. Quoted in Memorandum, supra note 5, at 17 n.38.

16. Id.

17. Id. at 18.

18. Id. at 20.

19. GPW *supra* note 3, at art. 4(A)(3).

20. Id. at art. 4(A)(2).

21. Dana Milbank, "In Cheney's Shadow," *Wash. Post*, Oct. 11, 2004, Charlie Savage, "Cheney Aide Is Screening Legislation," *Boston Globe*, May 28, 2006, Ron Hutcheson, "Quiet Force Behind Bush Policies," *Philadelphia Inquirer*, Mar. 20, 2006.

22. See Memorandum to John C. Yoo, Deputy Assistant Attorney General, Office of the Legal Counsel, United States Department of Justice, from William H. Taft, Legal Adviser, Re: Your Draft Memorandum of January 9 (Jan. 11, 2002), quoted in Robert J. Delahunty & John Yoo, "Statehood and the Third Geneva Convention," 46 Va. J. Int'l L. 131 (2006). Mr. Taft's two-page letter is accompanied by a memorandum, stamped "Draft," prepared by him or his Office.

23. See Message to the Senate, *supra* note 12.

24. See, e.g., "Denied: A Shield for Terrorists," *N.Y. Times*, Feb. 17, 1987.

25. See Mary Elise Sarotte, "Transatlantic Tension and Threat Perception," 58 Naval War College Rev. 25 (2005); see also Eliot A. Cohen, "History and Hyperpower," 83 Foreign Affairs 49 (2004).

26. Robert Kagan, *Of Paradise and Power* 3 (2003).

27. Jeremy Rabkin, *The Case for Sovereignty: Why the World Should Welcome American Independence* (2004).

28. Draft Memorandum for the President, From Alberto R. Gonzales, Subject: Decision Re Application of the Geneva Convention on Prisoners of War to the Conflict with Al Qaeda and the Taliban (Jan. 25, 2002).

29. Memorandum to the Counsel to the President & the Assistant to the President for National Security Affairs, From: Colin L. Powell, Secretary of State, Subject: Draft Decision Memorandum for the President on the Applicability of the Geneva Convention to the Conflict in Afghanistan (Jan. 26, 2002).

30. Letter to the President, from Attorney General Ashcroft (Feb. 1, 2002).

31. Memorandum for the Vice President, Secretary of State, Secretary of Defense, Attorney General, Chief of Staff to the President, Director of Central Intelligence, Assistant to the President for National Security Affairs, Chairman of the Joint Chiefs of Staff, Re: Humane Treatment of al Qaeda and Taliban Detainees (Feb. 7, 2002).

32. See, e.g., Waldron, *supra* note 10.

33. President's Weekly Radio Address, May 13, 2006, available at http://www.whitehouse.gov/news/releases/2006/05/20050513.html.; Rice Says United States Does Not Torture Terrorists, Dec. 5, 2005, available at: http://usinfo.state.gov/is/Archive/2005/Dec/05-978451.html.; see also *infra* chapter 7.

34. 11 U.S. Op. Atty. Gen. 297, 1865 WL 1168 (U.S.A.G.).

35. "By universal agreement and practice the law of war draws a distinction between the armed forces and the peaceful populations of belligerent nations and also between those who are lawful and unlawful combatants." *Ex Parte Quirin*, 317 U.S. 1, 30–31 (1942).

36. Ben Fox, "Guards and Detainees Clash at Guantanamo," Associated Press, May 20, 2006.

Chapter 3

1. David Johnston & David E. Sanger, "Fatal Strike in Yemen Was Based on Rules Set Out by Bush," *N.Y. Times*, Nov. 6, 2002; see also Walter Pincus, "U.S. Strike Kills Six in Al Qaeda," *Wash. Post*, Nov. 5, 2002.

2. Michael Powell & Dana Priest, "U.S. Citizen Killed by CIA Linked to N.Y. Terror Case," *Wash. Post,* Nov. 9, 2002; "7th Man Is Accused Of Role in Terror Cell With Al Qaeda Link," *N.Y. Times,* May 22, 2003.

3. See James Risen, "Bin Laden Aide Reported Killed By U.S. Bombs," *N.Y. Times,* Nov. 17, 2001; Thom Shanker & Carlotta Gall, "U.S. Attack On Warlord Aims to Help Interim Leader," *N.Y. Times,* May 9, 2002; Douglas Jehl, "Remotely Controlled Craft Part of U.S.-Pakistan Drive Against Al Qaeda, Ex-Officials Say," *N.Y. Times,* May 16, 2005.

4. Ellen Knickmeyer, "Zarqawi's Hideout Was Secret Till Last Minute," *Wash. Post,* June 11, 2006.

5. Bob Woodward, *Bush at War* 100–01 (2002).

6. James Risen & David Johnston, "Bush Has Widened Authority of C.I.A. to Kill Terrorists," *N.Y. Times,* Dec. 15, 2002.

7. Josh Meyer, "CIA Expands Use of Drones in Terror War," *L.A. Times,* Jan. 29, 2006; Chris Downes, "'Targeted Killings' In an Age of Terror: The Legality of the Yemen Strike," 9 J. Conflict & Sec. L. 277 (2004).

8. David E. Sanger & David Johnston, "Allies Think Iraqi Leader Eluded Death In U.S. Strike," *N.Y. Times,* March 24, 2003.

9. Kevin Sullivan & Rajiv Chandrasekaran, "Hussein's Two Sons Killed In Firefight With U.S. Troops," *Wash. Post,* July 23, 2003.

10. President Bush Discusses Progress in Iraq, July 23, 2003, available at http://www.whitehouse.gov/news/releases/2003/07/20030723-1.html.

11. Craig Whitlock & Kamran Khan, "Blast in Pakistan Kills Al Qaeda Commander," *Wash. Post,* Dec. 4, 2005.

12. Kamran Khan & Griff Witte, "Protests Spread Across Pakistan," *Wash. Post,* Jan. 16, 2006.

13. Exec. Order No. 12333, 3 C.R.F. § 2.11, at 200, 213 (1982).

14. Downes, *supra* note 7, at 278.

15. George Gedda, "Policy Against Assassinations Was No Barrier," *Philadelphia Inquirer,* July 24, 2003.

16. Thomas Powers, "Target Practice," *N.Y. Times,* July 13, 2003.

17. In 1941, British commandos attempted to kill German field marshal Erwin Rommel in Libya; in 1942, British-supported Czech partisans ambushed Nazi SS General Reinhard Heydrich; in 1943, American fighter planes intercepted and shot down a plane ferrying Japanese admiral Isoroku Yamamoto over the Pacific; in 1951, Navy planes killed 500 Chinese and North Korean senior officers at a planning conference in North Korea. These examples are taken from W. Hays Parks, Department of the Army Pamphlet 27-50-204, Memorandum of Law: Executive Order 12333 and Assassination, Army Lawyer 4 (Dec. 1989).

18. In April 1986, Libyan agents bombed a Berlin disco frequented by U.S. servicemen; two servicemen died in the explosion. Intelligence agencies stopped a second Libyan attack against the American embassy in Paris. President Reagan responded by sending American bombers against military and intelligence targets in Libya, including one which Colonel Qadhafi himself apparently used as a residence. As Abraham Sofaer, former judge and State Department legal adviser under President Reagan, later wrote, Qadhafi was not "personally immune from the risks of exposure to a legitimate attack. He was and is personally responsible for Libya's policy of training, assisting, and utilizing terrorists in attacks on U.S. citizens, diplomats troops, and facilities. His position as head of state provided him no legal immunity from being attacked when present at a proper military target." Abraham Sofaer, "Terrorism, the Law, and National Defense," 126 Mil. L. Rev. 89, 120 (1989).

19. See, e.g., Albert-Laszlo Barbasi, *Linked* (2003).

20. Esther Schrader, "Response to Terror," *L.A. Times,* Feb. 15, 2002.

21. Eric Schmitt, "Pentagon Says U.S. Airstrike Killed Women and Children," *N.Y. Times,* Mar. 13, 2002.

22. *9/11 Commission Report, supra* note 9. at 111.

23. Id. at 112–13.

24. Id. at 113.

25. Id.

26. Id. at 114 (quoting interview with unnamed head of CIA counter-terrorism unit).

27. Id. at 132.

28. Exec. Order No. 12333, *supra* note 13, at 200, 213.

29. Exec. Order 11905, 3 C.F.R. § 5(g), at 90, 101 (1977). There is some debate over whether the Carter and Reagan executive orders intended to broaden the definition of assassination. Ford's version prohibited "political" assassination. The Carter and subsequent Reagan versions dropped the word "political." Exec. Order 12036, 3 C.F.R. § 2–305, at 112, 129 (1979). One could argue that the deletion of "political" was meant to include individual killings not of a political nature, or that "political" was seen as surplus language and the deletion did not signify a change in meaning.

30. Sofaer, *supra* note 18, at 116–17; Parks, *supra* note 17.

31. Sofaer, *supra* note 18, at 118.

32. Alleged Assassination Plots Involving Foreign Leaders: An Interim Report of the Senate Select Comm. to Study Governmental Operations with Respect to Intelligence Activities (1976)

33. See, e.g., H.R. 15,542, 94th Cong., 2d Sess. § 9(1) (1976) ("Whoever, except in time of war, while engaged in the duties of an intelligence operation

of the government of the United States, willfully kills any person shall be imprisoned for not less than one year.").

34. Sofaer, *supra* note 18, at 119; William C. Banks & Peter Raven-Hansen, "Targeted Killing and Assassination: The U.S. Legal Framework," 37 U. Rich. L. Rev. 667, 717–26 (2003).

35. U.N. Charter, Ch. I, Art. 2(4).

36. U.N. Charter, Ch. VII, Art. 42.

37. U.N. Charter, Ch. VII, Art. 51.

38. See discussion in John Yoo, "Using Force," 71 U. Chi. L. Rev. 729 (2004).

39. Memorandum for the Attorney General, from Norbert A. Schlei, Assistant Attorney General, Office of Legal Counsel, Re: Legality under International Law of Remedial Action against Use of Cuba as a Missile Base by the Soviet Union 2 (Aug. 30, 1962), reprinted in 6 Green Bag 2d 195, 196 (2003).

40. Daniel Webster, Letter to Henry Fox, British Minister in Washington (Apr. 24, 1841) in Kenneth Bourne and D. Cameron Watt, eds., 1 British Documents on Foreign Affairs: Reports and Papers from the Foreign Office Confidential Print (Part I, Series C) 153, 159 (1986).

41. Myres S. McDougal, "The Soviet-Cuban Quarantine and Self-Defense," 57 Am. J. Int'l L. 597, 598 (1963); W.T. Mallison, Jr., "Limited Naval Blockade or Quarantine-Interdiction: National and Collective Defense Claims Valid Under International Law," 31 Geo. Wash. L. Rev. 335, 348 (1962–63).

42. Hugo Grotius, *The Laws of War and Peace*, bk. III, Sec. XVIII(2).

43. Parks, *supra* note 17, at 5.

44. Hague Regulation 23(b) makes it "especially forbidden" to "kill or wound treacherously individuals belonging to the hostile nation or army"; 23(c) makes it forbidden "to kill or wound an enemy who, having laid down his arms, or having no longer means of defense, has surrendered at discretion"; 23(d) makes it forbidden "to declare that no quarter will be given." Regulations Respecting the Laws and Customs of War on Land, 36 Stat. 2277, Annex to Convention (IV) Respecting the Laws and Customs of War on Land, Oct. 18, 1907, 36 Stat. 2295, 205 Consol. T.S. 277. See also U.S. Army Field Manual 27–10, The Law of Land Warfare, at para. 31.

45. Those orders prohibited assassination and declared that "the law of war does not allow proclaiming either an individual belonging to the hostile army, or a citizen, or a subject of the hostile government, an outlaw, who may be slain without trial by any captor, any more than the modern law of peace allows such international outlawry; on the contrary, it abhors such outrage." U.S. Army, General Orders No. 100, paragraph 148 (1863).

46. Michael N. Schmitt, "State-Sponsored Assassination in International and Domestic Law," 17 Yale J. Int'l L. 609, 633 (1992). Protocol I to the Geneva Conventions, which the United States refused to ratify in 1987, continues the

prohibition against "treachery" by prohibiting "resort to perfidy," which it defines as "acts inviting the confidence of an adversary to lead him to believe that he is entitled to, or is obliged to accord, protection under the rules of international law applicable in armed conflict, with intent to betray that confidence." Protocol Additional to the Geneva Conventions of 12 August 1949, and Relating to the Protection of Victims of International Armed Conflicts (Protocol 1), June 8, 1977, art. 37.

47. Army Manual, *supra* note 44, at art. 3.

48. Protocol I defines proportionality by prohibiting operations that can "be expected to cause incidental loss of civilian life, injury to civilians, damage to civilian objects, or a combination thereof, which would be excessive in relation to the concrete and direct military advantage anticipated." Protocol I, supra note 46, at art. 57(2)(a)(iii). The Navy manual defines proportionality as: "The employment of any kind or degree of force not required for the purpose of the partial or complete submission of the enemy with a minimum expenditure of time, life, and physical resources, is prohibited." Office of the Judge Advocate General, United States Navy, The Commander's Handbook on the Law of Naval Operations, § 5.2 (Jul. 1987).

49. See, e.g., Steven David, "Israel's Policy of Targeted Killing," 17 Ethics & Int'l Aff. 111 (2003).

50. Oran Ben-Naftali & Keren Michaeli, "We Must not Make a Scarecrow of the Law: A Legal Analysis of the Israeli Policy of Targeted Killings," 36 Cornell Int'l L.J. 233 (2003).

51. Israeli Ministry of Foreign Affairs, http://www.israelemb.org/faq_main_conflict.htm.

52. Eric Posner, "A Theory of the Laws of War," 70 U. Chi. L. Rev. 297 (2003); James Morrow, "The Institutional Features of the Prisoner of War Treaties," 55 Int'l Org. 971 (2001).

53. See, e.g., Geoffrey Best, *War and Law Since 1945* (1994).

54. Id., at 77.

Chapter 4

1. http://www.fbi.gov/hq/siocfs.htm.

2. Foreign Intelligence Surveillance Act of 1978, codified at 50 U.S.C. §§ 1801–1862.

3. 50 U.S.C. § 1805(a)(3).

4. FISA defines a foreign power, in part, as "a group engaged in international terrorism or activities in preparation therefor" and "a foreign-based political organization, not substantially composed of United States persons." 50 U.S.C. §§ 1801(a)(4), (5).

5. 18 U.S.C. § 1801(b)(2)(A); see also *In re Sealed Case*, 310 F.3d 717, 737–42 (For. Intel. Surv. Ct. Rev. 2002).

6. Bill Brubaker, "Bush Signs New Version of the Patriot Act," *Wash. Post*, Mar. 9, 2006.

7. http://www.whitehouse.gov/news/releases/2006/03/20060309-4.html.

8. Uniting and Strengthening America by Providing Appropriate Tools Required to Intercept and Obstruct Terrorism (USA Patriot Act) Act of 2001, Pub. L. No. 107–56, 115 Stat. 272, at § 213 (amending 18 U.S.C. § 3103a).

9. Fed. R. Crim. P. 41(d).

10. *Dalia v. United States*, 441 U.S. 238 (1979).

11. See U.S. Department of Justice, The USA Patriot Act: Myths v. Reality, http://www.lifeandliberty.gov/subs/add_myths.htm (discussing hawala case).

12. Id. (describing detonator and Zodiac gunman cases).

13. Quoted in id.

14. See, e.g., *United States v. Miller*, 425 U.S. 435 (1976).

15. Fed. R. Crim. P. 41(a).

16. Myths v. Reality, *supra* note 11.

17. These facts come from *The 9/11 Commission Report*, *supra* note 9, at 273.

18. Id. at 181.

19. Id. at 266.

20. Id. at 269.

21. Id. at 271.

22. Id.

23. 50 U.S.C. § 1804 (requiring a national security official to certify that "the purpose" of the surveillance is to obtain foreign intelligence information).

24. *In re Sealed Case*, 310 F.3d at 735.

25. U.S. Department of Justice, Procedures for Contacts Between the FBI and the Criminal Division Concerning Foreign Intelligence and Foreign Counterintelligence Investigations (1995).

26. Richard Posner, *Preventing Surprise Attacks* (2005).

27. Title III of the Omnibus Crime Control and Safe Streets Act of 1968, 18 U.S.C. §§ 2510–2522.

28. *United States v. Verdugo-Urquidez*, 494 U.S. 259, 273 (1990) (concluding that the Fourth Amendment did not protect nonresident aliens against unreasonable searches or seizures conducted outside the sovereign territory of the United States, because of serious consequences for use of armed forces abroad).

29. This conclusion is supported by the Supreme Court's recent "special needs" cases, which allow reasonable, warrantless searches for government needs that go beyond regular law enforcement. See *Vernonia School Dist. 47J v. Acton*, 515 U.S. 646, 653, 115 S.Ct. 2386, 2391, 132 L.Ed.2d 564 (1995) (random drug testing of student athletes); *Michigan Dep't of State Police v. Sitz*, 496

U.S. 444 (1990) (stopping drunk drivers); *United States v. Martinez-Fuerte*, 428 U.S. 543 (1976) (border control checkpoints).

30. See e.g., *United States v. Truong Dinh Hung*, 629 F.2d 908 (4th Cir.1980); *United States v. United States District Court*, 407 U.S. 297, 322 (1972).

31. *Katz v. United States*, 389 U.S. 347, 358 n.23 (1967); see also *Mitchell v. Forsyth*, 472 U.S. 511, 531 (1985).

32. 407 U.S. 297, 308 (1972).

33. 629 F.2d 908, 913 (4th Cir. 1980).

34. Id. at 913–14.

35. See also *United States v. Brown*, 484 F.2d 418 (5th Cir. 1973), cert. denied, 415 U.S. 960 (1974); *United States v. Buck*, 548 F.2d 871 (9th Cir.), cert. denied, 434 U.S. 890 (1977); *United States v. Clay*, 430 F.2d 165 (5th Cir. 1970), rev'd on other grounds, 403 U.S. 698 (1971).

36. *Vernonia School Dist. 47J v. Acton*, 515 U.S. 646, 652 (1995).

37. Id. at 653 (quoting *Griffin v. Wisconsin*, 483 U.S. 868, 873 (1987).

38. See, e.g., *Pennsylvania v. Labron*, 518 U.S. 938 (1996) (per curiam) (automobile searches); *Acton*, 515 v.s. at 653 (drug testing of athletes); *Michigan Dep't of State Police v. Sitz*, 496 U.S. at 455 (1990) (drunk driver checkpoints); *Skinner v. Railway Labor Executives' Ass'n*, 489 U.S. 602 (1989) (drug testing railroad personnel); *Treasury Employees v. Von Raab*, 489 U.S. 656 (1989) (drug testing federal customs officers); *United States v. Place*, 462 U.S. 696 (1983) (baggage search); *Terry v. Ohio*, 392 U.S. 1 (1968) (temporary stop and search).

39. See *Tennessee v. Garner*, 471 U.S. 1, 8 (1985).

40. *Haig v. Agee*, 453 U.S. 280, 307 (1981).

41. The courts have observed that even the use of deadly force is reasonable under the Fourth Amendment if used in self-defense or to protect others. Here, the right to self-defense is not that of an individual, but that of the nation and of its citizens. Cf. *In re Neagle*, 135 U.S. 1 (1890); *The Prize Cases*, 67 U.S. (2 Black) 635 (1862). If the government's heightened interest in self-defense justifies the use of deadly force, then it certainly would also justify warrantless searches.

42. *City of Indianapolis v. Edmond*, 531 U.S. 32 (2000).

43. Id. at 44.

44. Id. at 47–48.

45. Cf. Akhil Reed Amar, *The Constitution and Criminal Procedure: First Principles* 1–45 (1997).

46. Quoted in *In Re Sealed Case*, 310 F.3d at 720.

47. Transcript of Docket No. 02–001, United States Foreign Intelligence Court of Review (Sept. 9, 2002), http://fas.org/irp/agency/doj/fisa/hrng090902.htm.

48. *In Re Sealed Case*, 310 F.3d at 724.

49. Id. at 743.

50. Id. at 735.

51. Id. at 744.

52. Id. 744–45.

53. Id. at 746.

54. Id. at 742.

55. Eric Posner & Adrian Vermeule, "Accommodating Emergencies," 56 Stan. L. Rev. 605 (2003).

56. Id.

57. See, e.g. Geoffrey Stone, *Perilous Times: Free Speech in Wartime* (2005).

58. A task force commissioned by Attorney General Reno to investigate the mistakes in the Wen Ho Lee prosecution concluded in 2000 that the Wall obstructed the government's ability to successfully conduct foreign intelligence. *In Re Sealed Case*, 310 F.3d at 743 n.28 [citing Final Report of the Attorney General's Review Team on the Handling of the Los Alamos National Laboratory Investigation (May 2000)].

Chapter 5

1. James Risen & Eric Lichtblau, "Bush Lets U.S. Spy on Callers Without Courts," *N.Y. Times*, Dec. 16, 2005.

2. Tim Golden, "A Junior Aide Had a Big Role in Terror Policy," *N.Y. Times*, Dec. 23, 2005.

3. S. Res. 398, Relating to the Censure of George W. Bush, Mar. 13, 2006, 109th Congress, 2d Session; Statement of Senator Russ Feingold, On the President's Warrantless Wiretapping Program, Feb. 7, 2006, available at www.feingold.senate.gov/06/02/20060207 .html (hereinafter "December 2005 Briefing").

4. Shailagh Murray, "Senate Maverick's Motion Stirs Angry Debate," *Wash. Post*, Mar. 15, 2006.

5. George F. Will, "No Checks, Many Imbalances," *Wash. Post*, Feb. 16, 2006.

6. *United States v. Curtiss-Wright Export Corp.*, 299 U.S. 304 (1936).

7. U.S. Const. art II, section 2 (The President "shall have the Power, by and with the Advice and Consent of the Senate, to make Treaties, provided two thirds of the Senators present concur").

8. Richard A. Epstein, "Executive Power on Steroids," *Wall St. J.*, Feb. 13, 2006.

9. *Morrison v. Olson*, 487 U.S. 654, 705 (1988) (Scalia, J., dissenting).

10. John Yoo, *The Powers of War and Peace*, 30–45, 88–142 (2005).

11. Epstein argues that "commander in chief" is not textually a "power," but just a position. But the lack of the word "power" there does not seem significant. Other authorities enjoyed by the President, such as the power to nominate and then appoint federal officials with the advice and consent of the Congress, do not use the word "power" either. But the authority to appoint individuals is not a position, but indeed a right of the President, and an important one at that. The Treaty Clause, by contrast, does designate the President as having a "power," but the role of the President in both appointments and treaties are virtually identical. It does not seem as if there is anything significant in the latter's grant of a "power" and the former's silence on the matter.

12. Yoo, *supra* note 10, at 152–55.

13. See Risen & Lichtblau, *supra* note 1 (describing use of information obtained via wiretap to arrest suspect who plotted to destroy the Brooklyn Bridge).

14. See *supra* note 1.

15. U.S. Department of Justice, Legal Authorities Supporting the Activities of the National Security Agency Described by the President (Jan. 19, 2006).

16. Richard Posner, "A New Surveillance Act," *Wall St. J.*, Feb. 15, 2006; see also Richard Posner, *Preventing Surprise Attacks* (2005).

17. Posner, "A New Surveillance Act," *supra* note 16.

18. Heather MacDonald, "What We Don't Know Can Hurt Us," City Journal, Spring 2004.

19. 50 U.S.C. § 1804(a).

20. 50 U.S.C. § 1805(f).

21. See Financial Crimes Enforcement Network, www.fincen.gov, which administers the Bank Secrecy Act, 31 U.S.C. §§ 5311 et seq.

22. Leslie Cauley, "NSA Has Massive Database of Americans' Phone Calls," *USA Today*, May 11, 2006.

23. President's Radio Address, May 13, 2006, available at: http://www.whitehouse.gov/news/releases/2006/05/20060513.html.

24. Susan Page, "NSA Secret Database Report Triggers Fierce Debate in Washington," *USA Today*, May 11, 2006.

25. *Smith v. Maryland*, 442 U.S. 735, 744–45 (1979); *United States v. Miller*, 425 U.S. 435, 443 (1976).

26. William Safire, "You Are a Suspect," *N.Y. Times*, Nov. 14, 2002.

27. MacDonald, *supra* note 18.

28. December 2005 Briefing, *supra* note 3.

29. In the 1907 Hague Regulations, one of the first treaties on the laws of war, the leading military powers agreed that "the employment of measures

necessary for obtaining information about the enemy and the country is considered permissible." Interception of electronic communications is known as SIGINT, or signals intelligence, as opposed to HUMINT, or human intelligence. Writers on the laws of war have recognized that interception of an enemy's communications is a legitimate tool of war. According to one recognized authority, nations at war can gather intelligence by use of air and ground reconnaissance and observation, "interception of enemy messages, wireless and other," the capturing of documents, and the interrogation of prisoners. Morris Greenspan, *The Modern Law of Land Warfare* 326 (1959).

30. *Halperin v. CIA*, 629 F.2d 144, 158 (D.C. Cir. 1980).

31. *Totten v. United States*, 92 U.S. 105 (1876).

32. Exec. Order No. 2604 (Apr. 28, 1917) (World War I order); Exec. Order No. 8985 (Dec. 19, 1941) (World War II order).

33. Christopher Andrew, *For the President's Eyes Only* 124–25 (1995).

34. *The Prize Cases*, 67 U.S. 635, 670 (1863).

35. The President has the power "to direct the performance of those functions which may constitutionally be performed by the military arm of the nation in time of war," and to issue military commands using the powers to conduct war "to repel and defeat the enemy." *Ex Parte Quirin*, 317 U.S. 1, 28 (1942).

36. See, e.g., Louis Fisher, *Presidential War Power* 11 (1995); Michael J. Glennon, *Constitutional Diplomacy* 17 (1990); but see Yoo, *The Powers of War and Peace, supra* note 10, at 143–60.

37. *Johnson v. Eisentrager*, 339 U.S. 763, 788 (1950).

38 The Federalist No. 64, at 435 (Jacob E. Cooke ed. 1961) (John Jay).

39. See, e.g., *United States v. Waterman S.S. Corp.*, 299 U.S. 304 (1936); *Chicago & S. Air Lines v. Waterman S.S. Corp.*, 333 U.S. 103, 111 (1948). In a post–Civil War case, recently reaffirmed, the Court ruled that President Lincoln had the constitutional authority to engage in espionage. The President "was undoubtedly authorized during the war, as commander-in-chief . . . to employ secret agents to enter the rebel lines and obtain information respecting the strength, resources, and movements of the enemy." *Totten v. United States*, 92 U.S. 105, 106 (1876). On *Totten*'s continuing vitality, see *Tenet v. Doe*, 544 U.S. 1, 8–11 (2005).

40. Reprinted in Appendix A, *United States v. United States District Court*, 444 F.2d 651, 669–70 (6th Cir. 1971).

41. See *Nardone v. United States*, 302 U.S. 379 (1937) (interpreting Section 605 of the Federal Communications Act of 1934 to prohibit interception of telephone calls).

42. See Robert H. Jackson, *That Man: An Insider's Portrait of Franklin D. Roosevelt* 68–69 (2003).

43. Foreign Intelligence Surveillance Act of 1978: Hearings on H.R. 5764, H.R. 9745, H.R. 7308, and H.R. 5632 Before the Subcomm. on Legislation of

the House Comm. on Intelligence, 95th Cong., 2d Sess.15 (1978) (Statement of Attorney General Griffin Bell).

44. Most notably, Clinton Deputy Attorney General Jamie Gorelick testified before Congress that the Justice Department could carry out physical searches for foreign intelligence purposes, even though FISA at the time did not provide for them. Amending the Foreign Intelligence Surveillance Act: Hearings Before the House Permanent Select Comm. on Intelligence, 103d Cong. 2d Sess. 61 (1994). Clinton's OLC issued a legal opinion that the President could order the sharing of electronic surveillance gathered through criminal wiretaps between the Justice Department and intelligence agencies, even though this was prohibited by statute. Sharing Title III Electronic Surveillance Material with the Intelligence Community, OLC Prelim. Print, 2000 WL 33716983 (Oct. 17, 2000).

45. *United States v. United States District Court*, 407 U.S. 297 (1972).

46. *In re Sealed Case*, 310 F.3d 717, 742 (For. Intel. Surv. Ct. Rev. 2002).

47. See Tom Daschle, "Power We Didn't Grant," *Wash. Post*, Dec. 23, 2005.

48. A letter to Congress from law professors and former government officials, many of them longtime critics of the Bush administration's war on terrorism or opponents of presidential war powers, backed up Senator Feingold's statement of this view with the conclusion that there is no "plausible legal defense" of the NSA program, and that President Bush should have sought an amendment to the Patriot Act to allow it. They argued that "the President simply cannot violate criminal laws behind closed doors because he deems them obsolete or impracticable." Beth Nolan, et al., Letter to Congress on NSA Spying (Jan. 9, 2006). A similar conclusion is reached by the Congressional Research Service. See Congressional Research Service, Presidential Authority to Conduct Warrantless Electronic Surveillance to Gather Foreign Intelligence Information (Jan. 5, 2006).

49. *Hamdi v. Rumsfeld*, 542 U.S. 507, 518 (2004) (plurality opinion). Although a plurality opinion, five justices agreed on this point because Justice Thomas, in dissent, concluded that the President had the constitutional authority to detain enemy combatants and that Congress had authorized this. Id. at 587 (Thomas, J., dissenting). In fact, a federal law also prohibited the detention of American citizens without the authorization of Congress, in part as a response to the internment of Japanese-Americans in World War II. Civil libertarians argued that the AUMF was insufficient to overcome this federal antidetention act.

50. As Hamilton wrote in the Federalist, "[E]nergy in the executive is a leading character in the definition of good government. It is essential to the protection of the community against foreign attacks." The Federalist No. 70 (Alexander Hamilton). This point applies to the war context directly. Wrote

Hamilton: "Of all the cares or concerns of government, the direction of war most peculiarly demands those qualities which distinguish the exercise of power by a single hand." The Federalist No. 74 (Alexander Hamilton). Future Supreme Court Justice James Iredell argued that "[f]rom the nature of the thing, the command of armies ought to be delegated to one person only. The secrecy, d[i]spatch, and decision, which are necessary in military operations, can only be expected from one person." Jonathan Elliot, ed., 4 *The Debates in the Several State Conventions on the Adoption of the Federal Constitution 107* (1836); 2 Joseph Story, *Commentaries on the Constitution of the United States* § 1491 (1833) (in military matters, "[u]nity of plan, promptitude, activity, and decision, are indispensable to success; and these can scarcely exist, except when a single magistrate is entrusted exclusively with the power").

51. See Charlie Savage, "Three Democrats Slam President Over Defying Statutes," *Boston Globe*, May 2, 2006; "ACLU Sues to Stop Illegal Spying on Americans, Saying President is Not Above the Law," Jan. 17, 2006, available at: http://www.aclu.org/safefree/nsaspying/23486prs20060117.html.

52. John Locke, *The Second Treatise of Government* § 148 (1690).

53. The Federalist No. 23, at 147 (J. Cooke ed., 1961) (Alexander Hamilton).

54. Id.

55. The Federalist No. 70, *supra* note, 50 at 471.

56. The Federalist No. 74, *supra* note, 50, at 500.

57. President Andrew Jackson expressed the same view in 1832, vetoing a bill that he regarded as unconstitutional even though the Supreme Court had upheld it as constitutional. "It is as much the duty of the house of representatives, of the senate, and of the president to decide upon the constitutionality of any bill or resolution, just as with the Supreme Court when the law arises in a case before them," he wrote. Abraham Lincoln, in the case of *Dred Scot*, famously announced in his first inaugural that thenceforth, he would not follow the rule that a slave would not be free once in Northern territory, though he chose to obey the Supreme Court's order in the *Dred Scot* case itself. President Franklin Roosevelt evaded Congress's Neutrality Acts and provided aid and comfort to the allies before Pearl Harbor.

58. For representative works arguing that Congress has sole control over when to begin wars, see Fisher, *supra* note 36, at 203; John Hart Ely, *War and Responsibility: Constitutional Lessons of Vietnam and its Aftermath* (1993); *supra* note 36, 81 (1990); Louis Henkin, *Constitutionalism, Democracy, and Foreign Affairs* 109 (1990); Harold Hongju Koh, *The National Security Constitution: Sharing Power After the Iran-Contra Affair* 158–61 (1990). My argument in response can be found in Yoo, *supra*, note 22, at 143–81.

59. See, e.g., John Hart Ely, Suppose Congress Wanted a War Powers Act That Worked? 88 Colum. L. Rev. 1379 (1988).

60. *Fleming v. Page*, 50 U.S. (9 How.) 603, 615 (1850).

61. For a standard historical source on the period see Robert Dallek, *Franklin D. Roosevelt and American Foreign Policy*, 1932–1945 (1979). See also Robert Divine, *Roosevelt and World War II* (1969); Gaddis Smith, *American Diplomacy During the Second World War* (1965); Frederick W. Marks III, *Wind Over Sand: The Diplomacy of Franklin Roosevelt* (1988); Warren F. Kimball, *The Juggler: Franklin Roosevelt as Wartime Statesman* (1991).

62. Marc Trachtenberg, "The Bush Strategy in Historical Perspective," in James Wirtz and Jeffrey Larsen, eds., *Nuclear Transformation: The New U.S. Nuclear Doctrine* (2005).

63. This history is recounted in John Lewis Gaddis, *Strategies of Containment: A Critical Reappraisal of American National Security Policy during the Cold War* (rev'd ed. 2005); John Lewis Gaddis, *We Now Know: Rethinking Cold War History* (1998).

64. The Framers clearly intended to replicate the British model of the executive, which was in both theory and practice hemmed in by the parliamentary power of the purse. Pressed during the Virginia ratifying convention with the charge that the President's powers could lead to a military dictatorship, James Madison argued that Congress's control over funding would be enough of a check to control the executive.

65. "Congress cannot anticipate and legislate with regard to every possible action the President may find it necessary to take or every possible situation in which he might act," the Supreme Court has said. "Such failure of Congress . . . does not, 'especially . . . in the areas of foreign policy and national security,' imply 'congressional disapproval' of action taken by the Executive." *Dames & Moore v. Regan*, 453 U.S. 654, 678 (1981) [quoting *Haig v. Agee*, 453 U.S., 280, 291 (1981)].

Chapter 6

1. *Hamdi v. Rumsfeld*, 542 U.S. 507, 519 (2004).

2. *Rasul v. Bush*, 542 U.S. 466 (2004).

3. *Hamdi*, 542 U.S. at 543.

4. *Johnson v. Eisentrager*, 339 U.S. 763 (1950).

5. These facts come from the opinions issued by Judge Ellis during Lindh's trial. See *United States v. Lindh*, 212 F. Supp. 2d 541 (E.D.Va. 2002); *United States v. Lindh*, 227 F. Supp. 2d 565 (E.D.Va. 2002).

6. *Lindh*, 212 F. Supp. 2d at 553–58.

7. 18 U.S.C. § 2339A—§ 2339B.

8. *Lindh*, 227 F. Supp. 2d at 571.

9. *Hamdi*, 294 F.3d 598 (4th Cir. 2002).

10. *Hamdi*, 542 U.S. at 511–12.

11. *Hamdi*, 296 F.3d 278, 279, 283 (4th Cir. 2002)

12. *Hamdi*, 542 U.S. at 513.

13. *Hamdi*, 316 F. 3d 450, 459 (4th Cir. 2003).

14. *Id.*, at 475.

15. These facts are taken from *Padilla v. Hanft*, 423 F.3d 386 (4th Cir. 2005); *Rumsfeld v. Padilla*, 542 U.S. 426 (2004); *Padilla v. Rumsfeld*, 352 F.3d 695 (2d Cir. 2003) *Padilla v. Rumsfeld*, 233 F. Supp. 2d 564 (S.D.N.Y 2002).

16. On Feb. 24, 2004 then White House counsel Alberto Gonzales described the Padilla process in a speech before the American Bar Association's Standing Committee on Law and National Security. 150 Cong. Rec. S2701, S2703–S2704 (daily ed. Mar. 11, 2004) (reprinting speech).

17. See *Padilla v. Hanft*, 423 F.3d 386 (4th Cir. 2005) (reprinting order).

18. *Padilla v. Rumsfeld*, 233 F. Supp. 2d 564 (S.D.N.Y. 2002).

19. *Padilla v. Rumsfeld*, 352 F.2d 695 (2d. Cir. 2003).

20. Brief of Louis Henkin, Harold Hongju Koh, and Michael H. Posner as Amici Curiae in Support of Respondents, *Rumsfeld v. Padilla*, 542 U.S. 426 (2004), 2003 U.S. Briefs 1027; 2004 U.S. S. Ct. Briefs LEXIS 299.

21. See also Brief of Janet Reno, et al., Amici Curiae in Support of Respondents, *Rumsfeld v. Padilla*, 542 U.S. 426 (2004), 2003 U.S. Briefs 1027; 2004 U.S. S. Ct. Briefs LEXIS 293.

22. See generally Lt. Col. G. Lewis & Capt. J. Mewha, History of Prisoner of War Utilization by the United States Army 1776–1945, Dep't of the Army Pamphlet No. 20–213 (1955).

23. *Ex Parte Quirin*, 317 U.S. at 30–31.

24. As the Supreme Court observed long ago, that power includes the discretion to direct the military "in the manner he may deem most effectual to harass and conquer and subdue the enemy." *Fleming v. Page*, 50 U.S. (9 How.) 603, 615 (1850). The Constitution's "grant of war power," the Court has said on another occasion, is not limited just to actual battlefield operations, but also "includes all that is necessary and proper for carrying [it] into execution." *Johnson v. Eisentrager*, 339 U.S. 763, 788 (1950).

25. *Ex parte Milligan*, 71 U.S. (4 Wall.) 2 (1866).

26. Milligan had lived "in Indiana for the past twenty years, was arrested there, and had not been, during the late troubles, a resident of any of the states in rebellion." Id. at 131.

27. Id. at 121.

28. Id. at 120–21.

29. These facts are taken from Louis Fisher, *Military Tribunals & Presidential Power: American Revolution to the War on Terrorism* (2005) and David Danelski, "The Saboteurs' Case," 1 J. S. Ct. Hist. 61, 61–63 (1996).

30. *Ex Parte Quirin*, 317 U.S. 1 (1942).

31. Id. at 37–38.

32. Id. at 37.

33. Id. at 45.

34. They argued that the Supreme Court "has never sanctioned military jurisdiction over an individual who was not a soldier in a recognized army or found in an area of active combat or under military occupation or martial law." Respondent's Brief on the Merits, *Rumsfeld v. Padilla*, No. 03–1027 (Apr. 12, 2005), at 2004 WL 812830 (U.S.).

35. Their argument also ignores Supreme Court precedent established in *Quirin*. Only an "association" with the enemy need be shown. A capture need not be in the midst of an act of hostility or in the theater of war. "It is without significance that petitioners were not alleged to have borne conventional weapons." *Quirin*, 317 U.S. at 37. They don't need to be carrying weapons. "It is without significance that . . . their proposed hostile acts did not necessarily contemplate collision with the Armed Forces of the United States." Id. Whether attacks planned are on the military or on civilian targets is irrelevant. Wearing uniforms, or being in the United States rather than at the front, doesn't matter either. Id. at 35.

36. Harvard law professor and former Clinton Justice Department official Philip Heymann writes that "a country cannot be free if the Executive retains the power, on its own determination that certain conditions are met, to detain citizens for an indefinite period." Philip B. Heymann, *Terrorism, Freedom, and Security: Winning without War* (2003).

37. Padilla's lawyers told the Supreme Court that "unlike a traditional war, the 'war on terror' may never end, and there is no clear point at which prisoners must be released." Respondent's Brief on the Merits, *Rumsfeld v. Padilla*, No. 03–1027 (Apr. 12, 2005), at 2004 WL 812830 (U.S.).

38. While this recent quote comes from the Geneva Conventions, it codifies centuries of historical practice requiring POWs to be released when peace came. GPW, art. 118, Aug. 12, 1949, 6 U.S.T. 3316, 75 U.N.T.S. 135 (entered into force Oct. 21, 1950).

39. Civil libertarians even went so far as to file a brief in the 2004 Supreme Court detainee cases on behalf of Mr. Korematsu, whose detention was upheld in the Supreme Court case of his name in 1944. *Korematsu v. United States*, 323 U.S. 214 (1944).

40. The Act declares that "No citizen shall be imprisoned or otherwise detained by the United States except pursuant to an Act of Congress." 18 U.S.C. § 4001(a).

41. Respondent's Brief on the Merits, *Rumsfeld v. Padilla*, No. 03–1027 (Apr. 12, 2005), at 2004 WL 812830 (U.S.).

42. In fact, when Congress passed the Act, some legislators questioned whether it might conflict with the President's powers in war, and the floor managers assured them that it would not have that effect. See, e.g., 117 Cong. Rec. at 31555–57 (statement of Abner Mikva). Before the *Hamdi* and *Padilla* cases, no court had ever construed this 1972 law to apply to the detention of the enemy in war, or to infringe on the President's commander-in-chief powers. Before the terrorism cases, every court to interpret the Anti-Detention Act applied it to the civilian prison system. See *Howe v. Smith*, 452 U.S. 473, 479 (1981); *Lono v. Fenton*, 581 F.2d 645, 648 (7th Cir. 1978); *Seller v. Ciccone*, 530 F.2d 199, 201 (8th Cir. 1976); *Marchesani v. McCune*, 531 F.2d 459, 461 (10th Cir. 1974); *Bono v. Saxbe*, 462 F. Supp. 146, 148 (E.D. Ill. 1978).

43. Another federal statute, 10 U.S.C. § 956(5), appropriates funds to the military for "the maintenance, pay and allowances for prisoners of war" and "other persons in the custody of the [military] whose status is determined by the Secretary to be similar to prisoners of war," and "persons detained in the custody of the [military] pursuant to Presidential proclamation." As the Fourth Circuit observed in *Hamdi*, "[It] is difficult if not impossible to understand" how Congress could appropriate funds for combatants "similar to prisoners of war without also authorizing their detention in the first instance." *Hamdi*, 316 F.3d at 467–468.

44. In 1909, Justice Oliver Wendell Holmes came to the same conclusion in a case brought by a citizen detained by the governor of Colorado in an uprising. *Moyer v. Peabody*, 212 U.S. 78 (1909). Holmes found that, under Colorado's constitution, the governor had the power to "suppress insurrections" and that this included the lesser power to detain. This power meant the governor "shall make the ordinary use of soldiers to that end; that he may kill persons who resist, and, of course, that he may use the milder measure of seizing the bodies of those whom he considers to stand in the way of restoring peace." Id. at 84. When the executive is authorized "with regard to killing men in the actual clash of arms," Holmes wrote, "the same is true of temporary detention to prevent apprehended harm." Id. at 85. Holmes also made the point that detention was appropriate as it was for the prevention of future harms, not punishment for past acts. "Such arrests are not necessarily for punishment, but are by way of precaution, to prevent the exercise of hostile power." Id. at 84–85.

45. For the rich academic debate on delegation of legislative authority to administrative agencies, see Larry Alexander & Saikrishna Prakash, "Reports of the Nondelegation Doctrine's Death are Greatly Exaggerated," 70 U. Chi. L. Rev. 1297 (2003); Eric Posner & Adrian Vermeule, "Interring the Nondelegation Doctrine," 69 U Chi. L. Rev. 1721 (2002); Gary Lawson, "Delegation and Original Meaning," 88 Va. L. Rev. 327 (2002); John F. Manning,

"The Nondelegation Doctrine as a Canon of Avoidance," 2000 S. Ct. Rev. 223, 228; Cass R. Sunstein, "Nondelegation Canons," 67 U. Chi. L. Rev. 315, 321–22 (2000).

46. *Haig v. Agee*, 453 U.S. 280, 292 (1981).

47. See, e.g., *INS v. St. Cyr*, 533 U.S. 289, 306 (2001); *Fernandez v. Phillips*, 268 U.S. 311, 312 (1925).

48. See *United States v. Lindh*, 2002 WL 1298601 (E.D.Va. 2002) (allowing defense to submit questions to be asked of enemy combatants); *United States v. Moussaoui*, 365 F.2d 292 (4th Cir. 2004) (ordering government to provide written substitutions to take place of live depositions of enemy combatants).

49. Brief of Louis Henkin, Harold Hongju Koh, and Michael H. Posner as Amici Curiae in Support of Respondents, *Rumsfeld v. Padilla*, 542 U.S. 426 (2004), 2003 U.S. Briefs 1027; 2004 U.S. S. Ct. Briefs LEXIS 299.

50. And only one President, Abraham Lincoln, has ever refused to obey a writ of habeas corpus. At the beginning of the Civil War, President Lincoln ordered a suspension of the writ. Only Congress appears to have this power, which the Constitution recognizes in Article I, Section 9's description of limitations on the legislature. Congress was not even in session for the first months of the Civil War. Lincoln's administration justified the suspension on the ground that the Constitution allows the suspension of the writ in the passive tense, without specifically identifying which branch may do so. In *Ex Parte Merryman*, Chief Justice Roger Taney issued a writ ordering the military to release John Merryman, a Maryland resident suspected of supporting Confederate efforts to prevent Union troops from moving south through Maryland to defend Washington, D.C. *Ex Parte Merryman*, 17 F. Cas. 144 (C.C.D. Md. 1861) (Taney, C.J.) (No. 9,487); see also Michael Stokes Paulsen, "The Most Dangerous Branch: Executive Power to Say What the Law Is," 83 Georgetown L. J. 217 (1994). The general holding Merryman refused to accept Taney's order, and it was not until 1862 that Congress enacted a law suspending the writ of habeas corpus and establishing procedures reviewing military detentions. It was the *Merryman* case and his suspension of habeas corpus that prompted Lincoln to utter his famous rhetorical question in his special message to Congress in July 1861: "Are all the laws, but one, to go unexecuted, and the government itself to go to pieces, lest that one be violated?" Chief Justice Rehnquist took the first words of the famous quote for the title of his book on civil liberties in wartime. William H. Rehnquist, *All the Laws But One: Civil Liberties in Wartime* (1998).

51. *Johnson v. Eisentrager*, 339 U.S. 763, 779 (1950).

52. Id. at 778.

53. Id. at 779.

54. Id.

55. In the 1990 *United States v. Verdugo-Urquidez*, the Supreme Court refused to hear a case against the United States brought by a Mexican citizen whose home had been searched without a search warrant by American agents. 494 U.S. 259, 273 (1990). In rejecting the Fourth Amendment claim, the Court emphasized that aliens could not claim the benefit of the Constitution for conduct outside the United States—such aliens were not part of the "we the people" who benefited from the Fourth Amendment. Further, the Court found that allowing such claims "would have significant and deleterious consequences for the United States in conducting activities beyond its boundaries," not just in drug cases as in *Verdugo-Urquidez*, but in the use of the armed forces abroad "for the protection of American citizens or national security."

56. http://www.defenselink.mil/news/Jul2004/d20040707factsheet.pdf.

57. Guy Taylor, "Military to Keep Freeing Prisoners," *Wash. Times*, Oct. 21, 2004.

58. *Eisentrager*, 339 U.S. at 779.

59. Justice Thomas, who observed that "the courts simply lack the relevant information and expertise to second-guess determinations made by the President based on information properly withheld," agreed with this approach. See *Hamdi*, 542 U.S. at 583 (Thomas, J. dissenting).

60. 542 U.S. 426 (2004).

61. *Padilla v. Hanft*, 423 F.3d 386, 391 (4th Cir. 2005).

62. U.S. Department of Justice Press Release, Jose Padilla Charged with Conspiracy to Murder Individuals Overseas, Providing Material Support to Terrorists, www.usdoj.gov/opa/pr/2005/November/05_crm_624.html.

63. See *Hamdi*, 524 U.S. at 516–24. Justice O'Connor wrote the plurality opinion, which the chief justice, Justice Kennedy, and Justice Breyer joined.

64. Id. at 518.

65. According to their opinion, "detention to prevent a combatant's return to the battlefield is a fundamental incident of waging war." Id. at 519. The Court also said that "[T]he purpose of detention is to prevent captured individuals from returning to the field of battle and taking up arms once again." Id. at 518.

66. "A citizen, no less than an alien, can be 'part of or supporting forces hostile to the United States or coalition partners' and 'engaged in an armed conflict against the United States,'" said the justices. Id. at 519.

67. Id. at 519–22.

68. Its only concern was that detention might go too far if hostilities continued for "two generations," but it did not explain why. Id. at 520.

69. At the outset of the Civil War, the Court deferred to the President's determination that the Confederate States' secession amounted to a decla-

ration of war, and observed that the President may determine the level of force to use. In the *Prize Cases*, the Court explained that the President, as the commander in chief and not the Court, had the power to decide whether to treat the Southern states as "belligerents." *The Prize Cases*, 67 U.S. (2 Black) 635, 670 (1862). The Court did not question the merits of his decision, but stated it must leave such an evaluation to "the political department of the Government to which this power was entrusted." Id. *Quirin* had decided that the President could detain American citizens without trial if they associate with the enemy. In the waning days of World War II, the Court found that the question of whether a state of war continued to exist—despite the apparent cessation of active military operations—was a political question. *Ludecke v. Watkins*, 335 U.S. 160, 169 (1948). ("Whether and when it would be open to this Court to find that a war though merely formally kept alive had in fact ended, is a question too fraught with gravity even to be adequately formulated when not compelled.").

70. Although Justice O'Connor's opinion drew only a plurality of the Court, Justice Thomas's dissent agreed with the plurality on these essential points.

71. *Hamdi*, 542 U.S. at 533.

72. *Mathews v. Eldridge*, 424 U.S. 319, 335 (1976).

73. *Hamdi*, 542 U.S. at 533.

74. *Hamdi*, 542 U.S. at 531.

75. Id.

76. See Press Release, Statement of Mark Corallo, Director of Public Affairs, Regarding Yaser Hamdi (Sept. 22, 2004) (available at http://www.usdoj .gov/opa/pr/2004/September/04_opa_640.htm)

77. 542 U.S. 466, 481 (2004).

78. See id. at 478–79 ("[B]ecause 'the writ of habeas corpus does not act upon the prisoner who seeks relief, but upon the person who holds him in what is alleged to be unlawful custody,' a district court acts 'within [its] respective jurisdiction' within the meaning of § 2241 as long as 'the custodian can be reached by service of process'") (alteration in original) (internal citations omitted). This passage of the Court's opinion will surely be offered as evidence that judicial review for U.S.-held detainees knows no bounds.

79. *Hamdi*, 542 U.S. at 538 ("There remains the possibility that the standards we have articulated could be met by an appropriately authorized and properly constituted military tribunal . . . [M]ilitary regulations already provide for such process in related instances, dictating that tribunals be made available to determine the status of enemy detainees who assert prisoner-of-war status under the Geneva Convention").

80. The only case that came close, that of General Yamashita in World War II, made it to the Supreme Court only because his military trial was held in the

Philippines, at that time an American possession. *Ex Parte Yamashita*, 327 U.S. 1 (1946).

81. For a more detailed analysis of judicial shortcomings in national security, see John Yoo, "Courts at War," 91 Cornell L. Rev. 573 (2006); Julian Ku & John Yoo, "Foreign Competence: Formalism, Functionalism, and the Alien Tort Statute," 2004 S. Ct. Rev. 153 (2005).

82. The Detainee Treatment Act of 2005 states that "no court, justice, or judge shall have jurisdiction to hear or consider" either "an application for a writ of habeas corpus filed by or on behalf of an alien" detained by the Defense Department at Guantanamo Bay, or "any other action against the United States or its agents relating to any aspect of the detention." Pub. L. No. 109–148, 119 Stat. 2739. The Detainee Act also contains the McCain Amendment, which prohibits the cruel, inhumane, or degrading treatment of enemy detainees. I address the important constitutional and legal issues surrounding the McCain Amendment in the next chapter.

83. See http://www.law.yale.edu/outside/html/Public_Affairs/675/profsltr .pdf.

84. Congress's actions paralleled *Ex Parte McCardle*, in which the Court upheld an amendment to the federal habeas statute to prevent the Supreme Court from exercising jurisdiction over the claim of a military detainee in the Reconstruction South. 74 U.S. (7 Wall.) 506 (1869). If anything the Detainee Act is further within constitutional bounds than that act. In *McCardle*, Congress amended a habeas statute it had passed just one year earlier, in order to prevent the Supreme Court from addressing the constitutionality of Reconstruction. If the academic critics were correct that the act was unconstitutional, then expansion of the habeas jurisdiction by judicial interpretation would operate as a one-way ratchet—every time the courts expanded habeas jurisdiction, Article III would prevent Congress from reversing the decision. By this logic, changes to habeas procedure under the Anti-Terrorism and Effective Death Penalty Act of 1996, which sought to eliminate multiple and successive habeas petitions by the same convicted criminal, also would have violated the Constitution. 28 U.S.C.A. § 2244 (a),(b).

Chapter 7

1. Information from Abu Zubaydah comes from Michael Gordon, "New Confidence U.S. Has al Qaeda Leader," *N.Y. Times*, Apr. 1, 2002; Karl Vick & Kamran Khan, "Raid Netted Top Operative of al Qaeda," *Wash. Post*, Apr. 2, 2002; Walter Pincus, "Seized Materials May Help Thwart Future Attacks," *Wash. Post*, Apr. 3, 2002.

2. Karl Vick, "The Terrorists Next Door: Al Qaeda Suspects Posed as Traders Before Capture in Pakistan," *Wash. Post*, Apr. 4, 2002.

3. Walter Pincus, "Al Qaeda Suspect Said to Be Talking to Interrogators," *Wash. Post*, Apr. 13, 2002.

4. Al Qaeda Training Manual, http://www.au.af.mil/au/awc/awcgate/terrorism/alqaida_manual.

5. *9/11 Commission Report*, 161.

6. Id. at 145.

7. Most of the details of the formation and execution of the 9/11 attacks are directly attributed in the Commission Report's text and footnotes to their interrogations. See the note on Detainee Interrogation Reports, *9/11 Commission Report*, supra note 6, at 146.

8. Kamran Khan and Susan Schmidt, "Arrest of Comrade Led to Mohammed's Capture," *Wash. Post*, Mar. 3, 2003.

9. Remarks of Deputy Attorney General James Comey Concerning Jose Padilla, June 1, 2004, www.usdoj.gov/dag/speech/dag6104.htm.

10. R. Jeffrey Smith & Josh White, "Cheney Plan Exempts CIA From Bill Barring Abuse of Detainees," *Wash. Post*, Oct. 25, 2005.

11. See, e.g., Seymour Hersh, *Chain of Command: The Road from 9/11 to Abu Ghraib* (2004); John Barry, et al., "The Roots of Torture," *Newsweek*, May 24, 2004, at 26.

12. Dana Milbank, "In Cheney's Shadow," *Wash. Post*, Oct. 11, 2004.

13. Evan Thomas & Michael Hirsh, "The Debate Over Torture," *Newsweek*, Nov. 21, 2005, at 26.

14. Neil Lewis, "Red Cross Finds Detainee Abuse in Guantanamo," *N.Y. Times*, Nov. 30, 2004.

15. United Nations Committee Against Torture, Consideration of Reports Submitted by States Parties Under Article 19 of the Convention, Conclusions and Recommendations of the Committee Against Torture, United States of America, CAT/C/USA/CO/2 (May 18, 2006) (Advanced Unedited Version), at http://www.ohchr.org/english/bodies/cat/docs/AdvanceVersions/CAT.C.USA .CO.2.pdf; see also Colum Lynch, "Military Prison's Closure is Urged," *Wash. Post*, May 20, 2006.

16. Convention Against Torture and Other Cruel, Inhuman or Degrading Treatment or Punishment, Dec. 10, 1984, S. Treaty Doc. No. 100–20, 1465 U.N.T.S. 85 (hereinafter "CAT").

17. Id. at art 16.

18. President Reagan understood the treaty this way when he first sent it to the Senate: "The United States understands that, in order to constitute torture, an act must be a deliberate and calculated act of an extremely cruel

and inhuman nature, specifically intended to inflict excruciating and agonizing physical or mental pain or suffering." S. Treaty Doc. No. 100–20, at 4–5. The Reagan administration listed acts of torture that were encompassed in the August 2002 memo: The definition of torture "is usually reserved for extreme deliberate and unusually cruel practices, for example, sustained systematic beatings, application of electric currents to sensitive parts of the body, and tying up and hanging in positions that cause extreme pain." S. Exec. Rep. No. 101–30, at 14 (1990).

19. S. Treaty Doc. No. 100–20, *supra* note 18, at 4. The first Bush administration eventually submitted to the Senate a more extensive definition of severe physical and mental pain that became the 1994 criminal statute. OLC's second memo tried to argue, weakly, that the phrase "severe" in reference to physical pain was an effort to expand the definition of torture beyond the Reagan administration's definition. But there is no real reason to think the Reagan and Bush administrations had different definitions of torture, and executive branch officials at the time said as much to the Senate. The 2004 OLC opinion quotes a comment from the Senate report on the CAT as saying that the Reagan administration definition had been criticized "for setting too high a threshold of pain." The 2002 opinion addressed this statement by pointing to the testimony of State and Justice Department officials before the Senate that there was no difference between the Reagan and Bush understandings of the treaty, but rather that the Bush administration sought to make the Reagan understanding more specific. Convention on Torture: Hearing Before the Senate Comm. on Foreign Relations, 101st Cong. 10 (1990) (statement of Abraham Sofaer, legal advisor, Department of State); id. at 13–14 (statement of Mark Richard, deputy Assistant attorney general, Criminal Division, Department of Justice). In the face of these statements, the 2004 OLC opinion concludes that the Bush administration had a lower standard for torture than Reagan because "the common usage of 'excruciating and agonizing' pain is understood to be more intense than 'severe' pain," without any citation to authority. Memorandum for the Deputy Attorney General, Legal Standards Applicable Under 18 U.S.C. §§ 2340–2340A, Dec. 30, 2004 (hereinafter December 2004 OLC Opinion).

20. 18 U.S.C. §§ 2340(1). As the Senate attached this language to its advice and consent to the CAT in 1994, and the Clinton administration attached it to its document ratifying the treaty, it also defines the United States' international legal obligations under the treaty. S. Exec. Rep. No. 101–30, at 36 (1990); 1830 U.N.T.S. 320 (Oct. 21, 1994).

21. The difference between specific and general intent is a difficult one to understand, and it has been only imperfectly explained by the Supreme Court. Cf. *U.S. v. Ratzlaf*, 510 U.S. 135, 141 (1994); *United States v. Carter*. 530 U.S. 255, 269 (2000); *United States v. Bailey*, 444 U.S. 394, 405 (1980).

22. Even OLC in its second opinion made this error. See OLC December 2004 Opinion ("We do not believe it is useful to try to define the precise meaning of 'specific intent' in section 2340"). It refused because, in light of the President's policy prohibiting torture, "it would not be appropriate to rely on parsing the specific intent element of the statute to approve as lawful conduct what might otherwise amount to torture."

23. See, e.g., *Webster's New International Dictionary* 2295 (2d ed. 1935); *American Heritage Dictionary of the English Language* 1653 (3d. ed. 1992); IX *The Oxford English Dictionary* 572 (1978).

24. Memorandum for Alberto R. Gonzales, Counsel to the President, Re: Standards of Conduct in Interrogation under 18 U.S.C. §§ 2340–2340A, Aug. 1, 2002, at 6, (hereinafter OLC August 2002 memo).

25. 42 U.S.C. § 1395w-22(d)(3)(B).

26. Congress here had adopted an understanding of the CAT recommended by the Bush administration. The Reagan administration had not submitted an extensive definition of mental pain and suffering.

27. Bush administration critics like Georgetown law professor David Cole claim that reading the statute to prohibit only threats of imminent death, rather than any threats of death, shows that the Justice Department was bending the law to allow torture. His approach would have a lawyer ignore Congress's deliberate choice of the word "immediate" and ban any interrogator from *ever* referring to death as a possibility, because he prefers that on moral or policy grounds. A lawyer's job, however, is to interpret the words Congress chose, and not to elevate himself into the role of an elected official.

28. In sending the treaty to the Senate, the Reagan administration said: "Torture is thus to be distinguished from lesser forms of cruel, inhuman, or degrading treatment or punishment, which are to be deplored and prevented, but are not so universally and categorically condemned as to warrant the severe legal consequences that the Convention provides in case of torture." S. Treaty Doc. No. 100–20, at 3.

29. Id. at 15 (discussing *Case of X v. Federal Republic of Germany*).

30. Id. at 15–16. It is worth mentioning another important difference between Congress's antitorture law and the CAT. The CAT had defined torture as inflicting severe pain or suffering in order to achieve certain purposes, such as obtaining information or a confession, punishment, intimidation or coercion, or discrimination. Congress removed the purpose requirement. In this case, Congress's definition of torture was broader than the international definition. CAT, *supra* note 16, at art. 1.

31. The Supreme Court held in the 1990 *Verdugo-Urquidez* case that a warrantless search of the home of a Mexican drug cartel member suspected of murdering an American DEA agent did not violate the Constitution. Chief

Justice Rehnquist reasoned that the Framers didn't intend the Bill of Rights to extend to aliens abroad precisely because of the potential for interference with military operations, with absurd results, such as destruction of property being found, battlefield deaths questioned as wrongful killings, and searches held unreasonably without a warrant. The Eighth Amendment's prohibition on cruel and unusual punishment expressly covers only criminal sentences, not actions taken by the military in wartime. While the Due Process Clause was not at issue here, the logic of this case implies that it too does not apply to aliens abroad. Otherwise virtually every action of the military against an enemy would be subject to constitutional challenge.

32. Even if the Fifth and Fourteenth Amendments' Due Process Clause applied, it would not bar coercive interrogation in wartime. "Only the most egregious official conduct" which "shocks the conscience" will give rise to a due process claim, the Supreme Court has said. It has not defined exactly what "shocks the conscience" means, but lower courts have found police or prison guard use of force, unnecessary and disproportionate to the situation, motivated out of malice and sadism, to meet that standard. Due process would also take into account the government's goal of protecting the nation from attack. *United States v. Verdugo-Urquidez*, 494 U.S. 259 (1990); *Johnson v. Eisentrager*, 339 U.S. 763 (1950); *Ingraham v. Wright*, 430 U.S. 651, 664 (1977) ("An examination of the history of the [Eighth] Amendment and the decisions of [the Supreme] Court construing the proscription against cruel and unusual punishment confirms that it was designed to protect those convicted of crimes"). See *Rochin v. California*, 342 U.S. 165 (1952); *County of Sacramento v. Lewis*, 523 U.S. 833, 846 (1998). Courts have found physical violence such as rape, beatings, or shooting to violate due process, but not de minimis contact such as a slap, push, or shove. See, e.g., *Riley v. Dorton*, 115 F.3d 1159 (4th Cir. 1997); *Webb v. McCullough*, 828 F.2d 1151 (6th Cir. 1987).

33. 28 U.S.C. § 1350.

34. See, e.g., *Mehinovic v. Vuckovic*, 198 F. Supp. 2d 1322 (N.D.Ga. 2002); *Daliberti v. Republic of Iraq*, 146 F. Supp. 2d 19 (D.D.C. 2001); *Cicippio v. Republic of Iran*, 18 F. Supp. 2d 62 (D.D.C. 1998).

35. *Ireland v. United Kingdom*, ECHR (1978) series A, No. 25, para 167 (1978). The ECHR found the British methods had produced "intense physical and mental suffering to the person" which led to "acute psychiatric disturbances during the interrogation." It also found them to be degrading because they "arouse in their victims feelings of fear, anguish, and inferiority capable of humiliating and debasing them," which could break "their physical and moral resistance."

36. S. Treaty Doc. 100–20, *supra* note 18, at 4.

37. *Supreme Court of Israel: Judgment Concerning the Legality of the General Security Service's Interrogation Methods,* 38 I.L.M. 1471 (1999) (H.C. 5100/94, *Pub. Comm. Against Torture in Israel v. Gov't of State of Israel,* 53(4) P.D. 817).

38. Anthony Lewis, "Making Torture Legal," *N.Y. Review of Books,* July 15, 2004.

39. Jeremy Waldron, "Torture and Positive Law: Jurisprudence for the White House," 105 Colum. L. Rev. 1681, 1701 (2005).

40. The most well-known was a symposium on the Landau Commission Report published in 23 Israel L. Rev. (1989). There have been a number of collections published since 9/11, such as Sanford Levinson ed., *Torture: A Collection* (2004).

41. Model Penal Code § 3.02; Wayne R. LaFave and Austin W. Scott, 1 *Substantive Criminal Law* §5.4, at 627 (1986); *United States v. Bailey,* 444 U.S. 394, 410 (1980).

42. OLC August 2002 Opinion, *supra* note 24, at 41. Congress did not rule out the necessity defense, nor had Israel. Israel's Landau Commission concluded that if lives were at stake, an interrogator could apply "a moderate degree of physical pressure" in proportion to the danger, and could rely upon a defense of necessity if prosecuted. Israel's Supreme Court has also held that the necessity defense is available to interrogators engaged in coercion below torture. Israel S.Ct. GSS Opinion, at para. 34–37.

43. Anglo-American law has recognized self-defense to homicide since at least the time of the great eighteenth-century British jurist William Blackstone.

44. It must be necessary to use force to avoid the attack, the belief that force is necessary must be reasonable, the attack must be imminent, and the use of force must be proportional to the harm. LaFave & Scott, *supra* note 41, at 663–64; see also Model Penal Code § 3.04.

45. Michael Moore, "Torture and the Balance of Evils," 23 Israel L. Rev. 280 (1989). One complication is whether it can be claimed when the terrorist being questioned is not actually carrying out the attack himself, but merely has knowledge of it. Some scholars believe self-defense applies if the terrorist helped to create a situation where innocent lives may be lost.

46. *In re Neagle,* 135 U.S. 1 (1890).

47. Alliance for Justice, Lawyers' Statement on Bush Administration's Torture Memos, August, 2004, http://www.afj.org/spotlight/0804statement.pdf.

48. CAT *supra* note 16, art. 2.2.

49. LaFave & Scott, *supra* note 41, at 629–30.

50. December 2004 OLC Opinion, *supra* note 19.

51. It is a standard canon of statutory construction that laws which do not explicitly regulate the President or the military should not be read as doing so.

Interfering with executive authority over wartime operations has always been frowned on in the law. Laws against murder or property destruction do not apply to the military in wartime. Congress authorized the President broadly to use force to prevent future attacks on the United States without any express limitations of methods of interrogation or the conditions and procedures for enemy detention.

52. Alliance for Justice, *supra* note 47.

53. 343 U.S. 579 (1952).

54. Id. at 637 (Jackson, J., concurring).

55. Regulation of domestic production, Justice Black wrote for the Court, "is a job for the Nation's lawmakers, nor for its military authorities."

56. John Yoo, *The Powers of War and Peace* (2005).

57. Memorandum from Walter Dellinger, assistant attorney general, Office of Legal Counsel, U.S. Department of Justice, to Abner J. Mikva, counsel to the President, Presidential Authority to Decline to Execute Unconstitutional Statutes, 18 Op. OLC 999 (Nov. 2, 1994).

58. Placing of United States Armed Forces Under United Nations Operational or Tactical Control, 20 U.S. Op. OLC 182, 1996 WL 942457 (May 8, 1996). Cf. H. Jefferson Powell, *The President's Authority Over Foreign Affairs* (2002).

59. December 2004 OLC Opinion, *supra* note 19, at n.8.

60. Waldron, *supra* note 39, at 1715. A similar position is argued by Thomas Nagel. See Thomas Nagel, "War and Massacre," in *War and Moral Responsibility* 3 (Marshall Cohen et al. eds., 1974); Thomas Nagel, "Autonomy and Deontology," in *Consequentialism and Its Critics* 142, 156–67 (Samuel Scheffler ed., 1988). See also David Sussman, "What's Wrong with Torture?," 33 Phil. & Pub. Aff. 1, 2–3 (2005). For legal academics who hold similar views, see Rosa Ehrenreich Brooks, "The New Imperialism: Violence, Norms, and the 'Rule of Law'", 101 Mich. L. Rev. 2275, 2316–18 (2003); Seth F. Kreimer, "Too Close to the Rack and the Screw: Constitutional Constraints on Torture in the War on Terror," 6 U. Pa. J. Const. L. 278 (2003).

61. Sanford H. Kadish, "Torture, the State and the Individual," 23 Isr. L. Rev. 345, 346 (1989). Even the most absolutist defenders of individual autonomy from state action, like Charles Fried, Henry Shue, and many other legal scholars, will not rule out coercive measures in all cases. See, e.g., Henry Shue, "Torture," 7 Phil. & Pub. Aff. 124, 143 (1977) (arguing that those who undertook morally justified torture must explain their reasons as defendants in a criminal trial); Charles Fried, *Right and Wrong* 10 (1978); Richard A. Posner, "The Best Offense," *The New Republic*, Sept. 2, 2002, at 28, 30; Michael Walzer, "Political Action: The Problem of Dirty Hands," in *War and Moral Responsibility* 70 (Marshall Cohen et al. eds., 1974); Oren Gross, "Are Torture Warrants

Warranted?: Pragmatic Absolutism and Official Disobedience," 88 Minn. L. Rev. 1481 (2004).

62. Eric A. Posner & Adrian Vermeule, "Should Coercive Interrogation be Legal?," 104 Mich. L. Rev. 671 (2006).

63. In fact, it appears that our regulatory agencies do not strike the same balance across issues. See Eric A. Posner & Cass R. Sunstein, "Dollars and Death," 72 U. Chi. L. Rev. 537 (2005).

64. Philip B. Heymann, *Terrorism, Freedom, and Security: Winning Without War* 109–11 (2003). Sanford Levinson calls this a strategy of "deny the basic premise—i.e., the efficacy of torture—and, therefore, maintain the commitment because it is in fact costless to do so." Sanford Levinson, "Precommitment and 'Postcommitment': The Ban on Torture in the Wake of September 11," 81 Tex. L. Rev. 2013, 2028 (2003).

65. U.S. Army Interrogation Field Manual 34–52, at 1–1 (May 8, 1987).

66. United Nations Committee Against Torture: Consideration of Reports Submitted by State Parties Under Article 19 of the Convention, Second Periodic Reports of States Parties, Addendum, Israel 7, U.N. Doc. CAT/C/33/Add.2/Rev.1 (1997).

67. Israel High Court Opinion, at para. 5. Anecdotal evidence from other conflicts, such as French efforts against the Algerian independence movement, also suggests that actionable intelligence has been obtained by democratic governments using methods going well beyond coercive interrogation and into torture. See discussion in Levinson, *supra* note 64, at 2030.

68. Concluding Observations of the Human Rights Committee: Israel, CCPR/CO/78/ISR, at para. 18 (August 21, 2003).

69. The case is discussed in Alan Dershowitz, *Why Terrorism Works, Understanding the Threat, Responding to the Challenge* 137–38 (2002), and the *9/11 Commission Report*.

70. See, e.g., *9/11 Commission Report, supra* note 69, at 525–27 n.107.

71. Id. at 247 & 531 nn. 161–62.

72. See Press Briefing by White House Counsel Judge Alberto Gonzales, DoD General Counsel William Haynes, DoD Deputy General Counsel Daniel Dell'Orto, and Army Deputy Chief of Staff for Intelligence General Keith Alexander (June 22, 2004).

73. See *9/11 Commission Report, supra* note 69, at 248.

74. Action Memo, for: secretary of defense, From: William J. Haynes, II, general counsel, Subject: Counter-Resistance Techniques, Nov. 27, 2002, approved by SecDef, Dec. 2, 2002.

75. Shue, *supra* note 61, at 141; Heymann, *supra* note 2, at 110.

76. Heymann, *supra* note 64, at 112.

77. Waldron, *supra* note 39, at 1718–34.

78. Gross, *supra* note 61, at 1507–09; Seth Kreimer, "Too close to the Rack and Screw," 6 U. Pa. J. Const. L. 278 (2003); Mordechai Kremnitzer, "The Landau Commission Report–Subordinated to the Law or the Law to the 'Needs' of the Security Service?," 23 Isr. L. Rev. 216, 254–57, 261–62 (1989).

79. Frederick Schauer, "Slippery Slopes," 99 Harv. L. Rev. 361 (1985); Eugene Volokh, "The Mechanisms of the Slippery Slope," 116 Harv. L. Rev. 1026 (2003).

80. Heymann, *supra* note 64, at 110.

81. Posner & Vermeule, *supra* note 62, at 690.

82. Final Report of the Independent Panel to Review DOD Detention Operations (August 2004), www.au.af.mil/au/awc/awcgate/dod/d20040824 finalreport.pdf. (hereinafter Brown-Schlesinger Report).

83. The panel concluded, "No approved procedures called for or allowed the kinds of abuse that in fact occurred. There is no evidence of a policy of abuse promulgated by senior officials or military authorities."

84. Church Report, at 3 (March 10, 2005), available at http://www.defense link.mil/news/Mar2005/d20050310exe.pdf.

85. Brown-Schlesinger Report, *supra* note 82.

86. See Working Group Report on Detainee Operations in the Global War on Terrorism: Assessment of Legal, Historical, Policy, and Operational Considerations (Apr. 4, 2003) (hereinafter Working Group Report).

87. Id. at 63.

88. U.S. Army Interrogation Field Manual 34–52, at Appendix H (May 8, 1987).

89. Working Group Report, *supra* note 86, at 64. Two involved manipulation of the environment and diet, not to be done in any way that would harm the detainee. Interrogators might want to adjust the temperature or introduce an unpleasant smell, and could do this if they did not injure the detainee in any way and the interrogator accompanied the detainee at all times.

90. Id. at 65.

91. Id. at 70.

92. After receiving the working group report, he issued an order to the commander of the U.S. Southern Command on April 16, 2003, authorizing the use of twenty-four of the first twenty-six interrogation methods recommended by the working group. Memorandum for Commander, U.S. Southern Command, Subject: Counter-Resistance Techniques in the War on Terrorism (Apr. 16, 2003).

93. Posner & Vermeule, *supra* note 62.

Chapter 8

1. Military Order of Nov. 13, 2001, *Detention, Treatment, and Trial of Certain Non-Citizens in the War Against Terrorism*, 66 Fed. Reg. 57,833 (Nov. 16, 2001), at http://www.whitehouse.gov/news/releases/2001/11/20011113-27.html.

2. Editorial, "A Travesty of Justice," *N.Y. Times*, Nov. 16, 2001.

3. Letter to the Honorable Patrick J. Leahy, chairman, senate judiciary committee, Dec. 5, 2001, at http://highbury.law.yale.edu/outside/html/Public _Affairs/152/Leahy.pdf; the signers of the letter can be found at http://highbury .law.yale.edu/outside/html/Public_Affairs/152/OrigSig.pdf.

4. Neal K. Katyal & Laurence H. Tribe, "Waging War, Deciding Guilt: Trying the Military Tribunals," 111 Yale L.J. 1259, 1309 (2002).

5. George Lardner Jr., "Democrats Blast Order on Tribunals," *Wash. Post*, Nov. 29, 2001.

6. Opening Statement of Senator Patrick Leahy, chairman, senate judiciary committee, "DOJ Oversight: Preserving Our Freedoms While Defending Against Terrorism," Nov. 28, 2001, available at: http://leahy.senate.gov/press/ 200111/112801.html.

7. Id.

8. Dan Eggen, "Ashcroft Defends Anti-Terrorism Steps," *Wash. Post*, Dec. 7, 2001.

9. Department of Defense, Military Commission Order No. 1, Subject: Procedures for Trials by Military Commissions of Certain Non-United States Citizens in the War Against Terrorism (Mar. 21, 2002) (superceded).

10. Department of Defense, Military Commission Instruction No. 2, Subject: Crimes and Elements for Trials by Military Commission (Apr. 30, 2002).

11. Under the ICC, a prosecutor who loses a case can appeal the decision, this is not possible under the military commissions, or in a civilian U.S. criminal trial.

12. See Laurence H. Silberman, "Will Lawyering Strangle Democratic Capitalism?," Regulation, Mar.–Apr. 1978, at 15.

13. Jerry Markon & Timothy Dwyer, "Some Saw Moussaoui as Bit Player, Juror Says," *Wash. Post*, May 5, 2006.

14. Dan Eggen, "New Home is 'Alcatraz of the Rockies,'" *Wash. Post*, May 5, 2006.

15. *9/11 Commission Report*, 273–76.

16. Jerry Markon, "Moussaoui Pleads Guilty in 9/11 Plot," *Wash. Post*, Apr. 23, 2005.

17. Jerry Markon & Timothy Dwyer, "Moussaoui Repeatedly Ejected at Trial; Outbursts Mark Start of Jury Selection Process," *Wash. Post*, Feb. 7, 2006.

18. *United States v. Moussaoui*, 382 F.3d 453 (4th Cir. 2004); *United States v. Moussaoui*, 365 F.3d 292 (4th Cir. 2004); *United States v. Moussaoui*, 333 F.3d 509 (4th Cir. 2003).

19. Andrew C. McCarthy, "The Intelligence Mess: How It Happened, What To Do About It," 117 Commentary 11 (Apr. 1, 2004).

20. *United States v. Moussaoui*, 282 F. Supp. 2d 480, 487 (E.D. Va. 2003).

21. *United States v. Nixon*, 418 U.S. 683 (1974).

22. Id. at 712–13.

23. A federal law, the Classified Information Procedures Act, creates a similar process for allowing summaries of classified national security documents to be given to juries instead of the documents themselves. Classified Information Procedures Act (CIPA), 18 U.S.C.A. App. 3 §§ 1–16.

24. *United States v. Moussaoui*, 365 F.3d 292, 306 (4th Cir. 2003).

25. Id. at 313–17. An earlier appeal had dismissed the case on a technical jurisdictional ground, *United States v. Moussaoui*, 333 F.3d 5089 (4th Cir. 2003), which had generated substantial difference of opinion among the judges of the Fourth Circuit as a whole, but did not lead to a full en banc argument. *United States v. Moussaoui*, 336 F.3d 279 (4th Cir. 2003) (en banc) (denying motion for rehearing en banc).

26. Jerry Markon, "Moussaoui Pleads Guilty in Terror Plot," *Wash. Post*, Apr. 23, 2005.

27. Jerry Markon, "Judge Bars Moussaoui From Jury Selection," *Wash. Post*, Feb. 15, 2006.

28. Jerry Markon & Timothy Dwyer, "Moussaoui Unfazed as 9/11 Attacks Detailed," *Wash. Post*, Mar. 8, 2006.

29. Jerry Markon & Timothy Dwyer, "Moussaoui Says He Was to Fly 5th Plane," *Wash. Post*, Mar. 28, 2006; Dana Milbank, "A Terrorist's Grand Delusions," *Wash. Post*, Mar. 28, 2005.

30. Jerry Markon & Timothy Dwyer, "Moussaoui Tells Court 9/11's Toll Was Too Low," *Wash. Post*, Apr. 14, 2006. Even so, the trial still threatened to run aground. Judge Brinkema halted the proceedings and almost ended the death penalty phase when it was revealed that a career Transportation Security Administration lawyer had e-mailed transcripts of the trial to government witnesses and attempted to coach them in their testimony. While those witnesses were banned from testifying and the lawyer was cited for misconduct, the conduct almost derailed the Moussaoui case yet again. Jerry Markon & Timothy Dwyer, "Judge Halts Terror Trial," *Wash. Post*, Mar. 14, 2006.

31. Even after his conviction and sentencing, Moussaoui continued to play games. Facing transfer to a super-maximum-security prison, he filed a motion seeking to withdraw his guilty plea and asked for a new trial. He

claims now that he was not involved in the 9/11 plot, and was only sent to train for a second wave of attacks. He wrote that he now believes "it is possible I can receive a fair trial even with Americans as jurors." Jerry Markon, "Moussaoui Fails in Bid to Withdraw 9/11 Guilty Plea," *Wash. Post*, May 9, 2006.

32. President Bush Welcomes German Chancellor to the White House, May 3, 2006, available at: http://www.whitehouse.gov/news/releases/2006/05/20060503-15.html.

33. Ruth Wedgwood, "Al Qaeda, Terrorism, and Military Commissions," 96 Am. J. Int'l L. 328, 330–31 (2002).

34. Geoffrey Stone, *Perilous Times: Civil Liberties in Wartime* (2004).

35. Id. at 331–32.

36. Barbara Olshansky, *Secret Trials and Executions: Military Tribunals and the Threat to Democracy* (2006).

37. Thomas L. Friedman, "A Travesty of Justice," *N.Y. Times*, Nov. 16, 2001.

38. For a critical review of the history, see Louis Fisher, *Military Tribunals & Presidential Power: American Revolution to the War on Terrorism* (2005). A valuable source is Brian Baldrate, "The Supreme Court's Role in Defining the Jurisdiction of Military Tribunals: A Study, Critique, & Proposal for *Hamdan v. Rumsfeld*," 186 Mil. L. Rev. 1 (2005); see also American Bar Association Task Force on Terrorism and the Law, Report and Recommendations on Military Commissions (Jan. 4, 2002). Law professors have written on both sides of the issue. See also Curtis Bradley & Jack Goldsmith, "The Constitutional Validity of Military Commissions," 5 Greenbag 2d 249 (2002); David J. Bederman, "Article II Courts," 44 Mercer L. Rev. 825 (1993); Harold Koh, "The Case Against Military Commissions," 96 Am. J. Int'l L. 337 (2002).

39. William Winthrop, *Military Law and Precedents* 832 (2d ed. 1920).

40. Proclamation Suspending the Writ of Habeas Corpus Because of Resistance to Draft (Sept. 24, 1862), in 6 *Life and Works of Abraham Lincoln* 203 (Marion Mills Miller ed., 1907)

41. Winthrop, *supra* note 39, at 834, 853.

42. *Ex Parte Vallandigham*, 68 U.S. 243 (1863).

43. *Ex Parte Mudd*, 17 F. Cas. 954 (S.D. Fla. 1868)(No. 9,899).

44. *Military Commissions*, 11 U.S. Op. Atty. Gen. 297 (1865).

45. See Eli E. Nobleman, "Military Government Courts: Law and Justice in the American Zone of Germany," 33 A.B.A. J. 777, 777–80 (1947); Pitman B. Potter, "Legal Bases and Character of Military Occupation in Germany and Japan," 43 Am. J. Int'l L. 323 (1949).

46. A. Wigfall Green, "The Military Commission," 42 Am. J. Int'l L. 832, 833 (1948).

47. The facts of the Nazi saboteur case are recounted in David Danelski, "The Saboteurs' Case," 1 J. S. Ct. Hist. 61 (1996); Louis Fisher, *Nazi Saboteurs*

on Trial (2003); Michael R. Belknap, "The Supreme Court Goes to War: The Meaning and Implications of the Nazi Saboteur Case," 89 Mil. L. Rev. 9 (1980); Eugene Rachlis, *They Came to Kill: The Story of Eight Nazi Saboteurs in America* (1962); *Ex Parte Quirin*, 317 U.S. 1 (1942).

48. Danelski, supra note 47, at 65.

49. Id.

50. 7 Fed. Reg. 5101 (1942).

51. Danelski, *supra* note 47, at 69.

52. See U.S. Dep't of Defense, Military Commission Order No. 1, Procedures for Trials by Military Commissions of Certain Non-United States Citizens in the War Against Terrorism para. 5 ("Procedures Accorded the Accused") and para. 6 ("Conduct of the Trial") (Mar. 21, 2002), available at http://www.defenselink.mil/news/Mar2002/d20020321ord.pdf; Crimes and Elements for Trials by Military Commissions, 32 C.F.R. 11.3.

53. "By the Articles of War, and especially Article 15, Congress has explicitly provided, so far as it may constitutionally do so, that military tribunals shall have jurisdiction to try offenders or offenses against the law of war in appropriate cases." *Ex Parte Quirin*, 317 U.S. at 28.

54. *Ex Parte Yamashita*, 327 U.S. 1 (1946).

55. *Hiroto v. McArthur*, 338 U.S. 197 (1948); *Johnson v. Eisentrager*, 339 U.S. 763 (1950). In a 1952 case in which the wife of an American serviceman in occupied Germany was tried by military tribunal for murdering her husband, the Supreme Court again upheld military commissions as authorized by Congress. *Madsen v. Kinsella*, 343 U.S. 341, 348–49 (1952).

56. In fact, Congress reiterated the point again in 1996 in the legislative history to the War Crimes Act. The act, Congress observed, "is not intended to affect in any way the jurisdiction of any court-martial, military commission, or other military tribunal under any article of the Uniform Code of Military Justice or under the law of war or the law of nations." H.R. Rep. No. 104–698, at 12 (1996), reprinted in 1996 U.S.C.C.A.N. 2166, 2177.

57. Now codified at 10 U.S.C. § 821 (2004) ("The provisions of this chapter conferring jurisdiction upon courts-martial do not deprive military commissions, provost courts, or other military tribunals of concurrent jurisdiction with respect to offenders or offenses that by statute or by the law of war may be tried by military commissions, provost courts, or other military tribunals").

58. *Ex Parte Yamashita*, 327 U.S. at 11, citing *Quirin*, 317 U.S at 28.

59. *Quirin*, 317 U.S. at 37.

60. The Geneva Conventions, and their successor treaties (which the United States has not ratified), deal with civil wars and insurgencies which cover certain groups that are not nations. See, e.g., *Kadic v. Karadzic*, 70 F.3d 232 (2d Cir. 1995).

61. *Rasul v. Bush*, 542 U.S. 466, 483–84 (2004).

62. Detainee Treatment Act of 2005, Pub. L. No. 109–148, § 1005(e)(1), 119 Stat. 2739, 2742 (2005).

63. GPW art. 102, Aug. 12, 1949, 6 U.S.T. 3316, 75 U.N.T.S. 135 (entered into force Oct. 21, 1950).

64. See, e.g., Jordan Paust, "Antiterrorism Military Commissions: Courting Illegality," 23 Mich. J. Int'l L. 1 (2001); Jordan Paust, "Antiterrorism Military Commissions: The Ad Hoc DOD Rules of Procedure," 23 Mich. J. Int'l L. 677 (2002).

65. The critics claim that distinguishing between aliens and citizens violates core international law norms of equal treatment. This reflects a fundamental failure to understand the difference between war and peace. In peacetime, the United States does provide extensive due process and equal protection for aliens, as it should, and there is no difference between an alien or citizen before a federal court. Wartime, however, is different. Foreign enemies, almost by definition, are aliens, although al Qaeda is trying to change that by intensively recruiting American citizens. In wartime, the United States can and has detained and deported enemy aliens. It has seized the property of enemy governments and its citizens. It has sent its military forces to kill and destroy the enemy's armed forces. A nation at war could not carry out war at all if it had to treat citizens and aliens completely equally.

66. Paust, *supra* note 64, at 688–89.

Conclusion

1. *Hamdan v. Rumsfeld*, 2006 WL 1764793 (U.S.) (June 29, 2006).

2. Richard A. Posner, *Uncertain Shield: The U.S. Intelligence System in the Throes of Reform* 209-11 (2006).

3. Report of the Commission on the Intelligence Capabilities of the United States Regarding Weapons of Mass Destruction ch. 10 (2005).

INDEX